68765SHI

3

THATCHERISM

THATCHERISM

Edited and with an Introduction by

ROBERT SKIDELSKY

Chatto & Windus

LONDON

First published in 1988 by
Chatto & Windus
30 Bedford Square
London WC1B 3SG

A CIP catalogue record for this book
is available from the British Library

ISBN 0 7011 3342 2

Photoset by Rowland Phototypesetting Ltd
Bury St Edmunds, Suffolk
Printed in Great Britain by
Redwood Burn Ltd
Trowbridge, Wiltshire

To Joy

Contents

Acknowledgements   ix

Introduction   1

1   IVOR CREWE   25
Has the Electorate become Thatcherite?

2   ANTHONY KING   51
Margaret Thatcher as a Political Leader

3   DAVID BUTLER   65
The 1987 General Election in Historical Perspective

4   BEN PIMLOTT   79
The Future of the Left

5   PATRICK MINFORD   93
Mrs Thatcher's Economic Reform Programme

6   FRANK HAHN   107
On Market Economies

7   KENNETH MINOGUE   125
The Emergence of the New Right

8   BRIAN BARRY   143
The Continuing Relevance of Socialism

9   DAVID MARQUAND   159
The Paradoxes of Thatcherism

10   A. H. HALSEY   173
A Sociologist's View of Thatcherism

11   RALF DAHRENDORF   191
Changing Social Values under Mrs Thatcher

References   203
List of Contributors   209
Index   211

Acknowledgements

This book is based on a series of public lectures delivered at the University of Warwick between January and March 1988, and is a collaborative endeavour. My thanks go to all those who helped make it possible: first and foremost my colleagues in the Department of International Studies at Warwick who strongly supported the idea that the Department should sponsor a series of lectures on Thatcherism, and the Departmental Secretary, Mrs Joy Gardner, who handled the correspondence and administration of the project with her usual tact and sympathy. The Departments of Economics and Politics provided co-sponsorship and, together with the University, the additional finance without which it would have been impossible to proceed. I would like to thank them, and also the *Birmingham Post* which, in the person of Tom Quirke, upheld its fine record of serious journalism by following the series with close attention and printing large extracts from the lectures on its leader page. I must thank the contributors for coming; their audiences of faculty and students for responding to them so appreciatively and questioning them so pertinently; the University's Audio-Visual Centre for recording the lectures; and Mrs Dorothy Foster of the Politics Department for transcribing them. Finally, I am grateful to my publishers for getting the presses rolling so promptly. Nothing dates so soon as assessments of yesterday's political events; the Thatcherism here analysed is today's, and tomorrow's, news.

ROBERT SKIDELSKY

Introduction

ROBERT SKIDELSKY

This book started life as a series of lectures delivered at the University of Warwick in the spring of 1988. The aim of the series was threefold: to consider the nature and politics of Thatcherism; to explore the circumstances in which it came to power; and to assess the durability of the so-called Thatcher revolution. As it turned out, it was not possible to get a full coverage of all the intended themes. In particular, there is no substantial discussion of the circumstances which brought Thatcherism to power – the background of the 1970s. To remedy this omission is the purpose of the first, and longest, section of this introduction.

There are many ways to slice into the cake called Thatcherism. It can be thought of as a free-market ideology – part of a world-wide reaction against collectivism; it can be discussed as a personal style of political leadership. Some people have said there is no such thing as Thatcherism, because Mrs Thatcher's governments have not acted consistently in the way that Thatcherist principles, had they existed, should have caused them to act. (One is reminded of Tolstoy's disciples who accused the Master of not being sufficiently Tolstoyan.) Patrick Minford claims that Mrs Thatcher does have a vision, but is also a shrewd political entrepreneur who responds to market constraints and opportunities. Her vision is that of 'a world in which *small* businesses could compete freely for the favours of the individual *family* consumer; [in which] the State keeps law and order, including the elements of a moral order to protect family decency, and provide succour for the genuinely unfortunate who cannot help themselves.' At the same time, she zig-zags towards her goals. This seems to me about right. Mrs Thatcher is the only British Prime Minister whose name has given rise to an 'ism'. Thatcherism suggests both a set of beliefs and a momentum to reorder society according to those beliefs, driven by the commitment of a remarkable political personality.

My own way of coming to grips with Thatcherism is historical rather than abstract. It arose out of the political failures of the 1960s and 1970s. As I see it, its initial inspiration was negative: to stop governments, and particularly Conservative governments, from getting into political business which yielded no profits, only losses. Naturally, the agenda soon broadened and acquired positive economic content, because in modern developed societies governments are largely judged by the performance of the economy. If government could not manage or direct the economy successfully, who, or what, was to do it? A market ideology developed in answer to such questions. Mrs Thatcher was, of course, deeply concerned about Britain's relative economic decline, accelerating inflation, industrial disorder. But so were Heath, Wilson, and Callaghan. They were not less patriotic; nor did they strive less mightily to reverse these tendencies. Where she came to differ from them was in her analysis of what caused these things, and what needed to be done about them. She came to believe that the remedies they espoused, or were driven to, were, if not the main, at least a major cause of the distempers they faced. She came to reject the whole drift towards *dirigiste* and corporatist styles of governing, and proclaimed her intention to reverse it. The mounting difficulties faced by these styles, and the ungovernability they engendered, gave her her political chance in 1979. The voters were not imbued with her cause, but they realised that the old regime was bankrupt and that something new had to be tried. They were prepared to give her a chance.

We need, then, to distinguish between the nature of Mrs Thatcher's economic ideas and the circumstances which made them politically marketable. About the first I shall have little to say. There is nothing new in them: what is new is their capture of political power after a century of retreat. They come out of a tradition of political and economic individualism, overshadowed by a seemingly irreversible drift towards collectivism.[1] There have been classic modern statements on which Mrs Thatcher and her advisers have clearly drawn.[2] The organised form of the individualist counter-revolution is said to have started with a meeting of economists at Mont Pelerin in Switzerland in 1947, an event of increasingly hallowed memory to the New Right.[3] In Britain, the decisive event was the foundation of the Institute of Economic Affairs in 1957.

However, for many years this substantial restatement of the individualist case made little impression. In 1960 Daniel Bell proclaimed the 'end of ideology' and announced a 'rough consensus' of Western intellectuals behind the idea of a managed welfare-capitalism.[4] In Britain, a 'post-war settlement',[5] based on a Keynesian commitment to full employment, the welfare state, a 'mixed economy' of private and public sectors, and a halting drive to greater equality, which commanded the assent of both political parties 'and the majority of people listed in *Who's Who*',[6] seemed to have reconciled capitalism and socialism, individualism and collectivism, democracy and authoritarianism. What gradually undermined this consensus was that in the 1960s the so-called Middle Way started to shift to the Left. The crucial change, as David Marquand characterises it,[7] was the transition from 'arm's length' management of 'Keynesian social democracy' to 'hands on' intervention in its working.

This was a largely Labour Party reaction to the 'thirteen wasted years' of Conservative rule (1951-64), though the Conservatives themselves had started on the interventionist road. (A parallel move occurred in the United States when Kennedy and Johnson succeeded Eisenhower.) But it was not the shift to greater *dirigisme* as such which broke the post-war settlement; but the fact that it failed to work. The first signs of the reaction came in the Conservative manifesto of 1970, but it required the further experience of the 1970s to show that the 'post-war settlement' had become unviable.

To understand this whole evolution it is worth recalling the way Britain's problems were discussed in the 1950s. What especially excited alarm was the persistently slow per capita growth of the British G.N.P. as compared with that of its main European competitors: 2.2 per cent for the decade 1950-60, as against 6.5 per cent for Germany and 3.5 per cent for France. For the next ten years the analytic spotlight played on this problem of slow growth – its reasons and its cures. Three main kinds of explanation were given – political, structural, and cultural.

Political explanations concentrated on the impact of government policy on economic performance. The chief issue here was the alleged failure of the government's short-term demand-management, characterised by the famous stop-go cycle, to create a secure environment for the sustained investment needed for faster growth. One explanation highlighted the technical incompetence of the Conservatives in running the economy. A typical conclusion was that 'budgetary and monetary policy failed to be stabilising, and must on the contrary be regarded as having been positively destabilising'.[8]

A second explanation was directed at the influence of electoral considerations on economic management. T. W. Hutchison wrote that 'The second half of the fifties saw the first, exquisitely timed, example of the political business cycle, bringing the Conservatives a third electoral success running . . .'[9] On this view, it was not the ineptness, but the skill, with which Keynesian techniques were used, from the political point of view, which produced stop-go with its attendant evils.

According to the third line of argument, the decisive obstacle to growth was the priority given to the defence of sterling.[10] Between 1949 and 1967 employment and growth objectives had to be consistent with maintaining the pound's value at 2.80 dollars. The defence of sterling took place against the background of an inflation rate higher than that of Britain's leading competitors. This above-average inflation rate progressively increased sterling's overvaluation. At full employment too many imports were sucked in, too many exports priced out of world markets, leading to periodic balance of payments crises. The resulting deflationary measures slowed down investment and the rate of technical progress, thus contributing to slow growth over the period.

The important point to stress is that these critiques of government performance did not, as yet, produce a general theory of government failure, such as was to be developed by the 'public choice' theorists of the Virginia School a little later. At this time they simply led to the view that governments must try to do better. The instruments of management must be refined; perhaps new instruments were needed. As regards inflation two positions developed: the Phillips–Paish view that the economy should run at a somewhat higher margin of spare capacity (2-3 per cent rather than 1-2 per cent unemployment), and the idea that government should act directly to restrain costs by means of an incomes policy. The first being deemed politically and morally unacceptable, Conservative politicians in the early 1960s took the early, halting steps towards pay policy with Selwyn Lloyd's 'pay pause' of 1961. This was the start of the corporatist 'hands on' phase of post-war economic policy.

The second set of explanations for Britain's poor economic performance was structural. The Brookings Report on the British economy, published in 1968, concluded that although faults in demand-management may have had some harmful results, especially on the level of investment, the main reason for slow growth was to be found in inefficiencies at the micro-level.[11] From the early 1960s attention switched to failures on the supply-side. These criticisms, which go back to the nineteenth century,[12] included: the poor quality of British industrial management, amateur and relentlessly opposed to the acquisition of relevant knowledge; the poor quality of decision-making in the civil service, also associated with the amateur tradition ('Latin and Greek guarded entry into the administrative class . . . as effectively as the English language test guarded immigration into Australia'[13]); the educational system, with its dominant humanist tradition, hatred of 'stinks', socially stratified secondary schooling, and lack of provision for technical training; the trade unions with their restrictive practices (according to Michael Shanks, the unions were the 'greatest institutional barrier to Britain becoming a genuinely dynamic society'[14]); and finally excessive product-differentiation associated with a class system, the traditional diversity of Britain's export markets, and an individualistic, small-scale, in-dustrial structure dating from the Industrial Revolution – all of which were supposed to hinder the application of cost-reducing inventions, economies of scale, scientific marketing practices, etc.

As analysts of British retardation contemplated the massive resist-ances to change in all walks of life, they were increasingly forced back onto cultural explanations. Professor Phelps Brown castigated the 'culture of managers and workers' alike;[15] Max Nicholson sneered at obsolete British 'ideas systems'.[16] In the late 1950s the term 'Establishment' came to be used, in its modern sense, to denote, on the one hand, a narrow network of personal and family relationships dominating big business, the City, the civil service, and the universities and, on the other, the whole syndrome of amateur, anti-scientific values originating in the public schools and the ancient universities. Specifically, the class system, and the attitudes and resentments it engendered, were identified as a major structural cause of slow growth.

The grand inquest on the state of the nation, carried out by a bevy of Royal Commissions, led to major changes of policy in the 1960s. In economic policy the main switch was from full employment to growth: demand-management would operate in the context of medium-term planning for growth, the model being the French system of 'indicative' planning. The centrepiece of the strategy to achieve higher growth was to run the economy flat out, in the belief that rapid output expansion causes enough productivity growth and *ex ante* saving to avoid inflation and deterioration in the balance of payments. 'Go-go' would replace 'stop-go'. If, nevertheless, the balance of payments went into the red before the productivity growth came through, sterling should be devalued rather than stop the 'go'.

The Conservative governments of Harold Macmillan and Douglas Home had already started on this road by producing the Maudling boom of 1963-4 and by setting up a National Development Council in 1962, with representatives of government, employers, and trade unions. The incoming Labour Government of Harold Wilson in 1964 transferred the main planning functions from the N.E.D.C. to a new ministry, the Department of Economic Affairs, headed by the ebullient George Brown; it spawned miniature N.E.D.C.s for each major industry and region. The D.E.A. published a National Plan in 1965 projecting a 25 per cent increase in national output over the six years, or a compound per capita growth rate of 3.4 per cent per annum. The Maudling boom was continued by Wilson. From the fertile mind of Nicholas Kaldor came a succession of devices to encourage higher manufacturing output. His most celebrated innovation was the Selective Employment Tax (s.e.t.) announced in the budget of 1966, which aimed to switch resources from services to manufacturing – or, according to the theory on which it was based, from firms producing under increasing cost to firms showing economies of scale. There were also investment grants, and employment subsidies to manufacturing industry in the 'development areas'. Planning of incomes started when Brown got employers and trade union leaders to sign a Declaration of Intent in December 1964 promising to keep the growth of prices and wages within the limits of productivity growth. A Prices and Incomes Board was established under Aubrey Jones to keep price increases and pay awards within a 3-3½ per cent 'norm'.

As part of structural reform, new business schools – the first ever – were opened for management training. Technical education was expanded. The first systematic attempt was made to engineer occupational and social mobility through education – by expanding higher education and regrouping secondary education in giant comprehensive schools. An active labour market policy was promoted by an ambitious scheme of industrial training and guaranteed redundancy payments. A merger mania spread through business, assisted by an Industrial Reorganisation Corporation set up in 1966. The iron and steel industry was re-nationalised and consolidated. The civil service was shaken up by a series of internal reforms and the injection of new blood into the new ministries which the Labour Government set up. Tony Benn headed a new Ministry of Technology charged with promoting research and development. Under regional policy came the biggest restructuring of local government since the Municipal Corporation Act of 1835. Bigness, Organisation, Planning, Science, Technology – all obscurely related by Wilson to Socialism – were the catchwords of the hour.

That this 'break for growth' failed is a melancholy fact of history. Per capita growth showed no increase whatever in Wilson's six years in office. Investment in manufacturing actually declined as a percentage of total investment. All the economic policies broke down, one after another, and were scrapped or suspended before Labour left office. There were many explanations as to why this happened. They agreed on one point: that the government failed to develop a balance of payments strategy consistent with its growth targets. Singled out is Wilson's refusal to devalue the pound, in 1964 or 1966. The consequence of the Maudling 'go', in the absence of devaluation, was to produce the Wilson 'stop' in July 1966. The stop, in turn, destroyed not only any chance of achieving the National Plan, but also the incomes policy connected with its achievement. That policy was replaced by a 'freeze', followed by two years of severe restraint. This not unnaturally led to a wages 'explosion', which sent the inflation rate from 5 to 8 per cent and largely undid the effects of the belated devaluation of November 1967 and Roy Jenkins's austere budgetary programme.

Thus run the detailed explanations. What they ignore is that no one in fact knew how to achieve a sustainable higher rate of growth. The idea that you would get it by running the economy for a number of years at zero unemployment was not a piece of knowledge, but an untested theory, and a counter-intuitive one at that. It rested on the idea that productivity depends on output, not the other way round, and thus fitted the hubristic mindset of the mandarins and planners of the time who thought of growth as a function of a single macroeconomic variable under the control of the government. Peter Sinclair, reviewing the Wilson era, finds the most depressing feature to lie not in specific mistakes of policy but in the Government's 'extravagant claims of omnicompetence . . . Some of the economic problems were found to be intractable. Others could be disposed of, like the heads of the hydra, only at the cost of creating more numerous and more horrifying ones. Each of the problems became more serious as the decade wore on. The traditional instruments to deal with them seemed less and less effective. The battery of new devices rarely improved upon the old.'[17]

Whether the claims to omnicompetence were really believed by the politicians who made them or whether they were felt to be necessary for political survival is hard to say: probably a bit of both. Governments in those days were held to be answerable for all aspects of economic affairs,[18] so politicians may have felt impelled by political need to promise more than they believed they could achieve. On the other hand, they would not have raised expectations to the degree they did unless their experts had given them plausible grounds for believing that something like higher growth was fairly easy to accomplish. One can see also why higher growth became central to the political strategy of the Labour Party, by enabling the Party to promise a shift of spending towards the social services without alarming business.[19] The Wilson Government could talk responsibly about keeping public spending within the limits of what 'the nation could afford', and at the same time defining what was affordable by reference to the growth predictions of the National Plan.

The consequences of all this for the future of the post-war settlement were serious. Macro-economic management acquired an inflationary reputation which cumulatively undermined its legitimacy. The reliance on continually enlarging public expenditure to achieve the growth objectives gradually destroyed the delicate political equipoise between capitalism and socialism which had sustained the mixed economy. It also left the legacy of a bloated and virtually unmanageable public sector, which was to destroy the authority of governments in the 1970s. Efforts to contain the inflationary pressures generated by the 'dash for growth' led governments ever deeper into the mire of 'pay policies' for which there never seemed to be enough consent. Attempts to win trade union support for such policies by offering the unions more power and the workers more socialism made industry increasingly ungovernable, alarmed the business community, and increased the inflationary pressures which the pay policies were designed to contain. Far from establishing a 'virtuous circle' of expanding prosperity, the Maudling–Wilson 'dash for growth' produced a vicious circle of problems which trapped the economy in 'stagflation' and undermined the ability of governments to govern.

No summary of what went wrong in Britain in the 1970s can omit the impact of external events, and particularly the traumatic effects of the fourfold increase in oil prices early in 1974, which entailed a sharp reduction in living standards in all oil-importing countries. Nevertheless, although the impact was common, the speed and technique of adjustment varied enormously. In Britain, the oil shock hit an economy already out of control, and a method of governing already in tatters.

At the heart of the troubles of the 1970s was the increasingly

9

unmanageable relationship between the British state and the trade union movement. The growth of state responsibility for making the economy work went hand in hand with the growth of union power to prevent it from working. The development of this perverse relationship was most apparent under the rule of the Labour Party, whose paymaster the unions were. In essence the bargaining position of the unions in industry was strengthened partly to win T.U.C. support for pay restraint, in turn seen necessary to secure the growth which would deliver greater benefits to the working class. When the growth and the benefits failed to materialise what was left was simply enhanced union power which could be turned against the state – either as employer or policy-maker.

Edward Heath, Conservative Prime Minister from 1970-4, was the most conspicuous victim of this development. The Conservatives took office in 1970, pledged, in Heath's words, to 'change the course of history' – which meant, in effect, reversing the Labour Government's economic policies. Planning was to be dismantled; trade union power was to be curbed by changes in the law; incomes policy was discarded, and the government prepared to fight pay claims in the now bloated public sector one by one; 'lame ducks' were to be left to the mercy of the market.[20] This was the start of the reaction against corporatism, but it was very tentative. Michel Crozier wrote in 1970 that 'Blockages seem to be an essential characteristic of modern advanced societies.' But the only escape from 'blockages' he offered was 'improved collective capacities'.[21] This, it turned out, was to become the solution adopted by Heath.[22]

Faced, at the end of 1971, with what was seen as the politically intolerable level of one million unemployed, the Heath government expanded the budget deficit from zero where Jenkins had left it to £4 billion, cutting unemployment in half by December 1973, but doubling the inflation rate – from 6.2 per cent to 13.5 per cent. Attributing the price explosion to inflationary wage settlements – the Government had been forced to concede a 27 per cent rise to the miners in February 1972 – Heath responded in September 1972 with a statutory incomes policy, trying to win trade union support by increasing social security payments, subsidising rents and nationalised industry prices, bailing out the 'lame ducks', and so on. But these spectacular

U-turns brought no relief from rising inflation and growing industrial disorder as the unions, led by the miners, fought his pay policy. Heath was brought down in February 1974 when he asked the electorate 'Who Governs Britain?' at the precise moment when it was perfectly clear it was not him.

By the time Wilson took office for the third time in February 1974 the fires of inflation, already raging under Heath, were being fed by the enormous rise in oil prices. Yet the main lesson Labour seemed to have learnt from its own, and Heath's, experiences, was that the inducements offered to the unions to co-operate in industrial policy had been insufficient and needed to be increased. On paper, the programme on which Labour returned to power was the most radical in its history. The Joint T.U.C.–Labour Party Liaison Committee statement on Economic Policy of February 1973 had foreshadowed 'a wide-ranging and permanent system of price controls' especially on food; municipalisation of private rented property, public ownership of required building land, and the building of 400,000 council houses a year; free public transport in the major conurbations; large-scale redistribution of income and wealth by wealth taxes, gift taxes, and a steeply progressive income tax; the end of prescription charges, immediate rises in pensions, and the annual indexing of pensions; the expansion of investment and the control of capital by further public ownership, state supervision of private investment, and the control of overseas investment.

These pledges and others were embodied in the Party's 1973 programme. The Party promised to repeal Heath's Industrial Relations Act of 1971 and replace it with an Act conferring new legal rights on workers and trade unions. The leadership agreed at the 1973 Party Conference to the nationalisation of North Sea Oil and Gas, registered and unregistered ports, shipbuilding and ancillary services, aircraft production, and 'identifiable sections or industrial firms within the pharmaceutical, machine tool, construction, and road haulage industries'. Wilson spoke of setting up a State Merchant Bank and a National Housing Finance Corporation to act as a publicly-owned building society. A National Enterprise Board would be set up to take over and manage existing state assets, and to buy a controlling interest in key manufacturing sectors. The major companies left in the private sector would be obliged to sign 'planning agreements' with the government which would condition the receipt of aid and state contracts. 'A fundamental and irreversible shift in the balance of power and wealth in favour of working people' (Labour's Programme, 1973) was thus seen as a necessary condition of economic recovery and trade union assent to wage restraint.[23]

The inside story of the Wilson–Callaghan governments of 1974-9 has been excellently told by Bernard Donoughue,[24] and there is no reason to repeat it here. Basically Wilson's first year and a half (which included his re-election in October 1974) was spent in emasculating his party's radical industrial policy, fobbing off the anti-E.E.C. lobby with a referendum, and buying off the unions by conceding their wage demands. The education of his party apparently required letting the economic situation deteriorate to the point when pay policy and public expenditure cuts could be sold as being dictated by external events. A voluntary pay policy was agreed with the T.U.C. in July 1975; it required the sterling crisis of 1976 and the negotiation of an I.M.F. loan under humiliating conditions to bring public spending under control. The pay accord with the unions worked well for two years, helping to bring down the annual rate of inflation from over 20 per cent to 8 per cent; but a third year of perceived falling living standards was too much for the unions to stomach. When the government announced a 5 per cent 'norm' for 1978, the unions went on the rampage, the public sector unions leading, and the pay policy collapsed in the 'winter of discontent'. This was the immediate background to the victory of the Conservative Party in the 1979 election and the advent of Thatcherism.

Did the era of Keynesian social democracy have to end with garbage rotting in the streets, hospitals closed, and grave-diggers refusing to bury the dead? In retrospect it is clear that the disintegration of the 'consensus' started with the move from the 'arm's length' to 'hands on' approach in the early 1960s. This was associated with the move from unemployment to growth targets. The latter, unlike the former, involved planning the economy. Planning, in a free society, involved corporatism – governing industry with the 'consent' and participation of organised business and the trade unions. This initiated the process of government by bribery: the whole syndrome of threats and inducements, in which the threats became less and less credible, and the inducements more and more lavish, until Keynesian social democracy ended in industrial anarchy.

Admittedly this is an interpretation of the policy of 'inducements' which the Labour Party would not admit. Its own analysis of unemployment, inflation, and slow growth emphasised the deleterious effect on economic performance of class privilege and industrial and financial power. Thus the promise of social reform and greater union power was necessary to bind the workers to co-operation in industrial reconstruction.[25] What Labour ignored was that it needed business, as much as trade union, co-operation to make its policies work. Labour's radical programme of 1973 implied the elimination of the private sector as the major force in the national economy: not the best basis for exhorting business to 'invest in Britain'. The Labour leadership, of course, never accepted this programme, and tried to sweep it under the carpet as soon as it regained office. By this time the virtue had gone out of the Wilson years. Wilson Mark I probably believed in his 'scientific' programme. Wilson Mark II no longer believed what he and his colleagues in the 1970s were saying. They tried to buy off the Left in opposition, business and trade unions in power. They cynically raised the expectations of their followers, and then doused them at the behest of the I.M.F. No wonder society became neurotic.

If the cynicism of the Wilson–Callaghan Labour Party was a major factor in the collapse of Keynesian social democracy, one must repeat that at no time was economic and social knowledge enough for the state to direct a free society to the goals successive governments set themselves from the 1960s onwards. What remains open to question is whether a more modest version of the 'post-war settlement', with more modest employment targets, no growth targets, and paying constant attention to efficiency in labour and product markets, could have been sustained for longer. Certainly, as the record shows, such an approach was contrary to the spirit of the age. But to what extent the *hubris* was the direct legacy of Keynes is uncertain. The assumption of almost unlimited omnicompetence owed a great deal as well to the legacy of the war, the Fabian belief in 'rule by experts', and the claims to knowledge by the academic estate.

Modesty was not in the air. Had it been the Thatcher 'counter-revolution' would scarcely have struck with such devastating effect.

It was in these circumstances that a section of the Conservative Party concluded not just that particular policies of governments had been wrong, but that the whole approach to governing summed up in the phrase Keynesian social democracy was misconceived. For Mrs Thatcher the important signposts on her road to Damascus were probably Heath's U-turn over incomes policy in 1972 and his defeat by the miners in 1973-4. The lesson which she drew from these events, which was to be confirmed as the 1970s unrolled, was that the political cost of trying to run the country by means of deals with the trade unions was too great, and anyway was not open to Conservative governments. But the 'seminal text'[27] of the Conservative intellectual rethink was Sir Keith Joseph's speech at Preston on 4 September 1974. In this speech Joseph identified the full employment commitment as the error from which the whole drift towards ungovernability flowed.[28] Breaking this commitment was a necessary precondition for a more viable philosophy of government. It was the full employment commitment which forced governments to take the pay policy route. Hold unions responsible for the level of unemployment, argued Joseph, and governments could once more fulfill one of their defining tasks: maintaining the value of money by controlling its issue. Simultaneously the rationale for budget deficits disappeared, and they could now be viewed for what they were: important causes of the excessive growth of the money supply and rising prices. With public spending robbed of any macro-economic function, the way was cleared for its reduction as a percentage of G.N.P., making possible tax cuts which would improve the 'supply side' of the economy. A reduction in state spending and taxes automatically meant a reduction in the size of the state, and the threat to freedom implied by its growth. Implicit in all this was a return to the ethic of individual responsibility and prudent housekeeping: the classical moral and political virtues.

This tentative statement of a new governing philosophy was to receive increasing support in the 1970s from academic analyses of the failures of government, provided by both the political scientists and the economic liberals.

Until the 1970s the expansion of state responsibility was not seen as a problem, in Britain at least; rather it was regarded as solving problems. In technical language it would compensate for 'market failures'. It was only as the 1970s unfolded that the opposite view started to gain significant ground – that state interventions created more problems than they solved. The 'ungovernability' thesis, or the theory of the 'overloaded' state, was developed by political scientists like Richard Rose and Anthony King.[29] What these academics were saying was that the government's reach had come to exceed its grasp; that the state's responsibilities had become too great for the conditions of consent. According to King, Britain was becoming harder to govern because 'the number of dependency relations in which government is involved has increased substantially and because the incidence of non-compliance by other participants in these relationships has also increased substantially.'[30] This was the nemesis of corporatism. The ungovernability thesis challenged the main assumption of the 'hands on' school that government interventions to compensate for market failure provide a protective belt for the capitalist system. Rather they were seen as introducing lawlessness into the heart of the polity, undermining both capitalism and democracy.

A parallel, and to some extent convergent, attack on the philosophy of big government came from the economic liberals, who were initially concerned with the problem of explaining and controlling inflation. Monetarists attributed the observed tendency for given levels of unemployment to be associated with ever higher rates of inflation to the continuous attempts of 'Keynesian' governments to reduce unemployment below its minimum sustainable rate. More generally, inflation was a purely monetary phenomenon caused by governments printing too much money.

Why did governments exhibit this propensity? Economic liberals came up with two types of explanation, influenced by the work of the Virginia School. The first drew on the economic theory of democracy first suggested by Schumpeter, but developed by the Americans Anthony Downs, James Buchanan, and Gordon Tullock. Democracy was seen by these economists as a vote-buying system. The politician is an entrepreneur in votes; the voter is a consumer of competitively marketed political merchandise. The consumer is sovereign in both the economic and political market place; but in the latter, unlike the former, he is not subject to a budget constraint. As Samuel Brittan put it, 'The costs of the handouts, whether met through taxation or inflation, will not necessarily accrue to the groups who benefit from them.'[31] Spending programmes are thus easy to sell to the poor and relatively poor. Party competition for votes takes the form of spending promises which are not matched by comparable taxation commitments for fear of antagonising the better-off who will have to pay for them. This does seem to capture some of the political logic of the 1960s, when spending commitments at unchanged rates of taxation were supposed to be 'paid for' by growth of the economy. (Bureaucratic empire-building is an autonomous source of enlarging state expenditures in these economic models.)

The other source of 'excess demand' is what Brittan called 'the pursuit of group self-interest through coercive means in the market place'; particularly the conflict between trade unions and employers, or between trade unions themselves, for incompatible relative shares of the national product. In the absence of an accommodating monetary policy, this conflict yields a 'natural' rate of unemployment. But if this rate is too high for the given conditions of political consent, governments will attempt to lower it by financing any wage-rate yielded by producer group rivalry. This, then, is the second source of inflationary pressure. The link between the two is the 'excessive burden ... placed on the "sharing out" function of government'.[32] Peter Jay, then the influential Economics Editor of *The Times*, thought that, given the dependence of democratic governments on 'renewable popular consent',[33] inflation would probably accelerate till democracy was extinguished, since no government would be able to survive the unemployment cost of weakening the power of the trade unions.

Not just inflation, but 'stagflation' was attributed by the economic liberals to government intervention. The main idea was summarised in *The Times* of 4 January 1975: 'The price of maintaining full employment by more and more inflationary finance is not only accelerating inflation, but also a progressive diversion of economic resources into activities favoured by or dependent on inflation.' Thus Britain's declining competitiveness in international markets was directly linked to the 'hands on' strategy of speeding up the rate of growth by huge injections of public money into the economy.

We can see how the two critiques of the post-war settlement converged. The political scientists' claim was that in pursuit of elusive 'social consensus' governments had created ungovernable societies. The economic liberals went on to say that the only method of governing left open to them in these circumstances was the liberal use of the printing press. Monetarism offered a way out for both groups. Abandonment of the quest for consensus would automatically restore to government control of its budget. It would also restore conditions for faster growth. Governability, solvency, and faster growth could all be attained by a single variable: control of the money supply.

It was not accidental that these critiques of collectivism found their loudest echoes in the Conservative Party. For the ideas which had governed Britain in the 1960s and 1970s came largely from the Left of politics, while the new notes struck by the monetarists were in tune with a number of constants of Conservative thought. In the Labour Party the failures of Wilsonian planning in the 1960s and of Wilson–Callaghan 'social contracts' in the 1970s handed the ideological ascendancy to the left-wing of the Party. Conservative free market ideas were projected, therefore, not only against the old 'hands on' interventionism of the Labour Right, but as a defence against the drift of Labour Party thinking in the 1970s towards support for a siege economy on the East European model – a tendency which was the direct cause of the decision of a group of moderate Labour leaders to break away from the Party and form the s.d.p. in 1981.

A final cause of the collapse of the consensus, more difficult to pin down, has to do with the changing composition of both main parties. Partly this was a generational matter: the older generation of leaders was simply dying off. But also the social composition of the party *élite* was changing. The post-war settlement had been underwritten by the ability of established money and social position to work with a trade union baronage and a Wykhamist intelligentsia. This wary, but complacent and inefficient, corporatism had given way, by the 1970s, to the fierce ideological antipathy of two groups of lower middle-class *arrivistes* – those who had risen through the private sector, and those who had done the same through the public sector. The theory of 'embourgeoisement' has a long history, but few of its proponents in the 1950s foresaw that its political fruit would be polarisation, not convergence.

Most of the essays in this collection set out to expound, analyse, praise and criticise the nature and politics of Thatcherism. Here I select only certain leading themes for note.

For Ivor Crewe, it is Mrs Thatcher's 'statecraft', rather than any social or ideological realignment of forces, that is responsible for her political triumphs. 'Mrs Thatcher's warrior style – setting objectives, leading from the front, confronting problems, holding her position – did make a major impact.' He concludes that 'cohesion, purpose and success take precedence over policy and ideology in voters' eyes: that is the lesson of Mrs Thatcher's and Thatcherism's astonishing success.' Anthony King, too, emphasises the personal style of Mrs Thatcher, exploring the techniques she has employed to place her stamp (or foot) on her government: her use of fear, the balance in her personality between extreme caution and risk-taking, her 'declaratory' manner of making policy. This stress on Mrs Thatcher's 'statecraft' and 'political personality' as keys to her success leads both writers to question the durability of 'Thatcherism'. Crewe uses opinion poll data to show that Mrs Thatcher's values have no hold on the electorate which has, if anything, become less Thatcherite since 1979; King emphasises the lack of strong collegial support for her in the Conservative hierarchy. John Campbell has predicted that the active life of Thatcherism will be limited to 'the span of [Mrs Thatcher's] own career'.[34]

Two different issues need to be disentangled. It is perfectly possible to have a social realignment without an ideological realignment. It happened earlier this century when the Labour Party replaced the Liberal Party without the (enlarged) electorate becoming more socialist. In the 1960s and 1970s most of Labour's distinctive aims and values were not shared by the electorate; this did not prevent the Party ruling for fourteen out of twenty years. There is clearly some evidence of social realignment today, with the Conservative share of the working-class vote going up. This reflects both a long-term trend towards 'embourgeoisement' and deliberate policy (the drive for 'popular capitalism'). Nor is there very much Labour can do to reverse it. As Ben Pimlott points out, it is stuck with its working-class constituency and trade union connection. Socialism in Britain has meant 'labourism'. Thus social forces may favour the Conservatives for some time to come, without the electorate (or even the Conservative Party) embracing Thatcherism.

However, the more important point is that 'statecraft' and 'ideology' cannot be separated so easily. As I have suggested, the statecraft of Mrs Thatcher was a response to the statecraft of the 1960s and 1970s. That fell into disrepute, not because the leaders were weak (Macmillan, Wilson in his prime, Heath, and Callaghan were all 'strong' leaders) but because they were trying to work an unworkable system. The question then is: do Thatcherite ideas offer a formula for a successful statecraft independent of the personality of the present Prime Minister? So far Thatcherism has kept the authority of Mrs Thatcher's governments intact, because it has prevented it from being systematically eroded by attempting projects (like incomes policy) which cannot succeed. And this lesson can hardly have been lost on those who aspire to govern after her departure.

The deeper question is whether Thatcherism is valid as a long-term economic and social philosophy. One must distinguish between doing things which had to be done in order to pull the country round, and a permanent way of doing things. Can *laissez-faire* economics be made to work better today than it did in the past? And to what extent does any economic system require the inspiration and support of moral order?

Two essays by Patrick Minford and Frank Hahn deal directly with the economics of Thatcherism. Minford gives a sympathetic account of Mrs Thatcher's promotion of 'popular capitalism' and her efforts to move the British economy closer towards the competitive ideal; Hahn, on the other hand, is contemptuous of Thatcherism's 'textbook market economics', though he sees more point in its 'political economy' – particularly its emphasis on entrepreneurship, and on the connection it makes 'between the institutions of a market economy and the citizens' liberty'.

Hahn's demonstration that markets can fail is coupled with an attack on a certain kind of market-friendly political rhetoric for damaging people's beliefs in the validity of collective mechanisms. 'Thatcherism,' he writes, 'by successfully promoting Thatcherite beliefs, has made [Keynesian] policies that much less likely to succeed. It has thereby reduced the influence we collectively can exert on our economic destinies.' It is not completely clear here what is being claimed. Is it that the collective mechanisms needed to compensate for market failures have been ruled out of court politically? Or is it that they will work only if people believe in them? The two are not the same. Antibiotics will clear up bacteriological infections, whether we believe they will or not: superstition, however, may prevent us from taking them. Thatcherism may be seen as a kind of superstition about the working of the economy, whose hold on government and opinion prevents the adoption of policies which, if they were adopted, would improve economic well-being. On the other hand, Hahn's language suggests that the *outcomes* of collective policies depend on agents' belief in them. In this view of things, agents' beliefs are self-fulfilling by causing them to modify their behaviour in such a way as to make the beliefs come true. Thus the government may believe that increasing the budget deficit will cause output and employment, but not prices, to rise. If agents believe that the result will be a rise in prices, but not employment, they may demand larger nominal rewards for their activities than they would had they held the opposite belief, thus falsifying the government's prediction and confirming their own. However, if this is so, we must also be prepared to entertain the hypothesis that the Thatcherite belief that unemployment is voluntary might, if generally accepted, lead workers (or their agents) to modify their behaviour in such a way as to make their unemployment far less likely. And if they do that, do we need 'collective mechanisms' in this area?

The difficulty that Thatcherism would appear to face is that the belief that unemployment is the worker's fault is not widely held, and indeed runs counter to other beliefs which are. This causes Minford difficulty on the Thatcherite side of the argument. He was one of the economists who advised the incoming Conservative government of 1979 that a policy of gradually reducing the rate of growth of the money supply would gradually bring down prices without causing much unemployment *if* the monetary targets were believed.[35] Now he admits that 'the government tried very hard to meet its targets; but the markets never really believed they would . . . This failure of credibility increased the *costliness* of counter-inflationary policy.' This is putting it mildly. 'The decline in industrial output between June 1979 and December 1980 was the fastest in recorded history. Industrial production fell by 14 per cent while unemployment increased by two-thirds.'[36] Minford now concedes that 'gradualism was unlikely to succeed'; that what in fact brought down the inflation rate was the *unintended* deflationary shocks which resulted from choosing a mistaken monetary indicator. It should however be remembered that there were many at the time (notably the late Lord Kaldor) who argued that the *only* way deflation can work is by creating depression and unemployment. An interesting question is this: if the Kaldor (or Keynesian) view of the matter had been unchallenged in 1979 would Mrs Thatcher and her advisers have ever embarked on the course of *deliberately* adding a million or more to the unemployment figures? One can see that, false though monetarism may have been, it was needed for the purpose of Mrs Thatcher's political experiment.

In economics, then, there must be a question mark over the staying power of Thatcherism. Keynesian expectations have been discredited, but Thatcherite expectations have not supplanted them. In sociology the same thing seems to be true. As Crewe documents, Thatcherite values are not yet widely accepted. The question arises: do we need a Thatcherite 'culture' to make Thatcherite economics work? Adam Smith would have answered no: market economics is 'natural' to man. Weber would have said yes: a market system requires a particular kind of rationality, historically inspired by a 'Protestant ethic'. Most of our contributors who address this issue side with Weber: economics and morals should be congruent with each other. But this, as David Marquand points out, involves Thatcherism in the attempt to engineer changes in social attitudes which is strikingly at odds with its championship of the sovereignty of individual choice.

Kenneth Minogue has described what a Thatcherite culture might look like. Essentially it would be one rid of the 'bourgeois guilt' which makes the rich and successful highly susceptible to moral blackmail by the poor and unsuccessful. The overthrow of the 'guilt culture' is a necessary condition of an enterprise society and reassertion of individual responsibility. But, as Marquand suggests, the attempt to fit people for life under Thatcherism involves an attempt to reshape values and institutions as heroic as anything attempted in the name of socialism: 'Thus the paradox of the strong, intrusive state and the free economy is built into the neo-liberal project itself'. Ralf Dahrendorf cites a whole series of Thatcherite attacks on institutions like the trade unions, local government, universities, and the B.B.C. which oppose Thatcherite values. In such pictures of Thatcherism, individualism and political authoritarianism appear as complements, not opposites. There is something slightly hysterical about these strictures. Any attempt to reshape attitudes involves the reshaping of institutions. Dahrendorf's objections might have been voiced by any supporter of the 'old corruption' in the eighteenth century; and as Halsey reminds us, what we have been seeing is no more than 'small practical steps' to alter the balance between individualism and collectivism.

Even if Thatcherism does succeed in creating an 'enterprise culture' the question remains whether such a culture can harmonise society. Recently Mrs Thatcher and her colleagues have taken to stressing the Christian duty which individuals owe to their neighbours. The drive to wealth creation and self-betterment needs to be balanced by a proper sense of social responsibility.

But if one wants socially concerned behaviour one has to have a social philosophy which connects individuals to each other; otherwise the rise in wealth and poverty are likely to proceed in tandem. Whether Christianity can do the job of reconciling selfishness to society as it did in the nineteenth century is highly doubtful; certainly Thatcherism has not come up with a secular equivalent.

Socialism, of course, in its ethical aspects, was such an equivalent; and Halsey still hopes it can do the job today. He is clear that economic socialism – acceptance of the use of collective mechanisms to solve social problems – requires 'socialisation – the encouragement of common moral sentiments leading to cooperation and peaceful competition through all the attachments of family, neighbourhood, community, and country . . .' However, the socialist bits of the British economy are rapidly being dismantled; and socialism the world over is on the defensive. It should also be noticed that socialist thought has been as hostile as has capitalist practice to such 'attachments' as family and country. Traditionally, it was the Right which favoured unconditional attachments, the Left which questioned them. More generally, the breakup of such attachments has been the driving force behind modernity. So it is rather late in the day to talk about restoring 'common moral sentiments'. The fading of the socialist hope for the 'transformation of human nature' is reflected in the essay by Brian Barry, who explicitly repudiates any such aim. Barry's argument for socialism rests squarely on the postulate of enlightened self-interest. His argument is technical, not moral. Barry points out that we cannot rely on the existence of social sympathy to maintain a generously funded system of social welfare. 'Where does this leave us?' he asks. 'Fortunately, it leaves us still in a good position. The [compulsory] insurance model is, I wish to say, the implementation of the socialist principle with regard to social security'. Collective mechanisms, he argues, can be shown to be more efficient at satisfying individual wants in a number of areas than can markets. And this ought to be sufficient to commend them to the rational citizen.

Many of the contributors to this volume clearly share my own ambivalence about Thatcherism. Thatcherism may have been necessary to break out of the corporatist and bureaucratic impasse of the late 1970s; but the analysis was oversimple, the means crude and mean. More fundamentally, Thatcherism as an economic and social philosophy – as a basis for the long-term government of Britain – is seriously one-sided. In this respect it resembles the Manchester Liberalism of the early nineteenth century which energised the economy but had to be tamed, moralised, and intellectually refined before it was fit to establish a new social order.

ONE

Has the Electorate become Thatcherite?

IVOR CREWE

How are we to assess Mrs Thatcher's election hat trick? Does it reflect an enduring realignment to the Right – the forging of a new popular Conservatism – or merely a remarkable, yet temporary, run of political luck? And how are we to assess the role of the electorate? Has it voted in Conservative governments because it is Thatcherite, or Thatcherite governments because it preferred the Conservatives?

Taking the measure of Mrs Thatcher's achievement, let alone explaining it, is less than easy. In one sense it is spectacular. There have been landslides before, but not two in succession built on such a wide margin of the popular vote. Macmillan's 100-seat majority in 1959 came from a lead of under 6 per cent; Thatcher's 100-seat majority in 1987 from over 11 per cent. The result is the replacement of the alternating two-party system, under which Mrs Thatcher was first elected, by a dominant one-party system under which she or her successor will almost certainly be re-elected. Only an extraordinary turnround of votes could bring Labour to office in four years' time. Put it this way: Labour needs a national swing of 6 per cent to become the single largest, albeit minority, party in 1991, and of 8 per cent to win a bare absolute majority; but since 1945 the largest swing at a single election has been 5 per cent, and the largest swing to Labour a mere 3 per cent. Moreover, if the electoral system continues to lose its exaggerative properties, as it has for the past quarter century, the swings required will be larger still. The choice available to the British electorate in 1991-2 is not between a Conservative government and a Labour government, but between a Conservative government and a hung Parliament.

Yet in another sense there has been no Conservative achievement at all. As her opponents frequently point out, Mrs Thatcher has won her landslides by default, on the cheap. By historical standards the 42 per cent Conservative vote in the 1980s is low, well below the levels achieved by Churchill, Eden and Macmillan in the 1950s, or even by Douglas-Home in 1964, when he *lost*. There has been no ground-swell of Conservative support: its vote has slipped, not surged, since 1979. Mrs Thatcher owes her power to a divided opposition and an unproportionate electoral system, as Baldwin did between the wars.

This is to dismiss and explain away her victories a little too easily. For one thing, 42 per cent of the vote in the genuine three-party contests of the 1980s is a superior achievement to 44 per cent in the two-and-a-bit contest of 1979. For another, the depiction of the Alliance as the splitter of an undiminished Left vote is thoroughly mis-leading. The fact that the s.d.p. broke away from the Labour Party does not mean that the Alliance's voters were temporarily exiled Labour supporters waiting until it was safe to return home. They leaned towards the Conservatives rather than towards Labour at both elections. Without the Alliance as safe harbour many Labour refugees in 1983 would have sailed on to the Conservatives, prob-ably producing an even larger Conservative majority. The Alliance muffled rather than magnified the scale of Labour's defeat.

A strange alliance of Thatcherites, Owenites and *Marxism Today* Euro-communists regard the elections as more than a succession of landslides. They constitute an enduring transformation – social, ideological, and cultural – of the party system, the 'Great Moving Right Show' of Stuart Hall's nightmare.[1] Parallels are drawn with Roosevelt's New Deal Democratic ascendancy in the 1930s, or de Gaulle's dominance in the 1960s. In each case there is a towering political leader; a sense of national renewal; a shift in the social balance of power; an alteration in the terms of political debate – and a twenty-year ascendancy for one party.

To historically-minded sceptics the three elections look more like a tremor than an earthquake. Normal political life has been tempor-arily disrupted, but the political landscape remains geologically intact. Each election, they argue, is a discrete event, subject to strictly temporary political factors; parties are remarkably adaptable to new social soils and political climates; trends are always reversible. The

1906 Liberal landslide was obliterated by 1910 and reversed by 1918; 1931 was followed by 1945; 1959 by 1964 and 1966. They remember hearing that 'Labour Must Lose' before. Why should it be any more true now?

At this point we need to digress into a sub-plot of the story: the failure of academic political science to account adequately for Mrs Thatcher's victories. By the late 1970s the conventional wisdom was that the February 1974 election had brought to an end a quarter century of stable, balanced two-party politics and ushered in a new era of partisan dealignment. The failures of successive governments, the fragmenting class structure and the non-partisan style of television were weakening old party loyalties. There were third party breakthroughs and a new electoral volatility. Many more voters were up for grabs.

New models of the voting decision sprouted alongside the old class and party identification approaches. All assumed that, as old class and party attachments waned, party policies and performance would count for more. Voters were becoming rational consumers, abandoning their old corner-shop loyalties for the big party supermarkets. Emphasis varied only on the narrow question of precisely what voters judged the parties by: some said it was the substance of party policies, others the government's overall record, others again the voter's personal economic interests. But whether vote decisions were based on advertised claims, record of service, or free giveaways, woe betide the party that ignored the revealed preferences of the electoral market place.

The first two Conservative victories did considerable damage to these theories. The 1979 victory put paid to the familiar proposition, popularised by spatial analogies of party competition,[2] that a consensual, middle-of-the-road electorate like the British would inevitably punish a party that abandoned the middle ground, and that party leaders, knowing this, would not engage in such reckless adventures in the first place. Sir Keith Joseph had already rejected this conventional wisdom in his important speech at Preston in October 1974, arguing that the middle ground was 'defined not by reference to popular feeling but to splitting the difference between Labour's position and the Conservatives';[3] Conservatives should instead seek the 'common ground' – what most people thought and desired – because the people 'were far closer to Conservative instincts on many issues'. Mrs Thatcher continued this anti-consensus line in the 1979 campaign. 'I am a conviction politician,' she announced. 'The Old Testament prophets did not say "Brothers, I want consensus." They said "This is my faith and vision. This is what I passionately believe. If you believe it too, then come with me."' And British voters did.

Spatial analogies then made way for so-called retrospective or performance voting models. Voters did not compare party promises; rather, they judged the Government's overall record, especially on the economy. Elections were lost by governments, not won by oppositions. Mrs Thatcher owed victory in 1979 to the Winter of Discontent, not to her radical manifesto.

Then the econometricians got to work. By correlating various monthly economic indicators with party support in the monthly opinion polls they came up with precise statistical formulae: one influential model concluded that government support was a simple function of the inflation and unemployment rates – what Americans call the 'misery index' – and that 'for every increase in unemployment of 10,000 the Government loses nearly one per cent of its popular vote.'[4]

This retrospective economic model appeared to work in the rest of the democratic world. In the post-1973 recession, the misery index took a massive toll. Between 1977 and 1983 the party in office was defeated at the polls in every democracy with a tradition of alternating government. The only exception was Britain in 1983. After four years of government, inflation had come down from 9 per cent to 5 per cent, but unemployment had tripled from 5 per cent to 13 per cent. The misery index rose from 14 to 18. The econometric equation produced a Conservative vote of *minus* 156 per cent! But the electorate re-elected the Conservatives with a handsomely increased majority.

So-called consumer models of voting fared no better. In overwhelming numbers voters pronounced that unemployment was the most important issue and that they preferred Labour as the party to deal with it. In fact, the 1983 election study shows that if the electorate had voted for the party they said they preferred on the single issue they said mattered most to them the result would have been a dead heat: Conservative 35 per cent, Labour 35 per cent, Alliance 31 per cent.[5] The same exercise in 1987 would almost certainly have placed Labour ahead. Clearly voters were moved by something other than party policies or performance in 1983: but what?

The idea of a fundamental partisan realignment is attractive because it offers a possible solution to this puzzle. The failed models of short-term influences on voting decisions all assumed that voters arrived at their preferences autonomously and that the distribution was spontaneous. They underestimated the capacity of parties to reshape the distribution by altering voters' expectations and economic interests. The idea of realignment recognised that it was not only the parties that shifted their position on the electoral battleground; the ground itself could be moved.

Political commentators frequently claim that a social realignment underpins the Conservative ascendancy. Thatcherism is both creator and beneficiary of a new social order and, within it, of a new working class. In fact three quite separate claims are being made. The first is that gradual, inexorable mutations in the social structure have benefitted, and will continue to benefit, the Conservatives. The second is that Thatcherism has accelerated the process by deliberately recreating the social structure in its favour. The third is that, over and above these changes, Thatcherism has a special appeal to important sections of the working class. All three claims are true, but all three need qualifications.

Certainly social trends are on the Conservatives' side. Almost all the expanding groups in the British electorate are predominantly Conservative, almost all the contracting groups predominantly Labour. The working class has become Britain's newest minority. Manual workers now constitute a mere 45 per cent of the labour force; exclude the self-employed, foremen and supervisors, and they dip to under a third. By the next election they will be outnumbered by the professional and managerial salariat, there will be fewer trade union members than shareholders, and owner occupiers will exceed council tenants by five to two in the electorate and by almost two to one among the working class. These trends alone have been worth a swing from Labour to Conservative of at least 5 per cent since 1964.[6]

But this is only part of the story. For reasons that are not entirely clear, region and community have been exerting a steadily stronger electoral influence. And here too the Conservatives are at an advantage. Migration from the Labour-voting north to the Conservative-voting south and from inner city to suburbia and commuter village will continue apace. By 1991 the urban/rural balance of population will have reverted to that of 1901, and Birmingham, Coventry and Norwich will fall in the northern half of the electorate. Even electoral demography is Conservative: increasing longevity combined with the decline in the 1970s birthrate means that job- and welfare-dependent new voters will be outnumbered, for the first time, by the fixed and investment income old voters. The greying rentier class will matter more than the employed – let alone unemployed – youth vote. Mix in the under-registration of poll-tax evaders – on balance, Labour supporters – and the revision of constituency boundaries (probably *after* the next election) and it is not too fanciful to envisage a Conservative-dominated system akin to Japan or Italy until the end of the millenium.

One must not be too mechanistic. There are counter-trends: women are entering the labour force in growing numbers and, partly as a result, trade union membership has started to reverse its post-1981 decline: there is scope here for the radicalisation of a hitherto Conservative group, white collar women, although the half-hearted industrial action in schools in 1985-7 and the anti-strike majority in the Royal College of Nurses ballot in March 1988 do not suggest that this will happen overnight. We should not automatically assume, either, that voting patterns must remain the same within each social group. Labour voters do not immediately abandon lifelong loyalties on moving south or buying a council house. And fluctuations of political fortune could counteract the social trends. The fact that Labour's vote dropped 13 per cent, not 5 per cent, between 1964 and 1987 suggests that political, not social factors, are primary: if Labour can underpoll its structurally given vote by 8 per cent it can, presumably, overpoll it by 8 per cent too. Social trends do not preclude a Labour victory, let alone guarantee unending

Conservative rule. It is not impossible to climb to the top of a downward moving escalator, just difficult.

Whether Thatcherites can be said to have *created* a new social base remains to be seen. Herbert Morrison promised to build the Conservatives out of London; have the Conservatives privatised and gentrified themselves back in again? Cause and effect are difficult to disentangle. Certainly council house owners voted Conservative in 1987 in larger numbers (40 per cent) than council house tenants (25 per cent), but then they were Conservative before they bought the house. Panel surveys refute the idea that voters switch from Labour to Conservative after buying their council house or, for that matter, their shares. House- and share-owners do not become Conservatives; rather Conservatives become house- and share-owners.

Other structural consequences of Thatcherism have hurt rather than helped the Conservatives. The squeeze on the public sector has alienated the administrating, educating and caring classes; the unemployed have swung sharply anti-Conservative. Indeed, a truly radical Thatcherism, which eliminated the subsidies and restrictive practices of its own core supporters, could be its own electoral undoing. Will farmers stay loyal when price supports are dismantled? Will doctors remain warm admirers once they have to be more accountable? Will mortgagees hold solid when tax relief is abolished? We shall see.

What of the final claim, that Mrs Thatcher, like Disraeli a century ago, has created a new Conservative working class, but this time a self-advancing post-industrial one rather than a self-effacing pre-industrial one? Thatcherism, it is said, has a special appeal to the working class because it speaks to their actual experience in language (and, nowadays, accents) it understands about unwanted strikes, work dodging, welfare cheating and crime on the streets.

It is on this issue that there is some academic controversy. Anthony Heath and his colleagues argue that over the long-term, and after taking the ups and downs in party fortunes into account, the readiness of the two main classes to vote for the enemy party rather than their own has not increased but merely shown a trendless fluctuation. Much of the debate is essentially a technical one about definitions, measurement and statistical inference.[7] What is beyond dispute is that the Conservative vote in the working class, however defined, grew at a faster rate than in the electorate as a whole, while the Labour vote declined at a faster rate in the working class than the electorate as a whole. Two comparisons make the point. The first is between the elections of 1959 and 1987. At both the Conservative message was essentially the same – 'Britain's Great Again. Don't Let Labour Wreck It' – [8] and at both they were returned with a one hundred majority. However, their share of the vote was 6.6 per cent lower in 1987 than 1959. This drop is the product of opposite changes in the two classes. Among manual workers the Conservative vote was actually 5 per cent higher in 1987 than in 1959, whereas among non-manual workers it fell 12.5 per cent, i.e. twice the national average. The Labour vote fell by 10 per cent in the electorate as a whole, but by 16 per cent among manual workers and only 3 per cent among non-manual workers. In 1959 Labour still enjoyed a massive 57 to 30 majority among manual workers; by 1987 it had contracted to a slim 41 to 35 per cent majority.[9]

The second comparison is between 1979 and 1987. Again, the change in overall party fortunes must be discounted before exploring class patterns. In the electorate as a whole there was a 2.2 per cent swing to the Conservatives over the eight years, but the classes diverged. In the middle classes the swing was zero; in the working class over 4 per cent. Quite simply, the Conservative advance over both the long and short term has been entirely within the working class. How has it been done? And how, in particular, was it done when segments of the working class were bearing the brunt of the recession?

At this point New Right and Neo-Marxist Left unite in a common answer: Thatcherism has fashioned an ideological realignment within the electorate. Sir Keith Joseph and Mrs Thatcher, Stuart Hall claimed in 1979, had 'constructed a new hegemonic project' in which free market doctrines and authoritarian populism would be fused into a new 'reactionary common sense'.[10] Peregrine Worsthorne said the same in better English: Thatcherism meant 'bitter-tasting market economics sweetened and rendered palatable by great creamy dollops of nationalistic custard';[11] in a word, Powellism. Of course, these two elements of Thatcherite Conservatism are not always compatible. Free market capitalism and chauvinism did not always walk hand-in-hand, as the Westland affair showed. But they were indissolubly linked. In the eyes of the Left the recession created by the monetarist experiment of 1979–81 required a more repressive state and authoritarian mood to contain the resistance, symbolised by the enlargement and enrichment of the police to deal with striking miners and inner city rioters. In the eyes of the Right, the unavoidable deprivation of economic security in the working class made it all the more essential to satisfy their moral and cultural prejudices, to avoid adding moral insult to material injury. The appeal to authoritarian populism, in other words, was needed to secure a prior consent for the truly important crusade on the economic front. Hence Mrs Thatcher's populist forays, supported by the sensationalist tabloid press, on immigration, law and order and foreign policy before the 1979 election.

Future historians will probably say that the Thatcher governments were both more authoritarian and more populist than their predecessors: tighter immigration controls, changes in the rules of evidence, the deporting of refugees, table-banging at Brussels, the *Real Lives* and Zircon affairs, and Clause 28 all come to mind. But the survey evidence fails to reveal any parallel trend in the electorate (see Table 1). True, it portrays a public that was already taking a hard line on immigration control, the death penalty and crime before 1979, as the simmering discontents brought to boil by Powellism in the previous decade suggest. In these respects there was a Thatcherite consensus before Thatcher. But this mood did not spread or intensify; on the contrary, the picture is one of a slow, halting advance for tolerance and liberalism. In 1974 the British Election Study asked respondents about a series of social trends: had they gone too far or not far enough? The identical questions were repeated in 1979 and, by Gallup, in November 1987. Between 1974 and 1979 the electorate grew slightly more conservative about pornography, modern teaching methods, racial equality, sexual equality and the availability of welfare benefits. But between 1979 and 1987 public sentiment reversed direction. The proportion of social conservatives fell by 33 per cent on 'the availability of welfare benefits', 14 per cent

Question: 'We would like to ask your views on some of the general changes that have been taking place in Britain over the last few years. Thinking first about . . . would you say that this has gone much too far, a little too far, is about right, has not gone far enough, or has not gone nearly far enough?'

year	gone too far	about right	not gone far enough	change 1974-79	change 1979-87
The right to show nudity and sex in films and magazines					
1974	64	30	6		
1979	66	29	5	+ 2	
1987	56	37	7		− 10
People showing less respect for authority					
1974	82	10	8		
1979	65	21	13	− 17	
1987	61	14	24		− 4
Change towards modern methods of teaching in schools					
1974	42	43	15		
1979	54	32	14	+ 12	
1987	40	32	27		− 14
Availability of abortion on the National Health Service					
1974	43	42	15		
1979	44	44	12	+ 1	
1987	36	47	17		− 8
Attempts to ensure equality for women					
1974	19	46	35		
1979	23	48	29	+ 4	
1987	12	43	45		− 11
The welfare benefits that are available to people today					
1974	34	42	24		
1979	50	33	13	+ 16	
1987	17	28	54		− 33

Table 1   Authoritarian Populism

on 'changes towards modern teaching methods', 11 per cent on 'attempts to ensure equality for women', 10 per cent on 'nudity and sex in films and magazines', 8 per cent on 'the availability of abortion on the N.H.S.', and 4 per cent on 'challenges to authority'.

Over a similar period support for the return of capital punishment – surely the core of authoritarian populism – fell by 12 per cent.[12]

Of course, the electorate remains socially illiberal on many issues, but less so in 1987 than in 1979. This does not suggest that public sentiment in these areas underlay or responded to the Conservatives' election wins. The most that can be claimed for the thesis of authoritarian populism is that between 1974 and 1979 Mrs Thatcher worked with rather than against the popular grain, softening them up for the true ideological crusade on the economic front.

A distinctive feature of Thatcherism is its pedagogic impulse. It has been at pains to educate the electorate about economic realities. Persuading the public to change economic expectations and assumptions is one of the few constructive economic roles it allows the state. Not since Gladstone has Britain been led by such an opinionated and evangelical Prime Minister as Mrs Thatcher. But there is precious little evidence that she has succeeded. Her missionary preaching has fallen on deaf ears. Let me now pepper you with polling evidence that the public has not been converted to economic Thatcherism – not to its priorities, nor to its economic reasoning, nor to its social values.

First, priorities. The Thatcherite refrain is that the reduction of inflation to near-zero levels is both a necessary and sufficient condition for bringing unemployment down in the long term. In 1980 the public agreed, just: 52 per cent wanted the government to give priority to curbing inflation, 42 per cent to cutting unemployment (see Table 2). By mid-1986, however, these priorities were massively rejected, by over six to one, and 75 per cent agreed that the government 'should always keep unemployment as low as possible, *even if this means some inflation with rising prices*'.

Mrs Thatcher believes in holding down government spending in order to facilitate tax cuts. But the electorate disagree: they want expansion of public expenditure, as Table 3 shows. The Gallup poll

Question: 'Which do you think the government should give greater attention to – trying to curb inflation or trying to reduce unemployment?'

month/year	curb inflation	reduce unemployment	don't know
10/76	54	36	10
(May 1979 election)			
6/80	52	42	7
11/80	30	62	8
1/82	23	70	8
11/82	21	73	6
5/83	22	69	9
(June 1983 election)			
7/84	18	75	7
6/85	14	78	8
8/85	16	77	7
2/86	15	78	7
5/86	13	81	6

Question: 'Do you think that the government should or should not always keep unemployment as low as possible, even if this means some inflation with rising prices?'

month/year	should	should not	don't know
7/84	75	16	10
6/85	75	16	10

Source Gallup Political Index

Table 2   Thatcherism's Economic Priorities: Curbing Inflation versus Reducing Unemployment

has asked at regular intervals whether, if forced to choose, they would prefer tax cuts – even at the expense of some reduction in government services such as health, education and welfare – or for these services to be extended even if this means some tax increases. In May 1979, when Mrs Thatcher entered Number Ten, there were equal numbers of tax-cutters and service-extenders. By 1983 there were twice as many service-extenders as tax-cutters; by 1987 six times as many. Of course, free market economists object that these are unpriced trade-offs, and thus almost meaningless questions. Surveys on welfare by the Institute of Economic Affairs suggest that, when offered a three-fold choice between universal welfare provision, selective provision for the poor, and the option of contracting out, universal provision has declined in popularity since 1963 and the plurality now opt for contracting out.[13] But the *trend* since 1978, when the survey was last conducted, parallels that in Gallup. Under Mrs Thatcher universal provision has revived in popularity, while contracting out has subsided.

Perhaps the public disliked the Government's economic medicine, but accepted that There Was No Alternative. Not a bit of it: in the public's eyes unemployment was neither justifiable nor inevitable (see Table 4). For example, in July 1984 a 56 to 44 per cent majority said that unemployment 'is always a bad thing' rather than 'sometimes necessary during a period of adjustment'; by June 1985 the majority had increased to 61 to 39 per cent. Similarly, a 56 to 44 per cent majority rejected the fatalistic proposition that 'high unemployment is something we shall just have to learn to live with as best we can' in July 1985; by December 1986 that majority had grown to 62 to 37 per cent. Indeed, the public turn out to be unreconstructed Keynesians.

Asked 'How likely do you think it that a cut in taxes would help reduce unemployment?' only 26 per cent replied 'very' or 'fairly' likely; 63 per cent said 'not very' or 'not at all' (October 1987). On the other hand, 85 per cent thought that 'spending more on building roads, houses, hospitals, etc would help to reduce employment?' and only 10 per cent demurred. Tough Thatcherite talk about the futility of throwing taxpayers' money at unemployment and about

Question: 'People have different views about whether it is more important to reduce taxes or keep up government spending. How about you? Which of these statements comes closest to your view?'
● cut taxes, even if this means some reduction in government services, such as health, education and welfare
● things should be left as they are
● government services such as health education and welfare should be extended, even if it means some increases in taxes

month/year	cut taxes	no change	extend services
10/78	29	26	45
(1979 election)			
5/79	37	26	37
3/80	25	27	47
3/81	22	25	53
2/82	22	27	52
2/83	24	23	52
(1983 election)			
10/83	18	23	53
5/84	15	27	58
11/84	13	26	62
2/85	17	19	63
2/86	17	20	63
6/86	17	14	64
9/86	9	18	68
5/87	12	21	61
10/87	11	19	66

Source Gallup Political Index

Table 3   Thatcherism's Economic Priorities: Taxes versus Social Services

Question: 'Do you think the current economic situation is the kind of problem that no government can really solve, or do you think it could be solved if a government really tried to apply the right measures?'

month/year	cannot be solved	could be solved	don't know
9/84	34	66	(10)
9/85	25	75	(9)

Question: 'Do you think unemployment is always a bad thing or can it sometimes be justified as necessary during a period of adjustment?'

month/year	always bad	sometimes justified	don't know
7/84	56	44	(6)
6/85	61	39	(5)

Statement: 'High unemployment is something we shall just have to learn to live with as best we can.'

month/year	agree	disagree	(neither/ don't know)
7/85	44	56	(5)
11/85	48	52	(5)
12/86	37	62	(3)

Table 4 'TINA' (There Is No Alternative)

the creation of 'real' rather than 'paper' jobs on a base of zero inflation and a thriving private sector has so far made few converts.

As for Victorian values, Samuel Smiles fares no better than Milton Friedman (see Table 5). In 1977, before Mrs Thatcher came to power, Gallup reported that 35 per cent of voters thought that, if people were poor, their own lack of effort was probably to blame; by 1985 that figure had fallen to 22 per cent and 50 per cent blamed 'circumstances'. Asked in November 1987 whether the unemployed

Question: 'Why, in your opinion, are there people who live in need? Here are four opinions – which is the closest to yours?'
- because they have been unlucky
- it's an inevitable part of modern progress
- because there is much injustice in our society
- because of laziness and lack of willpower

month/year	bad luck	inevi- table	injustice	laziness/ no willpower
1976	19	20	12	50
9/83	14	28	36	25

Question: 'In your opinion, which is more often to blame if a person is poor – lack of effort on his own part, or circumstances beyond his control?'

month/year	circum- stances	lack of effort	both	(don't know)
1/77	32	35	33	(6)
3/85	50	22	28	(3)

Statement: 'When someone is unemployed it is usually his or her own fault.'

month/year	agree	disagree	(don't know)
5/86	10	90	(9)
11/87	13	87	(10)

Question: 'Which of these two statements comes closest to your own opinion?'

	8/87	6/86
'Benefits for the unemployed are too low and cause hardship'	53%	45%
'Benefits for the unemployed are too high and discourage people from finding jobs'	26	35
neither	20	21
(don't know)	(7)	(8)

Table 5   Victorian Values

have usually themselves to blame, only 13 per cent agreed; 87 per cent disagreed.

Thus Mrs Thatcher's message of self-reliance has fallen mainly on deaf ears. In 1984 Gallup asked voters whether they thought the Government's most important job was to provide good opportunities for everyone to get ahead, or whether its job was to guarantee everybody steady employment and a decent standard of living. Only 30 per cent said they were content with good opportunities; 65 per cent wanted a Government guarantee. The proportion believing in self-reliance was actually higher when the identical question was put under Mr Attlee's Government in 1945.[14]

Finally, Thatcherism claims to have instilled a new sense of national pride, to have put the Great back in Britain; but surveys suggest otherwise. In 1985 Gallup asked voters whether they had more or less pride in Britain than five years earlier: only 18 per cent said they had more pride now; 42 per cent said they had less. More recently, only 18 per cent said they believed Britain as a nation was on the way up; 50 per cent thought it was standing still, while 32 per cent thought it was on the way down. The strong sense abroad that Britain is no longer the sick man of Europe does not appear to have penetrated opinion at home.

The electorate, in other words, is hardly suffused with Thatcherite values on either the economic or moral plane. Not surprisingly, therefore, it has consistently opposed a raft of specifically Thatcherite policies and decisions. Table 6 presents a long list of which these are examples:

	Approve	Disapprove
Abolition of G.L.C.	21%	79%
Banning of trade unions at G.C.H.Q.	31%	69%
Privatisation of British Gas	43%	57%
Privatisation of British Telecom	44%	56%
Community charge	29%	71%
Privatisation of electricity and water supply	28%	72%
Attempt to prevent publication of *Spycatcher*	35%	65%

Abolition of Greater London Council *Question:* 'Do you approve or disapprove of the Government's decision to abolish the Greater London Council?' (Londoners only)

approve 21%   disapprove 79%   (don't know 19%)

G.C.H.Q. *Question:* 'Do you think that the Government is or is not justified in proposing to ban trade unions at the secret communications headquarters at Cheltenham?' (Feb 1984)

justified 31%   unjustified 69%   (don't know 10%)

Cruise *Question:* 'Do you think Britain should or should not allow American Cruise missiles to be based in Britain?'

month/year	should	should not	(don't know)
11/83	45	55	(11)
2/84	42	58	(13)
5/84	36	64	(14)
9/85	44	56	(11)

British Gas *Question:* 'The Government is proposing to sell off British Gas, which supplies all main gas in this country, by offering shares to the general public and private companies. Do you think this is a good idea or a bad idea?' (Nov 1985)

good idea 43%   bad idea 57%   (don't know 17%)

British Telecom *Question:* The Government is proposing to sell British Telecom, by offering shares to the general public and private companies. Do you think this is a good idea or a bad idea?'

good idea 44%   bad idea 56%   (don't know 14%)

Falklands *Question:* 'Do you think that Britain should or should not go on spending £140m per year on the Falklands?' (Oct 1987)

should 35%   should not 65%   (don't know 9%)

Spycatcher *Question:* 'Do you support or oppose the Government's attempts to prevent the publication of Peter Wright's book *Spycatcher* in Britain?' (Sept 1987)

      support 35%   oppose 65%   (don't know/neither 28%)

Privatisation of Electricity and Water *Question:* 'Do you agree or disagree with the Government's proposal to privatise the electricity and water industries, that is, sell shares in them to the public?' (Nov 1987)

      agree 28%   disagree 72%   (don't know 10%)

Community Charge *Question:* 'Do you agree or disagree with the Government's proposal to replace local government rates levied on every house with a community charge, that is, a poll tax to be paid by every adult in a house?' (Nov 1987)

      agree 34%   disagree 66%   (don't know 13%)

Question: 'From what you know of the proposals, do they sound a good idea or a bad idea?'

	good idea	bad idea	(don't know)
Feb 1986	54%	46%	(16%)
Jan 1988	28%	72%	(14%)
Apr 1988	30%	70%	(12%)

National Health Service *Question:* 'Some people say that the National Health Service needs more money. Other people say that more money is not necessary, just a reorganisation. Which of these two views comes closest to your own?' (Feb 1988)

      Needs more money   77%
      More money not necessary 23%
      Don't know   6%

Budget *Question:* 'Do you approve or disapprove of the following measures in the Budget: Top rate of income tax cut from 60p to 40p, in the £? (March 1988)

      Approve   35%
      Disapprove   65%
      Don't know   7%

Table 6   Attitudes to Particular Government Decisions since 1983

Question: 'Are you satisfied or dissatisfied with . . . as Prime Minister?'

Period	Prime Minister	% satisfied (mean)	range low	high
1945-51	Attlee (Lab)	47	37	66
1951-55	Churchill (Con)	52	48	56
1955-57	Eden (Con)	55	41	70
1957-63	Macmillan (Con)	51	30	79
1963-64	Douglas-Home (Con)	45	41	48
1964-66	Wilson (Lab)	59	48	66
1966-70	Wilson (Lab)	41	27	69
1970-74	Heath (Con)	37	31	45
1974-76	Wilson (Lab)	46	40	53
1976-79	Callaghan (Lab)	46	33	59
1979-82	Thatcher (pre-Falk)	36 ⎫	25	46
1982-83	Thatcher (post-Falk)	47 ⎬ 39	44	52
1983-87	Thatcher	39 ⎭	28	53

Source: Gallup Political Index

Table 7   Popularity of Post-war Prime Ministers

So Conservative success remains a puzzle. Voters oppose the Government on the vast array of its specific policy initiatives. They say they prefer Labour on the issues that matter. Their economic values are solidly social democratic, their moral values only half-Thatcherite, and on both fronts they have edged to the Left since 1979. There has been no ideological sea change. The economic record might account for 1987, but not 1983. The changing class structure explains only a fraction.

What jigsaw pieces are left? Mrs Thatcher herself? The long-running 'satisfaction' ratings in the polls suggest that Mrs Thatcher has been the second most *un*popular prime minister since the war, surpassed only by Edward Heath (see Table 7). Admittedly, this is a crude measure because it ignores intensities and combines assessments of performance with those of personality. The truth is more complicated. In effect, she is *both* intensely admired and deeply loathed, like Britain's other peacetime warrior prime minister, Lloyd George. Not much liked as a human being, she is widely if grudgingly respected as a leader, the opposite of Harold Wilson. Therein lies her electoral appeal, and it offers a clue to solving the electoral puzzle.

For policy-based party preferences to be translated into votes, a prior condition is probably crucial: the party in question must be regarded as 'fit to govern'. In 1983 and 1987 both Labour and the Alliance fell at this first hurdle, allowing the Conservatives to win because the voters judged that indeed There Was No Alternative – no governing alternative. This primary judgement by the voters has been neglected in the surveys, which ask respondents which party is better on this or that policy, but not 'which is better at governing?' *tout court*. The ingredients of 'fitness to govern' include strong leadership within party as well as over country; party unity; clarity of policy goals; and personal probity.

Thatcherism's 'statecraft', to use Bulpitt's happy term, [15] is at least as distinctive as its economic and cultural prejudices and is the neglected element of its electoral success. Mrs Thatcher's warrior style – setting objectives, leading from the front, confronting problems, holding her position – *did* make a major electoral impact in both 1983 and 1987. So did her austerely centralist conception of the role of government: that it should rule untrammelled by organised interests, or by other governments, whether local or European; and that within the Government she should be unimpeded by doubting ministers or officials.

The results of a set of questions on Thatcherism as statecraft asked in the B.B.C.'s 1983 and 1987 election surveys are revealing (see Table 8). Voters were asked, for example, whether it was better for government to stick firmly to their beliefs or meet opponents halfway; whether it was better for governments to be tough or caring in economically hard times; whether governments by themselves could do much to create prosperity; whether governments should involve major interests in making decisions or keep them at arm's length. Voters turned out to be fairly evenly split overall, with anti-Thatcherites in a slight majority in 1983 and an increased majority in 1987; there was certainly no consensus for Thatcherism. Of course it

Question: 'When dealing with political opponents, what is better –
sticking firmly to one's political beliefs, or trying to meet them
halfway?'

month year	sticking to beliefs	meet half way	neither, both, don't know	balance of approval for 'Thatcherism'
6/83	50	39	11	+ 11
5/87	45	48	7	− 3

Question: 'In difficult economic times, what is better – for the
government to be caring or for the government to be tough?'

	tough	caring	neither etc	
6/83	46	34	20	+ 12
5/87	36	50	14	− 14

Question: 'When governments make decisions about the economy,
what is better – to involve major interests like trade unions and
business, or to keep them at arm's length?'

	keep at arm's length	involve interests	neither etc	
6/83	28	60	12	− 32
5/87	22	69	9	− 47

correlated with the vote, but much more closely with the 1983 vote
than with that of 1979. In other words, it was an important
component of vote-switching between the two elections.

There is an important technical point to make here. Responses to
attitude questions can be expected to correlate with party preference
if the questions deal with policies that have been associated with one
party or another for many years, or if they call for an evaluation of
the government's record. The Thatcherism scale does not fall into
this category. It contains neither specific policy references, nor does it
call for a judgement of the government's performance; rather it is

Question: 'It is sometimes said that no government of any party can in fact do much to create economic prosperity, that it is up to people themselves. Do you agree or disagree?'

	agree	disagree	neither etc	
6/83	48	37	15	+ 11
5/87	39	48	13	− 9

Question: 'In its relations with the rest of the world, what is better – for Britain to stick resolutely to its own position, or for Britain to meet other countries half way?'

	stick to own position	meet half way	neither etc	
6/83	30	58	12	− 28
5/87	28	63	9	− 35

	1983	1987
Average percentage supporting Thatcherite position	40.4%	34.0%
Average percentage opposing Thatcherite position	45.6%	55.6%

Table 8:   Thatcherism as a Style of Governing

concerned with the more abstract issues of statecraft. Yet it is strongly associated with the constancy and switching of votes between 1979 and 1983 (see Table 9). Take 1979 Conservative voters as an example. Among the majority who remained Conservative in 1983 there was a clear majority of Thatcherites (+ 37 per cent). But among the minority who switched to Labour (− 39 per cent) or the Alliance (− 21 per cent) they were outnumbered by anti-Thatcherites. The differences are very sharp. There is a similar, but reverse, pattern among 1979 Labour voters. Not surprisingly, perhaps, Thatcherites were in a small minority among Labour

Vote in 1979	Vote in 1983		
	Con	L/SDP	Lab
Con	+ 37	− 21	− 39
L/SDP	+ 12	− 23	− 88
Lab	+ 25	− 53	− 48
Did not vote	+ 27	− 43	− 61
Too young	+ 13	− 43	− 38

Note: Cell entries are the percentage majority of 'Thatcherites' over 'anti-Thatcherites', as defined in Table 8. For example, among those voting Conservative in both 1979 and 1983 the proportion of Thatcherites exceeded the proportion of anti-Thatcherites by 37%.

Table 9: Thatcherism as Statecraft and the Flow of the Vote 1979-83

loyalists (− 48 per cent) and indeed among Labour defectors to the Alliance. But a not insubstantial block switched right across to the Conservatives, and among them there was a clear Thatcherite majority (+ 25 per cent). Attitudes to Thatcherism as statecraft had a powerful discriminating impact in the 1983 election.

Whether a distinctive statecraft can form the basis of an enduring party realignment, however, seems doubtful. Style of government is bound up with the personality of the Prime Minister, and this Prime Minister, who so much prefers to bypass than reform political institutions, will bequeath few structural legacies for continuing the style after her departure. Could a Labour prime minister emulate Mrs Thatcher's style of government and get away with it? That too seems doubtful. For a Conservative leader has resources of support not available to Labour leaders: a far stronger constitutional position within the party; more patronage; a party ethic of unity and loyalty; and the replacement of the old parliamentary generation of gentlemenly amateurs by a new generation of professional players. Strong government is an electoral card dealt only to Conservative leaders.

Almost every government defeated at an election in this century lost authority before it lost office. Governments defeated at the polls forfeit votes for lack of authority, not authority for lack of votes. This is evidently true of four of the five defeats of government since the war – 1951, 1964, February 1974 and 1979. Among electors, policy and ideology have been mere cloaks for applying a *coup de grace* to a government already crippled by failure, division, scandal or sheer exhaustion. Cohesion, purpose and success take precedence over policy and ideology in voters' eyes; that is the lesson of Mrs Thatcher's and Thatcherism's astonishing success.

TWO

Margaret Thatcher as a Political Leader

ANTHONY KING

Almost everything that is ever said or written about Margaret Thatcher has a very high normative content. Almost every commentator is in the business of praising Mrs Thatcher or blaming her, of extolling her virtues or heaping abuse on her head. One reason why people take sides when they contemplate the present Prime Minister is that she has a strong public personality, and one that is the opposite of emollient. But another reason, equally important, is that people judge her in terms of her political, social and economic objectives. If they broadly approve of those objectives, they tend to think well of her; if they disapprove, they tend to think ill of her.

This is natural. All of us judge people partly in terms of their personalities and their values and goals. Nevertheless, in this essay I want to look at the Prime Minister, *as* Prime Minister, from a different angle. I want to look at her as a political operative, a political technician, someone whose job it is to match *her* political means to *her* political ends. After all, military analysts and historians ask of a military commander, 'Was he a great general? Was he a brilliant strategist? Was he skilful as a commander of men? How did he comport himself on the field of battle?' They only secondarily ask whether, in the war in question, he was fighting on the right side. It is in that spirit – a spirit of almost clinical detachment – that I intend to approach Mrs Thatcher's leadership here.[1]

Let me begin by asserting a proposition that will strike most readers as almost wilfully perverse. I want to assert that during most of this century the British Prime Ministership has *not* been a very important political office – prestigious certainly, desirable probably, but not in the end desperately important.

Here are some snippets of evidence – not conclusive, but suggestive – to support this bizarre-seeming contention.

Item. On 3 January 1988, Mrs Thatcher became the longest-serving Prime Minister of the twentieth-century. She came out on the doorstep of Number Ten and made a little speech in front of the television cameras. But was it in fact on 3 January, precisely, that she set her record? No one quite knows, because, as a number of journalists noted at the time, there are considerable doubts about when exactly Mr Asquith, the previous record-holder, became Prime Minister and also about when exactly he relinquished the office. As far as his becoming Prime Minister is concerned, strong arguments can be advanced in favour of dates anywhere from 5 April to 8 April 1908. As to when he stood down in 1916, a good case can be made out for 5 December, but an equally good case can be made out for 7 December.[2] The details do not matter, of course; but I offer the thought that, if the Prime Ministership were as important an office as it is often made out to be, there would not be any such doubts: historians would long since have felt compelled to settle the issue one way or the other, just as American historians are concerned to know, almost to the second, when Lyndon Johnson succeeded John F. Kennedy following the latter's assassination in 1963. The Presidency matters in the American system in a way that, in the British system, the Prime Ministership, usually, does not.

Another item, related. Ask any student of politics about the academic literature on the American Presidency and he or she will say that, quite apart from anything else, there is an enormous amount of it: several shelves of books, huge numbers of academic articles. Compare the literature on the British Prime Ministership. It scarcely exists: a few books, a very few articles. The most recent full-length book by an academic on the Prime Ministership was published as long ago as 1956, in the time of Sir Anthony Eden.[3] There are, to be sure, good reasons why the Prime Ministership is difficult to study: confidentiality is of the essence of the office (and not just under Mrs Thatcher). But confidentiality and secrecy are equally a problem in the United States. And much can be written about either country without the writer's needing to have access to state secrets. If the Prime Ministership in Britain had historically been of overweening importance, political scientists would surely have gone to the trouble of telling us more about it.

Yet another item, perhaps more telling than the others. One reason why people tend to exaggerate the Prime Ministership's importance – in addition, of course, to their tendency to focus on the wartime premierships of Lloyd George and Churchill – is that they naturally conflate changes of *Prime Minister* with changes in the *party in power*. Wilson comes to power in 1964 and again in 1974 – and important policy and other consequences follow. Likewise, Heath comes to power in 1970 – and important consequences follow. But are these consequences to be attributed to Wilson's and Heath's having become Prime Minister? Or are they to be attributed to the fact that in both cases, not only did someone new move into Ten Downing Street, but a new party, till then in opposition, became the government? Is it, in other words, the personality or the party that matters? There is good reason to think that, most of the time, it is the party that is more important.

Consider the following. There have, in this century, been twenty-two transfers of power from one Prime Minister to another. Of these twenty-two, slightly more than half – twelve – have coincided with a change in the party in power; the rest have taken place within the lifetime of a single party government, as a consequence of the party, for whatever reason, changing its leader.[4] Focus on this second category: for example, Salisbury to Balfour in 1902, Campbell-Bannerman to Asquith in 1908, Churchill to Eden in 1955, Eden to Macmillan in 1957, Macmillan to Home in 1963, Wilson to Callaghan in 1976. What is striking about almost all of these changes of Prime Minister – taking place while the same party remained in power – is that they did *not* result in major changes of policy or in very pronounced changes in the way in which the government was conducted. There have been exceptions, of course; the change from Stanley Baldwin to Neville Chamberlain in 1937, for instance, brought about considerable changes in policy and style. But these have been exceptions. Change the Prime Minister in Britain without also changing the party in power and, in general, nothing much happens. The Prime Minister turns out not to be (so to speak) the crucial variable. The importance of the office, to repeat, has been exaggerated.

Assume for the moment that this line of argument is correct. Why is it correct? What is there about the office of Prime Minister that limits – or has historically limited – its importance? There are, I think, three reasons, one familiar, the other two perhaps less so.

The first, familiar reason is that, under Britain's constitution, such as it is, the 'best' decisions – the most authoritative, those of the highest political quality – are taken, not by any minister acting alone, but by a collegial body, our equivalent of the Soviet politburo: the Cabinet. The Prime Minister is supposed to act on policy matters – and usually does act – only with the consent of, and in the name of, the Cabinet. Not only that, but the British Prime Minister, unlike the heads of government of many other countries, has only a very restricted basis of authority deriving from statute law. The British Prime Minister, unlike his or her colleagues, has almost no statutes to administer personally; there are almost no statutes – there may be none – that require him or her personally to take specific actions. In short, the British sytem is meant to be, and to a considerable degree is, a collegial system.

The second reason why Prime Ministerial power in Britain has historically been limited relates to the fact that a British Prime Minister – like the prime ministers of most other countries, but unlike the American or French presidents (impeachment apart) – is always vulnerable, in principle, to being sacked. Prime Ministers in the past have fallen – a fact that Prime Ministers in the present never forget, however invulnerable they may seem at any given moment. The result is that most Prime Ministers, in dealing with their Cabinets and their parties, tend to be cautious. They tend not to take policy initiatives; they tend not to go public with their personal views; they tend, in Cabinet, to advance their personal views very circumspectly. They are circumspect because, if they seek to give a lead on any given issue and they are defeated on that issue in Cabinet or elsewhere, they lose twice: they lose on the issue itself, but they also lose some portion of their authority. A man or woman who has been defeated once can be defeated again. Defeat may become routine. And routine defeat is not only debilitating in itself: it exposes the vulnerability of the holder of the office. Most Prime Ministers, as Richard Neustadt once pointed out, do not go about clad in riding boots and spurs: they are usually to be seen wearing sneakers.[5] Think, to take an admittedly extreme case, of Harold Wilson.

The third reason why Prime Ministerial power has historically been restricted is probably the least familiar. It is simply that most Prime Ministers, most of the time, have not sought to be powerful. Specifically, they have not had policy goals and agendas of their own distinct from those of their party or their Cabinet colleagues. They have not 'led' because they have not had anywhere distinctive that they wanted to go. Think of most post-war Prime Ministers – Attlee, Churchill, Macmillan, Wilson and so on – and it is clear that, most of the time, their own objectives were the objectives of their party or government, and that they regarded themselves principally as the managers of their government's and their party's political business: maintaining party unity, preventing Cabinet resignations, winning the next election, or whatever. Of course several of them had goals of their own – Macmillan, long before most of the rest of his colleagues, wanted Britain to join the Common Market – but these goals were almost always very limited, very specific. A Prime Ministerial policy agenda broad in scope and distinct from that of the Prime Minister's government or party: that has been very rare – indeed unknown, I think, in this century.

What, then, is one to say, against this background, about Margaret Thatcher? The short answer will already have occurred to every reader: she is different, *very* different. She has a broadly-based policy agenda of her own, an agenda distinct from that of most members of the Conservative Party. More to the point, she is determined that her agenda will be her Government's agenda and is therefore willing to assert herself – and willing to take risks with her authority and her own personal position – on an unprecedented scale. And she is successful. She has put her own personal stamp on the actions of her Government: it is a totally different government from what it would have been had anyone else been at the head of it since 1979. Try rerunning the history of the last eight years with, say, William Whitelaw, or Sir Geoffrey Howe, or Francis Pym, or Sir John Nott as

Prime Minister, and the point is made. To be sure, she has probably been defeated more often in her own cabinet than any other twentieth-century Prime Minister, especially in her first two years and in the months immediately following the Westland affair; but, although she has lost more often than most (probably all) of her predecessors, she has also won more often – far more often. This is, in simple truth, *her* government.

Two questions arise. Why does she do it? And how does she do it? Both are intriguing; but because the 'why' question has been asked and answered so much more often than the 'how' question, it is on the 'how' question that I want to concentrate here.

In setting out to provide a partial answer to that question, let me begin – some will say, 'How could one begin anywhere else?' – with Machiavelli. A famous chapter of *The Prince*, Chapter 17, is entitled: 'Cruelty and compassion; and whether it is better to be loved than feared, or the reverse'. Machiavelli is talking about the relationship between the prince and his subjects, but much of his analysis can be made to apply equally to the relationship between the prince and his close circle of colleagues, supporters and advisors. Ivor Crewe writes elsewhere in this volume on the relationship between Mrs Thatcher and the British people. The focus here is on how Mrs Thatcher succeeds *within* government: that is, on her relations with her own Cabinet, her other ministers and civil servants and Conservative M.P.S.

Is it, asks Machiavelli, better to be loved than feared, or the reverse?

The answer [he says] is that one would like to be both the one and the other; but because it is difficult to combine them, it is far better to be feared than loved if you cannot be both . . . Men worry less about doing an injury to one who makes himself loved than to one who makes himself feared. The bond of love is one which men, wretched creatures that they are, break when it is to their advantage to do so; but fear is strengthened by a dread of punishment which is always effective . . . I conclude that since men love as they please but fear when the prince pleases, a wise prince should rely on what he controls, not on what he cannot control.

But Machiavelli is not as unsubtle as that passage, taken by itself, implies. He adds:

> The prince should nonetheless make himself feared in such a way that, if he is not loved, at least he escapes being hated. For fear is quite compatible with an absence of hatred . . . If . . . it proves necessary to execute someone, this should be done only when there is proper justification and manifest reason for it.[6]

How does the present Prime Minister match up to these standards? The answer is: admirably. Mrs Thatcher is, in her personal dealings, a considerate person. She has no trouble in winning the affection and loyalty of those in her immediate circle, principally at Number Ten Downing Street. This should never be forgotten. Nevertheless, it is perfectly clear that, in her relations with her fellow ministers, civil servants and Conservative M.P.s, her distinctive weapon – far more than in the cases of men like Churchill, Macmillan or Wilson – is fear. She seeks to control the content of public policy and, through it, Britain's destiny. She must therefore control her Government. She must therefore, following Machiavelli, seek to rely on what she can control, namely fear, not on what she cannot control, namely love – which, as Machiavelli says, men bestow as *they* please, not as the prince pleases.

Machiavelli cites the case of Cesare Borgia, and it possibly needs to be pointed out that, in Mrs Thatcher's case, the use of fear as a political weapon does not imply the use of the chopping block or the garrotte. On the contrary, those whom Mrs Thatcher politically executes can look forward to a knighthood, if they are lucky, to a life peerage, if they are still luckier. Twentieth-century Britain is an altogether gentler place than sixteenth-century Italy. Rather, Mrs Thatcher uses fear in two less malign ways that are nevertheless equally effective.

The first is by means of face-to-face fear: 'fear at first hand'. Her use of fear in this form is well known, and there is no need to go into detail here. Mrs Thatcher has a formidable personality, and she is capable of hectoring, cajoling, threatening, wrong-footing, bullying, embarrassing and even humiliating her ministers and officials. She is, in this respect, the Lyndon Johnson of modern British politics.

Johnson discovered that people will take a lot from as powerful a person as the President of the United States; Mrs Thatcher has made the same discovery about the British Prime Minister. She puts the fear of God into people, and they usually respond well. Of course, there is no need to use this particular weapon very often: fear of being on the receiving end of a Prime Ministerial tongue-lashing – or even merely of Prime Ministerial *froideur* – is usually adequate to the purpose.

One specific aspect of her use of face-to-face fear is worth mentioning. Mrs Thatcher long ago observed that most well-brought-up Englishmen – especially, though not only, if they went to a public school – have no idea what to do with a strong, assertive woman. Not only are they brought up not to be rude to women: they find it very difficult in general to deal with women in the same matter-of-fact, direct way that they deal with men. Women to them are mothers or nannies to be feared or sisters to be bullied (or, alternatively, adored); they are not colleagues and fellow-politicians, to be stood up to all the time and shouted at when necessary. The average Englishman of the middle and upper classes simply quails in the presence of a formidable female personality, torn between the desire to strike and the desire to sulk, not knowing what an appropriate response would be. Mrs Thatcher long ago noticed that such Englishmen found it hard to stand up to her – and conceived a considerable contempt for the whole tribe. As one of her former ministers, Sir John Nott, said in a recent television interview, she thinks all men are 'wimps' (presumably because they behave in such a wimpish way in her presence). Not all men are afraid of her as a woman, of course; but many are. It helps.

The other way in which Mrs Thatcher uses fear is related to an important change in the 'occupational sociology' of British politics. There was a time when a considerable number of Britain's politicians were not solely, or even primarily, politicians. Ernest Bevin was a trade union leader; Sir Stafford Cripps was a leading Q.C.; Oliver Lyttelton, the first Lord Chandos, was a leading industrialist; and so on. That time is not yet quite past, but it is rapidly disappearing. More and more of Britain's politicians are 'career politicians', in the sense that they regard politics as their primary occupation, their calling in life. Personal ambition for them takes the form of a desire to become a government minister, then, having become one, to rise up the ministerial hierarchy, then, having risen in the hierarchy, to become and remain a member of the Cabinet. Such people, such 'career politicians', if they sit on the government side of the House of Commons, obviously depend utterly on the Prime Minister of the day for the fulfilment or non-fulfilment of their ambitions. The Prime Minister can raise them to heaven or cast them into outer darkness. Britain's Prime Minister has, of course, always had the power to hire and fire ministers: it is the conjunction of this power with the rise of the ambitious career politician that nowadays makes the power of such transcendent importance.[7]

Mrs Thatcher knows this – or at any rate behaves as though she knows it. She has used her power to appoint and dismiss ministers to create a government almost entirely in her own image. More to the point, she has used the fear of not being appointed, and the fear, having been appointed, of being sacked, to discipline the scores of ambitious young men on the Conservative back benches and also the existing members of her administration. Any minister thinking of stepping out of line need only recall – or have recalled to him – the fates of Norman St John-Stevas, Mark Carlisle, Lord Soames, Sir Ian Gilmour, Francis Pym, Jim Prior (though he took care to jump before he was pushed) and, most recently, the once-loved John Biffen. Several of these men were not career politicians in the sense in which I have been using the term; they were part of an older, more detached tradition of British politics. They spoke out. They were turfed out. And it goes without saying that many of those who have remained inside the government have gradually altered their political views as time has gone on. Originally appointed as 'Heathites' or 'wets', they now boast of being in the Thatcherite mainstream. In this case, no names, no pack drill. As Machiavelli says, it is better, if one has to choose, to be feared rather than loved.

It is worth emphasising in this connection that Mrs Thatcher, far more than any other twentieth-century Prime Minister, has used her hiring-and-firing power single-mindedly to produce a team of ministers loyal to her person and, more important, to her policy agenda. Other Prime Ministers have used the appointment power to embrace within their government everyone in their party of outstanding ability, or everyone with a factional following in their party, or everyone who, left outside, might threaten them politically. The aim, historically, has been to produce a 'balanced' Cabinet – one in which all the tensions and divisions in the governing party have been reproduced – and also one with a broad appeal to the public. In insisting on having a Cabinet united in the pursuit of lines of policy determined by the Prime Minister, Mrs Thatcher is, as in so much else, unique.

A great deal more could be said in response to the question 'How does she do it?': about her capacity for work; about her ability to gauge accurately her own power and the power of other people; about her mountain-climber-like ability to combine extreme caution with a breathtaking willingness to take risks. Richard Neustadt, whom I quoted a moment ago, defines a head of government's 'professional reputation' as the belief in the minds of his fellow-politicians that he has the skill and will to use to the full all of the bargaining advantages afforded by his office.[8] Mrs Thatcher has a high professional reputation. She guards it. She enlarges it. She makes use of it. It has slipped only once (and then, as it turned out, only temporarily): during the Westland affair of 1985–6.

It would be tempting to explore all of these themes; but I want to use the rest of this essay to examine a different aspect of the present Prime Minister's pursuit of her policy goals.

Let me suggest, in the broadest and most general terms, that someone in authority can adopt one or other of two quite different approaches to the making of policy. (I refer to government, but the same is probably true of an industrial firm, a trade union or a university.)

The first approach can be called 'deliberative'. Using this approach, the policy maker defines his goals, narrowly or broadly. He then decides what needs to be done – and who needs to do it – if his goals are to be achieved. He asks and answers questions that have to do with feasibility and political costs and benefits. Are my goals technically achievable? What practical steps need to be taken if they are to be achieved? Who needs to take those steps? Is whoever needs to take them in fact willing to take them? Will pursuing these goals get in the way of my other goals? And so on. Deliberative policy-making, as its name implies, involves not merely forethought on the part of the policy-maker: it involves deliberating with other participants, and potential participants, in the business of deciding on the details of the policy and actually putting them into effect. Deliberative policy-making is bound to be an iterative process, a back-and-forth process, both intellectually and in political and administrative terms.

The second approach is quite different. It might be called 'declarative'. Using it, the policy-maker begins, not by deliberating, but by declaring publicly what his goals are, by nailing his colours to the mast in the most visible possible fashion. The goals having been publicly stated, it is then up to the policy-maker – or, more probably, his colleagues and subordinates – to decide how they are to be achieved in practice. Underlying this approach is the belief that public declarations maximise the chances of goal-achieving success. The policy-maker, having made a public declaration, is unlikely to back away from his goal. Everyone knows what the goal is. And everyone also knows what the man or woman in charge expects of them: total commitment followed by success. To fail to achieve the declared goal is to risk courting the policy-maker's wrath – and of causing his or her political defeat and humiliation.

The advantages of these two approaches – the deliberative and the declarative – are fairly obvious. In the deliberative case, the costs of the policy, as well as its benefits, will gradually become apparent; and, if the policy is not technically or politically achievable, that, too will become apparent. In addition, precisely because the process is deliberative, and precisely because efforts are made to ensure that all relevant factors are brought on board, the policy goal, if it is achieved at all, is likely to stay achieved, to 'stick'. The advantages of the declarative approach are the ones already indicated: if the person in authority can command sufficient support, the mere fact that the policy has been publicly declared increases the chances of its being adopted, of its not being sabotaged or its purposes subverted.

But the disadvantages of the two approaches are also fairly obvious. The deliberative approach is bound to be time-consuming. It is almost certain to be patience-consuming too. And, as the process of deliberation proceeds, the policy-maker's goals may subtly change. The entire policy may run into the ground, as people pay lip service to it while trying to undermine it or, alternatively, claim that their cooperation is essential to the policy while at the same time refusing to cooperate. The disadvantage of the declarative approach, as must be obvious, is that it is a *very* high risk approach. To declare that something is one's policy is not only to put one's policy in the firing line: it is to put oneself in the firing line. Indeed that is one of its purposes. But, if the policy fails, or if it cannot be implemented because it proves technically impossible or because sufficient political support is not forthcoming, then it is the policy-maker who, unmistakably, carries the can. Moreover, declarative policy making, precisely because it is public, boxes the policy-maker in. He or she cannot retreat from the declaration or policy without losing face – and 'face' in this connection means reputation: credibility and authority.

How does Mrs Thatcher fit into all this? One has to be careful about answering this question too hastily. The present Prime Minister's policy-making approach, despite what one might expect on the basis of her personal style, has frequently been extremely deliberative. It has been deliberative over the reform of tax policy, over the evolution of youth training policy, over the withdrawal of subsidies from loss-making state industries. It has been deliberative, not least, over the reform of trade union law, where the government's step-by-step approach has, from its point of view, been a brilliant success. Mrs Thatcher is a subtle, adaptable politician, more so than is often realised.

But of course her approach to government is frequently also of the declarative kind. We will retake the Falklands. The declaration of ends first, the means to follow. We will abolish the Greater London Council and the other metropolitan authorities. Again, declaration first, the mechanics later. We will abolish I.L.E.A. Ditto. Likewise, we will abolish the rates. The declaration was made as long ago as 1974, but the details of the policy are still being worked out. The Education Reform Bill is in many ways a similar case, though the Prime Minister's involvement in parts of it is only indirect. Moreover, and significantly, the ratio of declarative to deliberative policy making is clearly increasing. This kind of policy-making, having proved so successful in the past, notably over the Falklands and the G.L.C., and being so congenial to the Prime Minister's personality, is being used more and more in the present.

Does this matter? I think it does – or at least it may. Suppose one were the Prime Minister's chief political adviser, had her complete trust and was able therefore to talk to her completely freely. What ways of behaving, as Prime Minister, might one be warning her about?

One, of course, would be hubris. All successful people, especially those who have succeeded against the odds, are in danger of becoming isolated, over-proud and, worst of all, careless. Machiavelli, as usual, puts the point well: 'A prince should be slow to take action, and should watch that he does not come to be afraid of his own shadow; his behaviour should be tempered by humanity and prudence so that over-confidence does not make him rash or excessive distrust make him unbearable.'[9] How great the risk of hubris is to Mrs Thatcher it is hard for an outsider to say. On the one hand, she occasionally seems to show signs of it. On the other, her natural caution, one of the deepest laid elements in her personality, should never be overlooked.

Perhaps she also needs to be warned about the possibility that fear may turn into – may already have turned into – hatred. 'The prince,' as Machiavelli says, 'should make himself feared in such a way that, if he is not loved, at least he escapes being hated.' Absence of love means that a political leader, if he or she gets into trouble, has no reservoir of generalised affection to draw on, as Edward Heath discovered to his cost in 1975. The presence of positive hatred means that one's political enemies – and one's political enemies are always in one's own party – are waiting to take advantage of any stumbles or signs of weakness, however slight. But, again, it is impossible for an outsider to say for sure how widely Mrs Thatcher is hated in the Government and the Tory party. By Mr Heath certainly, but by who else? Just as her natural caution should never be overlooked, neither should her natural charm and her genuine concern for the well-being of many of her fellow politicians and their families. Machiavelli says that, if one decides to carry out an execution, it should always be 'when there is proper justification and manifest reason for it'. All of

Mrs Thatcher's political executions probably fall into this category. None seems to have been an exercise of purely personal spite.

But a serious warning would undoubtedly have to include, in addition, the risks of declarative policy-making. The attractions of this style are enormous: if one wants to move mountains, one probably has to announce in advance that mountain-moving is the name of the game. But the dangers are also enormous. Mrs Thatcher evidently sensed this at the time of the 1984–5 miners' strike, when she carefully avoided saying that her object was the total defeat of the miners until the strike was very nearly over – and won. But both the poll tax and the Education Reform Bill, neither very clearly thought through, pose evident dangers to the government and to Mrs Thatcher's personal position – especially the poll tax, which seems on the face of it a classic instance of how *not* to set about making public policy: the stakes are too high; the probability of failure is too great; the goal in itself is probably not worth it. And Mrs Thatcher is indubitably, inescapably identified with the whole enterprise.

At the beginning of this essay, I stated that my aim was to look at the Prime Minister *as* Prime Minister – in a detached way, as a political leader, quite apart from the specifics of her political and other goals. I have, for instance, my own views about the poll tax, just like everyone else; but my concern has been to look at the poll tax, not from my point of view, but from hers. I know whether I like it. Should she, from where she sits, like it?

But what about the deliberate use of fear as a political weapon, albeit within her own party and administration? Fear is not a morally attractive weapon; even Machiavelli acknowledges that. But is it sometimes a necessary weapon? Given the sheer scale of everything that Mrs Thatcher has wanted to achieve, could she have achieved it with only love and rational arguments as her weapons? Could the inevitable, and massive, resistances have been overcome without the use of fear? I wonder. I am inclined to doubt it. But it is at least a good question. I leave the reader with it.

THREE

The 1987 General Election in Historical Perspective

DAVID BUTLER

My essay is different from the others in this volume in that it does not direct itself to the particular impact of Mrs Thatcher or the way in which government has been changed by her. Yet I think it nests well enough among the rest because it deals with the basic pre-conditions of Britain's democratic politics as exemplified in the thirteen elections of the post-war period. I am concerned with the changing social and political forces that have made possible the rule of the current Conservative government and its three successive election victories.

What I am going to write about is, in a way, an egotistical story, for I have been in an indirect way concerned with all those thirteen elections. I was twenty-one in 1945 when, discharged from the army by an administrative mistake, I returned to Oxford and at once became involved in helping R. B. McCallum to write a book entitled, *The British General Election of 1945*. I have been writing about elections ever since and have been involved in each of the thirteen successive studies that Nuffield College has sponsored.

I want to draw your attention to the similarities and the differences that have characterised British elections over the last forty years. One of the few attractions of age is that it enables one to see things in a personal perspective; one begins to see directly how then turns into now. I have been concerned all my life with writing contemporary history, recording events while they're still alive, while the people at the centre of affairs can still react to what is said about them. I come from a family of historians and I am aware of the prejudice against contemporary history, the doubt whether anyone can write immediately after an event with the kind of detachment which should be possible about the distant past. I don't accept that stricture on writing about the present. I remember my grandfather A. F. Pollard, an established Tudor historian, talking to me as a small boy about Martin Luther with a passion and indignation that I have never managed to deploy about any of the politicians of whom I have approved or disapproved in my own contemporary world. I don't think that detachment presents a special difficulty. There are, of course, problems of perspective, but, having supervised people writing theses about the elections of 1880 and 1906, I have tried to assess whether I was better or worse off when writing immediately after an election and trying to establish the truth about it.

Many years ago in Peterborough Cathedral, I came across the grave of Bishop Mandell Creighton, who died in 1901. On his tombstone is the wonderful short epitaph: 'He tried to write true history'. I have often thought of that as an examination question. When last could anyone have unself-consciously written such words on a tombstone? We all know about the relativity of truth nowadays. Such simplicity must be taboo. Yet, if I try and ask the question of whether when looking back at writing *The British General Election of 1951*, my first book, I got nearer to the truth than my admirable pupil, Trevor Lloyd, did a few years later when writing about the Election of 1880, there are, of course, plusses and minuses to the account. But I am willing to defend the plusses as being slightly bigger than the minuses. I wanted to make that preface before considering writing about, and the substance of, the post-war general elections.

Many aspects of the elections remain unchanged: indeed they are astonishingly the same as in 1945. The Prime Minister still arrogates to himself or herself the right to dissolve Parliament at the moment of his or her choice, after which there are four weeks or so of the election campaign, Constituency election expenses continue to be strictly limited and the routine conduct of the campaign still echoes the Victorian rituals of canvassing and marking up the register and the polling day routines around the booths. Such activities remain unchanged. Moreover, the franchise has not been significantly altered since 1945, apart from lowering the age to eighteen.

But despite these notable continuities, the 1987 election was extraordinarily different from that of 1950. I remember Mr Attlee being driven around by Violet Attlee in the pre-war family saloon, with a large detective sitting in the back, but no other entourage at all, speaking night after night in big fifty-minute orations at mass rallies in the major centres, and during the day at street corner or market place gatherings. I remember Winston Churchill more regally going out by special train and making grand speeches three or four nights a week. It was a very different world from that which Gordon Reece and others have conjured up around Mrs Thatcher since 1979, and from that which Peter Mandelson provided for Neil Kinnock in 1987.

The party headquarters did not do much in elections forty years ago. They were routine administrative bodies sending out party literature to the constituencies and providing technical advice on election law. There was very little grand strategy involved. By an extraordinary chance, which has made all subsequent excitements in my life seem slightly anti-climatic, I was summoned down at the beginning of February 1950 to Chartwell to talk to Mr Churchill about an article I had written in the *Economist*. He couldn't quite remember why he'd asked me, but he thought he ought to put on a performance and for four hours he refought the Dundee by-election of 1908 and the grand days of 1940 and the *angst* of the 1945 election defeat. During those four hours he was not interrupted by phone calls from colleagues about the latest crisis or anything else that had happened. He didn't seem to be at the centre of any great web of activity. I am quite certain that if I had spent four hours with Mrs Thatcher or Mr Kinnock during this election, not only would they have been rather less congenial, but I would not have had such uninterrupted attention from the leader of a great party.

In 1950 the B.B.C. solved the problems of neutrality during election campaigns by a total silence, eschewing all coverage of the contest in its news bulletins. If you had listened to the radio consistently through the 1950, 1951 and 1955 elections the only thing you would have heard were absolutely formal reports like 'nominations closed today' or 'polling will take place next Thursday'. Of course, there were party election broadcasts – five twenty- or 30-minute slots allotted to the Conservative and to the Labour Party, and three to the Liberals. That was how the game was played in 1950. People got their news about elections from a highly partisan press, but a press that actually gave them far more solid news than popular newspapers offer today in their election reports. At that time the campaigns seemed to me to be, in a way, extraordinarily isolated. The two parties were manoeuvring on quite separate battlefields against straw armies of their own devising. There was virtually no interlocking between the rival campaigns. It was a very different world from the one we know today.

The turning point was 1959. It was in 1959 that we first saw many of the phenomena that we now recognise as the central characteristics of an election campaign. One of them occurred by accident – the daily press conference. Hugh Gaitskell had asked Dick Crossman to look after publicity, aided by Chris Mayhew, Tony Benn and Woodrow Wyatt. Something had to be done to keep Morgan Phillips, the rather *passé* general secretary of the party, quiet. They asked him to manage the daily press briefing which hitherto had comprised unimportant routine announcements of the leaders' schedules. Morgan Phillips seized the opportunity brilliantly and in a competitive way. For the first week of the election he got three times more column inches in the *Daily Telegraph* for Labour than the Conservatives could secure; this was because he was providing such good copy that even the *Daily Telegraph* couldn't refrain from splashing his story. He made the press conference into the central feature of the election day, a must for the journalists covering the campaign, and every other party followed suit. The journalists found that by moving across Smith Square from Transport House to Conservative Central Office, with the Liberals doing their best to get into the act somewhere nearby, they could within three hours each morning put together a full campaign story. The daily press conference did much to interlock the rival campaign in 1959 – and in every subsequent contact with journalists taking questions from one side to the other, usually spontaneously but sometimes spurred on by prods from within the party headquarters.

Another innovation of 1958-9 was the arrival of mass advertising. It had been thought for many years that political advertising was illegal because of Section 63 of the Representation of the People Act – 'No person other than the duly authorised agent may incur expenses with a view to promoting or procuring the election of a candidate'. It was believed that a newspaper advertisement saying 'Vote Conservative' would be construed as 'Vote for Bloggs in this constituency'. In 1951, at the instigation of the Labour Party, a test case was brought against the Tronoh-Malayan mining company which had placed a long and unreadable advertisement in *The Times* and other papers attacking socialist policy; the courts decided that, since the advertisement did not mention any specific candidates, it was legal. Coleman, Prentis and Varley, then the Conservative Party's advertising agents, put out what many regard as the most compelling party advertisements this country has seen: 'Life's better with the Conservatives. Don't let Labour ruin it'. This slogan was paid the compliment of almost verbatim repetition in the Conservatives' final campaign advertisements of 1987. But if 1959 saw the first of these nationwide poster campaigns linked to a limited amount of press advertising, it was only in the last three elections that press advertising has been used on a massive scale.

Another development of 1959 was the coming of private opinion polls. In this, oddly enough, Transport House was the initiator; Mark Abrams did private polling for the Labour Party which certainly had an impact on the nature and planning of their campaign. Competitive public opinion polls arrived at the same time. From 1945 to 1955 Gallup had provided the only serious poll and its findings were reported exclusively in the *News Chronicle*. In 1959 there were four rival polls regularly reported in the national press.

But far the biggest development in 1959 was the advent of television news coverage and of other kinds of broadcast reporting of the election. All the routine current affairs programmes, *Panorama* and the rest, gave up their time during the three weeks of the campaign to putting on reports or confrontations about particular issues and how they had been and should be treated by the parties. This transformed the nature of elections in a fundamental way. By 1964 a great majority of people were telling pollsters that they relied on television for most of their information about the election.

After 1959 the 1987 contest stands out as the next major landmark in electioneering. Most of the phenomena I am about to discuss were manifest in earlier campaigns; some of them go back to the

1960s, and most have their roots in 1979 or 1983. However, in 1987 they seemed to reach an altogether new peak and to involve all parties, and most notably the Labour Party which in the past had behaved as though there was something unclean about getting involved in huckstering. Labour showed itself reluctant to abandon Nye Bevan's belief that the art of the politician was to know about people and how to communicate to them, and that he should be above professional prompting about the subject. Bevan objected to private polls in 1959 on the grounds that 'you are taking the poetry out of politics'. By now the poetry has indeed been taken out of elections on a rather grand scale – and that is, in a sense, the central theme of this essay.

The most obvious characteristic of the last ten years has been that our elections have become more presidential. The Nuffield series of general election studies usually contain an admirable chapter by Martin Harrison which, among other things, chronicles the exact number of minutes given in news time to the party leaders. You will see in his tables the dominance of the two party leaders, particularly on television. The result is not necessarily that people vote for the persons of Margaret Thatcher or Neil Kinnock but, in so far as viewers receive an image of what the Conservative or Labour parties stand for, it is received through the top leaders's words. Of course Baldwin and Macdonald or Gladstone and Disraeli were the dominant figures in their party campaigns fifty or a hundred years ago, but the actual day-to-day message that the British electorate receives now comes, to a degree unknown before, through the words and the face and the character of the party leaders. A television news editor has only got so many camera teams, and he can only give twenty minutes to the election. He must have camera teams with the Conservative, Labour and Alliance leaders; he won't want additional expensive teams out covering secondary or tertiary figures since he can fill his news story with the message of the parties as expressed by their leaders. Even when the party leaders have tried to play down their role, or when, as in 1983, the Labour Party thought it inexpedient to emphasise its leader, there was little real choice. The story carried on television was, to an overwhelming degree, about the leaders.

A second change, more extreme in 1987 than ever before, was the increased amount of money spent. In real terms the party outlays were ten times greater than those of 1951, and nearly twice those of 1983. At the constituency level, elections have got cheaper and cheaper. Michael Pinto-Duschinsky has written an important book about the cost of politics over the last 150 years in which he shows the extraordinary reduction in real terms of constituency expenditure. However, in 1987 there was far more press advertising than ever before. In the last week of the campaign Lord McAlpine, the Conservative treasurer, worked on the principle that 'I would rather be a poor party in government than a rich party in opposition,' and, in a prodigal way, he authorised the spending of vast sums. Between 8 June and 11 June 1987, there were eleven full pages of Conservative advertising in *The Times*. Most of the other nationals carried an equal amount. Around £5 million was spent by the Conservatives on press advertising during the election. It is very doubtful whether it was worthwhile. I would very much like to see a ban on display advertising in the press during campaigns comparable to that on political advertising on television. I am in favour of freedom, but I believe that messages can be got across in other ways. A ban on press advertising would save a great deal of money – and of party indebtedness to the people and institutions who have the money to give. If there were such a ban, I don't see that there would be any loss in real communication; the only people to suffer would be the press tycoons.

A third feature of the 1987 election was that press partisanship got more extreme. This may sound very ivory-towerish, but I was appalled when, as a matter of duty, I read all the popular papers during the election. Reading *The Sun* and, to a slightly smaller extent, the *Daily Mirror* and the *Daily Star*, I was shocked by the total abrogation of the news reporting function by these papers. In so far as they covered politics, they behaved merely as partisan sheets selling the virtues of one side or the other. Of course, the press has always been partisan, but in the early 1950s it made more of an attempt at serious news coverage. Obviously in this I exempt those dailies that really tried to report the election, the *Independent*, the *Guardian*, the *Daily Telegraph* and *The Times*.

Another feature of 1987 was the increase in published opinion polls. About sixty nationwide surveys were reported in the press. Newspapers had discovered that £8–10,000 is a great deal of money to spend to pay for twenty column inches, the cost of a reputable poll today. However, it is a small sum to spend for receiving a mention on all the nightly news broadcast bulletins, as well as a mention in all the rival newspapers. Sometime in the 1960s the financiers of the press recognised this basic truth. Newspapers stopped making their polls exclusive stories. They now leak them to each other, and still more to the television bulletins, so that they get coverage for their polls in all the rival media, with full citation of their own names. This is what has encouraged an orgy of polling, which has emphasised more than ever before the appeal of the election as a sporting event. Racing tipsterism about the possible outcome takes precedence over the substantive arguments of politics. There was a front page story about the polls on well over half the issues of *The Times* during the election, whether reporting of *The Times*' own polls or of those of their rivals.

1987 also saw the further development of a phenomenon that has only been seriously manifest since the late 1970s – photo-opportunities and media events. Mrs Thatcher puts on wellington boots and tramps around the farm; Mr Kinnock goes to a bakery and wears a starched white hat. Leaders do all sorts of things that they would not do in ordinary life but which they know will, by their very oddity, produce photographs to which the news editors on i.t.n. or even the *Observer* will give full prominence. Who could resist shots of well-known, instantly recognisable public figures doing some-thing absurd, and doing it early enough in the day for the photo to be processed for presentation? Although one always hopes that the press will show some self-restraint, in 1987 the parties exploited this more systematically than ever before. The b.b.c. did try to lay down a policy decision not to use stories that had no actual content what-soever, but they could not always resist the temptation. There had been a moment of hope in 1979 when Mrs Thatcher issued a photo call to be seen at 8 a.m. in a field in Norfolk cuddling a new-born calf; the photographers got mutinous and started photographing the photographers who were photographing Mrs Thatcher and the new-born calf. For once a media occasion was sent up in ridicule. Nonetheless the press still buys into far too many of the photo-opportunities that they are offered. They occasionally mock them or protest; the public is becoming rather more cynical, but is not as sophisticated as one might like about such non-events, which throw no real light on who is most fitted to run the country and occupy a disproportionate amount of contemporary election coverage.

Another phenomenon which was particularly manifest in 1987 was the speeding up of the election due to the party managers' assumption that the television news editors were the most important people in the election, and that they would be very quickly bored with any one lead story, however important. What heads the news at lunchtime will seldom last till nightfall; a fresh lead is needed by 6 o'clock, and another by 9 o'clock, and the parties are ready to supply them. So if somebody raises a really interesting and important point at one of the morning press conferences, the story has got to be carried forward by the media people who are fixing the election in Smith Square. They will supply a comment to top the latest comment, or produce a brand new lead story. It is very seldom that the same theme will head the news through each successive bulletin of the day, even though most voters are only exposed to a single newscast. It is felt that something else must be found to stir things up. The first story, if it lasts at all, will be carried lower down the bulletin. In 1950 the big news item would have been a speech by Winston Churchill or Clement Attlee at 9 o'clock at night, unreported on the radio but carried extensively in the next morning's newspapers. Now no party leader ever speaks later than 7 p.m. because there is no point in doing so – it will be dead copy by next day. The leaders always arrange their schedule so that the film or the video-tape of anything they say or do is ready for the studios in time for the 9 or 10 o'clock T.V. bulletins.

Other technical innovations marked the 1987 election. The vodaphone arrived at press conferences, so that one would actually see journalists dictating their copy while the party leaders were speaking. There were, it is true, complaints from party officials in both the Kinnock and the Thatcher camps about the awful dead spots around the country where, for half an hour or so, the battle bus was out of range of the Cellnet and it was impossible to keep in touch with headquarters; were the other side to say something important, they could not secure an immediate authorised quote from the boss to be used in reply. No doubt by the 1991 general election the telephone radio network will have spread across the country, so that this little technological hiccough will be a thing of the past.

There was, it is clear, much more conscious manipulation in the 1987 election. John Desborough in Conservative Central Office and Peter Mandelson at Labour headquarters both did a splendidly professional job of ringing up friendly journalists, pushing to the top of the agenda a story which they thought had some mileage for their own parties.

At the constituency level there was a great development in the use of computers. In some cases they were exploited in a sophisticated way to organise polling day telling and knocking up. On both the Conservative and Labour side most marginal seats had computers, but they were seldom used very efficiently. Things will be different by next election, though they may not make much difference to the outcome.

There is an odd paradox at the end of this story, and it's not a narrowly British point. Immediately after the Westminster contest I went to Canberra for the Australian election, which also culminated on 11 July with their prime minister being elected to a third term in office (albeit a Labour Prime Minister). There I watched exactly the same things happening, though perhaps in not quite so sophisticated a fashion. Elections anywhere must be duller and flatter when accidents don't happen. In February 1974 the Conservatives got into a terrible mess when the 'Figgures figures' emerged late one afternoon, suggesting that the miners were underpaid, not overpaid, and nobody was available in Conservative Central Office to provide a rebuttal during that crucial period from 6 p.m. to 9 p.m. when television bulletins are being prepared and newspapers are putting their morning editions to bed. Nowadays every party takes full precautions against such misfortunes. In a technical sense, the Labour Party fought a particularly impressive campaign in the 1987 election. Peter Mandelson knew what he wanted on each day of the campaign: he communicated to all the leading figures in the Party what the theme for the day should be, and they didn't deviate from it. Except for some slight flutters at the end they were not diverted onto other issues. On both sides the whole campaign was so much more professionally packaged that those accidents that give life to an election didn't happen. It was the same in the Antipodes. Both here and in Australia, 1987 offered the dullest of the dozen or so elections I have so far observed in both countries. Politicians played safe, and in future they will probably play safer still. We are in a different world.

Hardly any seats changed hands in by-elections from 1945 to 1957, and not very many between 1957 and 1965. Since 1966 the proportions have changed enormously: one by-election in three has seen a change in party control.

Why is the British electorate so much more volatile nowadays? Let me offer four reasons. In the first place, the experience of the last twenty-five years has seen power changing hands four times. In the decade up to 1964 it was possible to believe that the nation's ills were the fault of the Tories. But when the Labour Party came to office in 1964, it soon seemed to adopt Conservative remedies, while the nation went from bad to worse in the international growth league. By 1970 it was possible to see the country's problems as all the fault of the Labour government. But when the Conservatives came back under Mr Heath they too made their U-turn and adopted Labour remedies. The same happened again when Labour came back in 1974.

Although it is easy to see why events in the 1960s and 1970s gave powerful encouragement to the voters' scepticism about whether any one party possessed a remedy for the nation's problems, what has occurred after 1979 may be a slightly different story. As these lectures show, Thatcherism has provoked some major problems. How far is it a basically new phenomenon? And how far is that phenomenon due to one person?

A second reason for increased volatility lies in the fact that the public has become more educated. In 1945 over 94 per cent of the electors had ended formal schooling at fourteen or earlier. Now the school leaving age is sixteen, and vastly more people go on to tertiary or further education. The more educated people are, the more they cherish the idea or the delusion that they are open-minded, and not bound by some primal party loyalty.

The third reason for volatility lies in the general cross-pressures of a changing society. In 1945 29 per cent of the British people lived in owner-occupied houses, and 70 per cent of the employed were manual workers. Today 66 per cent of people live in owner-occupied houses, and 51 per cent are in white-collar jobs. Almost every family has members on both sides of the class divide, cross-pressured rather than confirmed in their solidary class loyalties by their neighbours and their relations. This has made voters much more ready to switch.

The last, and far the most important, cause for increased volatility is the coming of television as the main source of communication. Since the mid-1950s when people have been asked where they got most of their news about politics from, 80 per cent have answered 'from television'. But what is television politics? The B.B.C. by its charter, and the I.T.A. by law, are required to maintain political balance. But what is balance? The television presenters usually offer talking heads in a 'balanced' discussion which tends to consist of two Oxbridge smoothies in a kid-glove argument first-naming each other, and in effect telling the British people that there is more in common between two elected persons of different parties than between an elected person and a non-elected person of the same party.

However, one reservation must be made about the 1987 election. It was a special situation. The end result (43%, 32%, 23%) for the three parties was more or less what the polls had been saying at the beginning. One could argue that it was a campaign which had no impact, but one could equally well point out that it was the first election in seven in which the party that was ahead in the polls did not slip back in the final outcome. In the seven contests from 1964 to 1983 it seemed to be one of the rules of the game that there would be some revulsion against the predicted landslide. The party that was ahead in the polls always fared worse than predicted when the votes were counted. That did not happen in 1987. That does not necessarily obviate the lesson of the previous seven elections. The phenomenon will probably manifest itself again as the years go by, simply because the voters have shown themselves increasingly changeable.

A long-term look at British elections since the war suggests that the most fundamental change in the British electorate over the last forty years has been this increase in volatility. Voters are much more prone to switch. The Gallup poll has conducted monthly polls since 1945. From 1945 to 1965 there were only two years in which the party lead switched within the twelve readings of each calendar year by as much as 10 per cent (which means only 5 per cent down for Labour and 5 per cent up for the Conservatives, or *vice versa*). Only in 1946 and 1958 did that fail to be the case. But from 1966 to 1986 only two failed to show a switch of over 15 per cent in the party lead, and in some years the switch was as much as 30 per cent. That points to a much more volatile electorate.

Television politics distances politicians from ordinary people, still more so the politicians try to seem matey. But television politics has also changed the style of political discourse. On television the politician, as an uninvited guest intruding into the ordinary domestic home, is forced to eschew the normal yaboo ruderies of the hustings or the House of Commons. He has to talk in mild terms, just as a husband and wife are constrained from quarrelling in public when they are guests in someone else's house. The adversarial quality of politics is diminished for the ordinary viewer, and one basic fact, familiar to all political scientists, is forced implicitly on the British public: that for democracy to work, 80 per cent of people have to be agreed on 80 per cent of the national agenda. If only 50 per cent agreed on only 50 per cent of the national agenda, people would resort to the barricades rather than accept an adverse outcome to an election. Because television has transformed people's attitudes to politics and politicians, the parties have far more difficulty in maintaining the firm loyalty of their voters.

The changes I have been describing may be as nothing to those that are to come. I don't pretend to foresee the nature of future electioneering. At the lowest level, a great deal more will be done with direct mail. There will be experimentation with telephone canvassing, innovations in sophisticated polling, and, if they can't be stopped, major developments in the techniques of advertising and subliminal persuasion, and the manipulation of the media. But I suspect that the consequence will be to make elections duller, rather than more interesting.

Let me end with two challenging questions. Firstly, what decides

British elections? I don't think the answer today is fundamentally different from the past. Let me offer a very simplistic reply to an infinitely complex question. The most important thing deciding the outcome of British elections has been a general perception of the competence of the rival parties to manage the economy. That, of course, is an enormous question begging an answer. What does one mean by 'the economy'? The art of politics is to define the economy and to measure economic success in terms that will be relevant and look good for your own party at the time of the next election. The key economic issue could be the balance of payments, which Harold Wilson, in a pyrrhic way, made his central theme in 1970. It could be the rate of inflation which the Conservatives, quite rightly from their point of view, made so major an issue in 1983 and 1987. What really matters in the economy can always be redefined. And that, maybe, is what decides elections.

Let me put a second, and final, question. What do elections decide? Do they decide anything? It may sound cynical, after a life largely devoted to the study of elections, to argue that elections seldom set the fate of the nation. But there are some worrying facts. Think of the major events of the last forty years: the convertibility crisis of 1947; the devaluation of 1949; the Korean war of 1950; the Suez crisis of 1956; the first try for Europe in 1962; the second try in 1967; the devaluation of 1967; the third try in 1972; the I.M.F. crisis in 1976; even the Falklands war of 1982. Not one of these phenomena was actually associated with an election, or a change of government. In almost all cases there must be a strong suspicion that if the other party had been in power at the time, events could have taken much the same course. I don't want to be too derogatory about my own trade, but perhaps it is a good thing in the end that when one examines elections and the changing ways in which they have been fought, their outcomes have made so limited a difference. However, I know that there are many who would argue that 1979 was an exception, and that the arrival of Margaret Thatcher was one of those rare occasions where the individual transcended history and changed the pattern of political evolution in this country. How far that is the case will be a subject of debate, not just in this series of lectures, but over many years to come.

FOUR

The Future of the Left

BEN PIMLOTT

The future of the Left is a question-begging title. There has never been a time since the 1930s when the prospects of the British Left have seemed bleaker. Will there always be a 'Left'? Centrist optimists and leftist pessimists abound. Yet there is a problem of identity.

For some, 'Left' is a cabal or faction. For others, it is a blanket term to describe all opposition to the centre and the right. For still others, it can only be understood in terms of ideas and principles. There are obvious connections between the three usages, but they are not the same; and confusion arises because writers and speakers frequently slip from one meaning to another, without a signpost.

Clearly in Britain there is no *essence* of Leftism: no single reference point or standard against which all claims can be judged. The term 'Left' is a quite modern immigrant, whose arrival and absorption into everyday language did little or nothing to change the political system within which it was applied. Its origins are French: supposedly it arose out of the seating arrangements of the Assembly of 1789. According to William Pickles, the word entered common parlance in Britain in the 1920s[1] – by which time the political spectrum to which it was applied (including an officially socialist Labour Party) was already well established. It is significant that as late as 1933 the O.E.D. defined 'left' in its political sense only in terms of 'those holding relatively liberal or democratic opinions', with no mention of socialism.

In nineteenth-century France, left and right described attitudes to the Revolution, with related domestic adhesions: not only change versus reaction, but also anti-clerical versus clerical and – later – state intervention versus non-interference. In Britain, there was no historic trauma to provide a dividing line, and the borrowing of often inappropriate continental applications merely added to the imprecision. The problem of church and state is a particular illustration of this. In some European countries, the church has been closely linked to the right. In Britain, despite a (Protestant) church closely linked to the Establishment, religion (including Anglicanism) is an important part of the socialist heritage.

The British usage of 'Left' has been full of such contradictions, which owe much to its foreign roots. The main value of the term – and its most common purpose – is *positional*, as in its earliest days. Having no core philosophy, it exists primarily in relation to non-Left parties and leaders. What constitutes non-Left is, of course, itself a matter of debate. While for most people 'Left' is a way of describing the Labour Party and its sympathisers, within the Labour Party itself – where 'Left' is imbued with sacred significance – there are many who do not regard the dominant forces inside the Labour fold as truly Left.

The importance of positioning cannot be over-emphasised. Since the aftermath of the First World War (if not before), the Labour Party has included a persistent tradition, often labelled 'Labour Left' to distinguish it from the mainstream, overall 'Left' of the party as a whole. In the early 1980s, what had always previously been a minority grouping became the most powerful one – producing an immediate semantic crisis. On the one hand, to be 'Left' involves struggle against an over-mighty enemy; on the other the Labour Left was itself divided. Hence journalists subdivided the Labour Left into consistencies, as of cheeses: 'soft' versus 'hard'. The changing identity of 'soft' left provides an interesting lesson in political psychology.

'Leftness' is an expression in political geography. But it also describes a mental attitude that can best be summed up as rebellion. Once power is acquired (in a party or the state), the momentum of rebellion is hard to sustain, especially as there are others who attack the new authority. So it has been with the soft left. For most members of the Labour Party, and certainly for all supporters of the hard Left, Neil Kinnock – once an extremist and the triumphant leader of the soft Left – is to be identified with the (Labour) Right. In this, Mr

Kinnock follows a long, almost unbroken, Labour leadership tradition. Of all Leaders since Labour became the official Opposition in 1922, only three (Henderson, Gaitskell and Callaghan) were not seen at the time of their election as standing to the left; at the time of their departure only one (Lansbury) was not seen among active Labour Party members as standing to the right. MacDonald, Attlee, Wilson, Foot and now Kinnock – whose combined regimes account for half a century of Labour Party history – have all lost the aura of leftness as their tenure of office progressed.

This may partly be a product of pragmatism or – as the 'true' Left would say – opportunism. But it is also an automatic consequence of authority. The Left's positioning is (almost always) in relation to existing leadership. Although it is not impossible for the party hierarchy to be to the left of the active rank-and-file, such a state of affairs is very hard indeed to imagine.

If Left is to be seen both as topographical and as a state of mind, the role of specific beliefs and ideas may be less crucial. Nevertheless ideas have always been important to the Left, and the dominant idea has been socialism.[2] This is not the only element: there have been other overlapping (and sometimes contrary) strands. The pacifist tradition within the Left has non-socialist roots, while the long-standing left-wing demand (derived from militant trade unionism) for free collective bargaining can have anti-egalitarian consequences. Early in this century, the division in the Labour Party was between the socialists – who in effect constituted the Left – and non-socialist trade unionists. Increasingly after the adoption of the socialist clause four of the party constitution, however, all active members of the Labour Party came to describe themselves as socialists, without necessarily altering their opinions. For many people, Left and Socialist and Labour became synonymous; while within the Labour Party itself, there remained an intense consciousness of the difference between degrees of leftness, as between 'real' and counterfeit socialism.

In one sense, because of the Left's positional nature, there will always be a 'Left' within the political system, and a 'left' within the Left. There is a tautological element here, as well as a psychological one. But in another sense of Left – ideological and sociological – the

Left is dependent for its survival on its roots, and for its political importance on its social and industrial base.

The collateral of British socialism and leftness has been trade unionism. Many unionists were slow in coming round even to a notional support of socialist doctrines, and socialist enthusiasts have always considered that within much of the trade union movement socialism does not go very deep. Nevertheless, what significance socialism has in British society has largely been derived from the sluggish, massive oppositional force which the organisations of the most proletarianised work force in the world have, from time to time, been able to provide. That is the major difference between the British socialist Left and, say, the beleaguered, marginal American equivalent.

The British Left may not have a future; or it may be unrecognisably different from its past. What is certain is that its fate is bound up with that of a labour movement of which the Labour Party is only a part. The key to understanding the British Left lies in an appreciation of the latent power, and above all the fundamental unity, of the single, union-based, class-conscious movement. The history of this movement is littered with quarrels, splits and expulsions. From the departure of the Marxist Social Democratic Federation from the original Labour Representation Committee in 1901 to the defection of the anti-Marxist S.D.P. eighty years later, there have been those who have dreamt of an alternative formation drawing away the labour movement's electoral base or building a movement of their own. All have failed, and occasional trade union breakaways have always eventually returned to the fold.

Since the earliest days, there has been a tendency for outsiders – and some insiders – to exaggerate the industrial power and to underestimate the underlying political strength of the labour movement, whose unity contrasts so sharply with the rival organisations of workers in some Continental countries. This strength derives from a relationship with a working-class constituency that is very deep. Like all political relationships, it is changing. But – despite the fondest hopes of some of Labour's critics – there is no sign that it is about to disappear.

Encouraged by journalists and market researchers, as well as by wishful-thinking politicians, a number of political scientists who ought to have a better sense of history have argued that support for political parties is today primarily determined by attitudes to 'policies' or 'issues'. Their case has been based partly on the increased fluidity of public opinion in the Seventies and Eighties, and partly on survey data which related answers to 'policy' questions to actual or intended voting behaviour. The argument, backed up by superficially impressive evidence, has had more than academic significance. The belief that the Labour Party was so out of tune with public opinion that a more poll-orientated rival could take over Labour's historic base encouraged the middle-ground optimism which precipitated the 1981 split. The s.d.p. and Alliance adventure certainly showed how unstable electoral opinion had become. It also revealed a serious weakening of Labour support. But the most important demonstration was of the long run resilience of Labour, in contrast to the extreme fragility of its rationally-constructed, voter-friendly progressive competitor.

There have been a number of reasons for Labour's survival. But the most important, paradoxically, has been its leftness. Labour has been protected by the polarised traditions of British politics which have continued to cast it as the most powerful alternative to the Right. Labour's position on the spectrum has never been usurped, largely because of its class profile, which offers a mirror image of popular perceptions of Conservatism, and because of a traditional, expected, set of attitudes. Various terms are applied to supporters of the political centre: for example, 'moderate' and 'sensible'. It is much harder to identify particular beliefs. By contrast, Labour and the Left immediately and vividly evoke a heritage. Labour is known to be against privilege, social hierarchy, capitalism, personal wealth, inequality, unregulated markets, the powerful, the Establishment, the upper classes, nationalistic fervour, military might; and in favour of equality, civil rights, state intervention, democracy, the working class, internationalism. Little in either list has changed in a hundred years, which is why the attitudes are so readily identifiable with the Left (and why Labour finds it so hard to disassociate itself from them). Many of them are supported by the centre too – but without the same oppositional persistence. If one thing has underpinned the ethos of the British Left, it has been the spirit of confrontation: Us against Them. At times of national restlessness, that has been an advantage.

But behind this ideological mood lies the physical and mystical reality of the labour movement, which the progressive centre can never match. To many observers, the expression is no more than that – and an unreal one to boot. 'Lack of movement' might seem a more appropriate label. To insiders it provides a culture and a simple faith. It was said of Arthur Henderson, architect of the modern Labour Party, that when he spoke of the Labour Movement you could hear the capital 'M'.[3] Much has changed since Henderson's day. The Labour Movement no longer describes the complex network of unions, co-operatives, women's organisations and other groups that loosely tie together a large part of British proletarian life. Nevertheless, the notion of a wide fraternity of shared hopes and values still has the power to unite and enthuse, far beyond the narrow circles of the politically or industrially active.

The cartoonist David Low used to represent the T.U.C. as a carthorse, symbolising obstinacy and conservatism, but also decency and strength. There is another image of the Labour Movement in human form – also brilliantly caricatured by Low: Ernest Bevin. Bevin, the union leader turned politician, represented in his massive personage the characteristic features of the Labour Movement in its era of ascendancy: verbose, bullying, bad-tempered, and as solid as a rock. The link between politics and unions which Bevin embodied is still summed up by his own famous malapropism, which reminded the politicians of their point of origin. The Labour Party, he declared, had grown 'from the bowels of the trade union movement'. As one writer has rightly remarked, Labour's 'bowel problem' – its historic link with the unions – is central to the party's modern crisis.[4] It is equally impossible to understand Labour or consider the future of the Left without appreciating the past and continuing importance of the trade union connection for Labour's electoral strength.

The Labour Party was not only founded with the help of trade union money and trade union members; it was not only, from its earliest days, constitutionally in the hands of large union votes. In addition, the unions provided its class identity, and gave it legitimacy in the areas of industrial concentration. It was, from the early days, emphatically a 'labour' body. The myth that some process of evangelical conversion was involved in winning votes for Labour has been successfully dealt with by the historian Ross McKibbin.[5] Labour triumphed during the critical period of Liberal disarray and a widening franchise less as a result of successful propaganda than because of the organising power of trades councils and the ability of an already established union movement to present Labour as a class party. Before 1945, Labour was able to offer voters little apart from vague aspirations which, during its brief periods of office, it proved singularly unable to meet. The increase in its support and its replacement of the Liberals reflected the strong sense of communion between party, unions and a class.

Have policy commitments ever played much part in determining the long-term trajectory of Labour support? It seems unlikely, though an identification of Labour with the proposals of the Beveridge report may have helped the party during the 'sea-change' of opinion towards the end of the Second World War.[6] The original aim of the Labour Representation Committee – as its title implied – concerned class and representation, not policy.[7] Despite the inclusion of a socialist commitment in the constitution, Henderson's 1918 reorganisation retained the same purpose. Neither indeed was Labour unique in giving policy a low place in its priorities. The Conservatives were similarly indifferent. It was the Liberals, squeezed between the socially-based juggernauts of Left and Right, who turned in desperation to policy development as a life raft. Most working-class voters failed to notice. Labour support grew for reasons unconnected with its policies, of which there continued to be few of any substance. 'Deficient in brains and starved of money', wrote Beatrice Webb in 1927, 'it is a miracle that the Labour Party grows in voting power.' The basis for the miracle was the labour movement, and its octopus embrace with the working class.

Beatrice Webb spoke of a 'slow social upheaval moving independently of organisation or leaders.'[8] Perhaps, recently, there has been an unpheaval in the opposite direction. That was the claim made in the mid-Eighties (as it had been made a quarter of a century before). Allegedly, the decline of class loyalty has produced a decline in class-based political attachment and an increase in issue-orientated voting.

Certainly, the huge changes in voting behaviour since the 1970 election, and especially since 1979, cannot be easily explained away. In 1983 and 1987 the Conservatives surpassed Labour in many areas as a party of the working class. In 1987 – despite Labour's partial recovery – the Conservatives obtained 36 per cent of the manual working-class vote nationally, only 6 per cent behind Labour with 42 per cent. Among skilled manual workers – the stratum from which the leaders of the Labour Movement had traditionally been drawn – the Conservatives did even better than in 1983, increasing their lead over Labour to 9 per cent. Even among the unemployed, the un-skilled and the semi-skilled, the Conservatives obtained almost a third of the total vote, while Labour could barely muster a half. At the time of writing (and following the spectacular collapse of the centre), Labour has recovered some lost ground. But even by the most hopeful interpretation it can no longer be regarded as 'the party of the working class' in the sense of the undisputed ruler of a particular social territory. After the last election, Professor Ivor Crewe sombrely concluded that his 1983 verdict that 'the working class was no longer largely Labour' and that Labour had become no more than a 'regional class party' had been amply confirmed. Furthermore, given the changing employment structure, demo-graphy and time were not on Labour's side. Yet Crewe's analyses, and those of others, also confirm that the social character of Labour's vote retains its ancient features: Labour remains, for good or ill, overwhelmingly a working-class party. Peter Pulzer's classic dictum that 'Class is the basis of British party politics' still holds for the Labour vote.

Obviously, if Labour cannot extend its social range and cannot even obtain the lion's share of the shrinking manual vote, it has no prospect of power. To be the party, as Crewe puts it, of 'a declining segment of the working class, the traditional working class of the council estates, the public sector, industrial Scotland and the north and the old industrial unions', and little else, is a position of stultifying weakness.[9] Yet there is also a positive side: there are circumstances in which a solid appeal to working-class voters in the traditionally working-class regions can have its advantages.

Indeed – as the sorry fate of the S.D.P. seems to demonstrate – the one thing worse than being a class party may be to be a national or classless one. Labour's governmental prospects depend on its ability to attract more support from the service sector working class of the South and South East, in particular. Yet there is something to be said for what Crewe calls Labour's 'old class fortresses'. Not only do they provide a vital concentration of support in hard times and hence (given our electoral system) a firmer parliamentary representation, so that Labour is better able to sustain a serious reverse than any other party. They also provide a moral base. The more Labour is pushed back into its ghetto, the clearer becomes it identity and – at least in theory – the clearer its purpose.

Behind that identity remains, as always, the trade union connection. Those who are concerned to widen Labour's appeal have wondered whether the link with the trade unions might not be weakened or even severed. The thought is scarcely new. After the 1959 election, a number of 'revisionist' leaders put forward a similar plan. It was even suggested that the party might change its name – 'Labour', it was felt, might put off socially aspirant voters.[10] The argument in favour of such a move is that opinion polls have repeatedly shown public hostility to trade unions (though also an acknowledgement of their necessity). The argument against breaking the link is that to separate Labour from its historic roots in order to increase its popularity among anti-union voters might in the end destroy the class consciousness and class loyalty that have been the party's mainstay.

At the end of a decade of decline in power, rights and membership, trade unions are not fashionable. Bewildered, divided and under siege, unions in Britain have been less confident and more uncertain about their goals during the Thatcherite era than at any time since the Second World War. Yet their role as an intermediary between Labour politicians and their working-class supporters should never be underestimated. Unions are widely believed to *lose* the Labour

Party votes. The extent to which Labour, in the long-run, gains from the union-class association is less frequently considered.

What is most noticeable, of course, is the extent to which Labour behaviour is directly affected by changing union concerns. Yet this may not always be to the party's disadvantage. Just as Labour's post-1979 crisis directly reflected trade union attitudes (mainly in reaction to the Callaghan Government during the Winter of Discontent), so the pressures of trade unionism during Mrs Thatcher's administrations have encouraged many unionists to make sacrifices in order to strengthen Labour's appeal. At the same time, the changing occupational structure – with white collar and service sector employment taking the place of manufacturing and mining – is affecting the shape of unionism, with a knock-on effect for Labour. White collar unionism does not necessarily mean less left-wing politics, as several recent union elections have demonstrated. But it is likely, in the long run, to entail a shift in the emphasis of the Labour Party's industrial interests – and in the nature of the working class it seeks to represent. The days when the T.U.C. – and hence the Labour Party – was overwhelmingly dominated by manufacturing, mining and other blue collar unions are past. In short, there is a trade union evolution in progress which will ensure a significantly different social image for Labour as well.

However, the pace of change is certainly slow; and in the meantime, there is the question of whether Labour Party politicians and members can autonomously change direction in order to perform better at elections – and in what direction they should seek to go.

The orthodox answer, the one supported by the psephological establishment and by the architects of Labour's own current policy review, is that the party should pursue a better match between the policies it advocates and the preferences of voters, as expressed in surveys of opinion. There are a number of reasons for being sceptical of this view.

One is that there is no direct evidence of it working in the past. Many forces come into play during elections. It is hard, however, to think of a post-war contest in which party commitments determined the outcome. Labour's three victories against Conservatives in office

– in 1945, 1964 and 1974 – seem either to have been reactive (against perceived Conservative failures) or to have reflected a wider shift in mood. A second reason is that public priorities on policy, and attitudes to policies themselves, change faster than it is possible even for a highly flexible party to meet. A third reason is that the market model of voting behaviour – in which voters are presented as consumers and parties as sellers – is misleading. A general election is not a market place because no actual exchange is involved: voters pay no price and receive nothing directly in return. Hence it is unrealistic for a party to hope to 'buy' support by making pledges.

These are not arguments for insensitivity to public feeling, or for ignoring the need for policy change. Rather, they indicate that to concentrate on what voters say to the polling organisations may be to start at the wrong end. If – despite the decline in instinctive class voting – electoral behaviour is still to be seen as intuitive rather than calculated, based as much on memory, emotion, taste and culture as upon material want or policy labelling, a party may do better to forget superficial expressions of opinion and consider instead what problems it wishes to solve and how to solve them. In medicine, diagnosis has to precede the prescription of remedies. So, too, in politics. Following a period of almost unprecedented peacetime institutional change, the difficulties involved in deciding what reforms need to be made is particularly acute. Hence a policy review that is a serious intellectual undertaking makes much more sense than one whose purpose is image adjustment. Equally sensible is the proposal for a labour movement think tank, which – properly staffed and funded – could provide a continuing source of ideas. 'Permanent policy review', instead of either permanent revolution or a once-and-for-all revision along supposedly popular lines, might well be the most promising approach.

Clearly, it also has its limits. If past election victories cannot obviously be attributed to policy bribes, they cannot be attributed to Fabian earnestness either. As Beatrice Webb observed, deeper and less accessible forces are involved in winning votes. Nevertheless, in looking for factors behind Labour's two most significant triumphs – in 1945 and 1964 – the role of practical ideas (as opposed to electoral window dressing) should not be discounted. The 1945 victory was preceded by the most intensive period of backroom intellectual activity in the party's history, as Elizabeth Durbin's excellent study *New Jerusalems* shows.

Of course, the discovery of Keynes and a coherent economic policy, linked to Labour's recent thinking on economic equality, did little directly to win the election. Yet it may not be an accident that Labour's electoral peak should have come at the same moment as the high point in what Professor Durbin calls British democratic socialism's 'rich tradition of designing realistic programmes'.[11] Both were a product of the restlessness engendered by the war and a 'never again' reaction to pre-war unemployment. Yet an enthusiasm for policy-making among socialist intellectuals and the sense they conveyed of being ahead of political rivals undoubtedly strengthened the confidence of the parliamentary leadership. A similar process occurred in the late Fifties and early Sixties, following the publication in 1956 of Anthony Crosland's *The Future of Socialism*.[12]

'Most of the political opinions of most men are the result,' wrote Graham Wallas, 'not of reasoning tested by experience, but of unconscious or half-conscious inference fixed by habit.'[13] Voting in Britain today remains as complex, and probably as ill-understood, as ever. Labour should be grateful for its union-linked social class ballast, and ought to avoid behaviour that risks losing it. It should also consider the possible role, among people outside Labour's normal supporters, of 'inference fixed by habit'. The point about genuine intellectual activity is not that it produces electorally tempting sweetmeats called 'policies' for the delectation of the voters, but that it gradually builds up an impression of a party of competence and conviction. In much the same way, with groups like the Institute of Economic Affairs and the Policy Studies Centre as engine rooms, the Conservatives picked themselves up after the débâcle of 1974.[14] The most convincing political leaders are frequently those with the best understanding of what they are saying, and the firmest belief in their own prescriptions. And after office has been obtained, the most effective ministers are often those who have been intellectually involved in serious policy formulation beforehand.

Labour is a working-class party, in terms of votes. Once upon a time, it was also the party of the progressive intelligentsia. As serious a disaster to the Left as the loss of votes and seats in the wake of the party's civil war was the evaporation of committed intellectual support. From the Thirties until the Seventies, leftness and Labour voting was – if not the norm – certainly extremely common among liberal-minded journalists, lawyers, academics, and civil servants, while the cultural world was dominated by it. The foundation of the S.D.P. in 1981 was the culmination of a long period of disaffection among such people. The importance of this numerically tiny layer of society is hard to overestimate – its influence on the media is immense, as it is also, directly, on the climate of opinion in and around government. Regaining the confidence of people who are the most susceptible to reasoned argument and the least available to bribery (because a Labour government would scarcely be to their personal advantage) is of particular importance. As the only alternative to illiberal Conservatism, Labour can play its positional, Left card. But it will also need to make a case that is both more coherent than in the past, and more inspiring.

Among the same group, as well as within the wider electorate, Labour's best strategy may not be to hide its traditional base, but to celebrate it, and to show defiantly, and also reasonably, how a Labour Government intends to help the working class's most deprived members. It should not discount either the altruism of many voters, or the advantage to the prosperous of a more united, less selfish, society.

For the Labour Party – as a trade-union based organisation – a campaign on behalf of the poor is not the most natural crusade. Although Labour has always expressed concern about those at the bottom (who happen to be its most reliable supporters) it has done so piously: the main energies of the movement have been fuelled by the interests of employed union members. The increase in unemployment since 1979, however, and the negative redistribution that has occurred in the same period, has necessarily widened the range of labour movement concerns. It has also (as survey evidence confirms) created a greater sense of unease among the voters.

In *The Next Left: The History of the Future*, the American socialist Michael Harrington comments on the existence in every western country of a 'sub-proletariat' of the unemployed, the precariously employed, immigrants and so on. 'Does one pension them off,' he asks, 'see to it that their material needs are met, but leave them floating and functionless? Or does one understand . . . that such an existence inevitably "marginalises" human beings?' He concludes that full employment is a necessity; and also that 'one of the essential tasks of the next Left will be to re-establish, in imaginative ways, the historic fact that increases in social justice are the very best stimulus for increased production'.[15] Arguably, the challenge in Britain for a proudly class-based party is not to target its appeal at the material desires of the better off (who are unlikely to be convinced, in any case, that Labour can offer them more than the present government) or to develop policy packages which will offend nobody. It is to provide imaginative proposals which link the requirements of social justice to those of economic efficiency, and call on every voter's sense of community and citizenship.

FIVE

Mrs Thatcher's Economic Reform Programme – Past, Present and Future

PATRICK MINFORD

Politicians sell products in the political market place. That market is changing continuously with evolving tastes and technology. Sometimes the same old product will succeed with some repackaging, like Butskellism in the 1950s and 1960s. Sometimes a political entrepreneur will perceive, or think he perceives, an opportunity for a new product to topple the reigning monopoly. Such is the story of the Thatcher reform programme, at heart an economic reform programme.

Looking back on three elections, it is tempting to see inevitability in Mrs Thatcher's success, arguing from the interests of the skilled working classes, the *de facto* floating voters. But though I am no political scientist, I am impressed with the failure of political scientists to see any such alleged inevitability before the event. I do not hold it against them, any more than I hold it against skilled investment analysts that they did not predict the rise and rise of Amstrad and Mr Alan Sugar, a more familiar type of entrepreneur. The truth surely is that there is a discovery process in political, as in normal, markets; the successful entrepreneur has the intuition to guess what *may* sell and to build on any initial successes with more of the same, while closing down his failures swiftly so as to cut losses.

I leave to political scientists the hard task of piecing together just why the Thatcher product sold so well in 1980s Britain; why working-class voters plumped for more economic freedom instead of more social insurance, and why the middle classes did not embrace the Alliance middle way as many Tory strategists deeply feared. My job in this essay is to describe the product, how it has evolved, what it has become, and how it may develop in the future.

But first I must allay concern about my choice of metaphor. If this is a product, are politicians mere salesmen out for more money? Of course not. The metaphor is precise. Politicians, like business entrepreneurs, are moved by an invisible hand to satisfy the common good; their motives are various and irrelevant. The rewards of success may take many different forms: money, power, satisfaction in being credited with helping one's fellowmen, a place in history, and so on. The same is true of business rewards: it is mere pastiche to suppose businessmen get rewards solely from money; think of the Chicago founders of museums and opera houses, enjoying the plaudits of grateful citizens. The main thing is that the rewards should be very large and variable to attract the best for the tasks involved.

Much has been written and spoken about Mrs Thatcher's and Keith (now Lord) Joseph's vision of a social market economy. Joseph's inspiration seems to have been not Victorian Britain, as is so often said, but the West Germany of the 1950s under Ludwig Erhard. Yet that particular vision has never been widely shared by Mrs Thatcher's allies; and we now see only too clearly that the German example is unattractively corporatist and flawed by massive regulation.

Since Mrs Thatcher's political judgements have guided the whole enterprise, it is relevant to ask what she has had in *her* mind as a guiding vision. True to her character as a woman of action, she has never been so unprofessional as to write it down or describe it too precisely. But my impression from her many interviews is of a world in which *small* businesses could compete freely for the favours of the individual *family* consumer; in this world the state keeps law and order, including the elements of a *moral* order to protect family decency, and provides succour to the genuinely unfortunate who cannot help themselves.

The vision of the small business freely competing to topple the corporate goliaths is basically Austrian, Schumpeter's arena of creative destruction; and it is clearly the antithesis of corporatism.

But the passionate concern with the decent family consumer surely owes much to her father's shop in Grantham, surviving by satisfying ordinary people's needs efficiently. The philosophy of helping (only) the deserving poor is not so much New Right as the folk wisdom of the British families whom Miss Roberts helped to serve; for them independence was the *sine qua non* of happiness and self-respect, and charity was wrung from the housekeeping budget.

Such an ideal was far from both the reality of the late 1970s and the ideals of its dominant centrist coalition. Nor was it in the form of a product that the British electorate would conceivably buy as an alternative to the existing system, mediocre as its results obviously were. Imagine the problems. It was a vision easily damned as *simpliste* by the intellectuals to whom traditionally the electorate looked for guidance. There were no role models elsewhere in the developed world. The United States under Carter was committed to moving in the direction of the British welfare state, and everywhere in Europe corporatism was supreme. Within Britain, vested interests were ready to pounce on any encroachment of privilege and were powerful in key parts of the Tory establishment; and there was an opposition recently in power and expecting its imminent return, determined not merely to oppose but even to reverse change. Parallels drawn with New Zealand or the United States, where similar revolutions have occurred, are misleading. In New Zealand the opposition was powerless to oppose the wearing of what should have been its own clothes, and the reformers had plenty of overseas examples to follow. The U.S. presidential system makes reform easier to initiate and more difficult to sustain; the President may get a clear folk mandate but Congress is designed to obstruct and diffuse its implementation. The difficulties of creating reform in Britain were unique.

The problem Mrs Thatcher faced was where to start and how to develop support for a programme of change that was as yet barely understood, let alone demanded enthusiastically enough to overcome the powers of defending interests. Mancur Olson[1] has made a centrepiece of his theory of the decline of nations the power of these interests to frustrate those of the ordinary small man; his argument, widely accepted by public choice theorists, is that the small man will not care about the imperceptible increment to his tax bill needed to satisfy the vested interest group, whereas of course the group members care passionately about the sizeable increase in their welfare. It follows that a political entrepreneur who wishes to advance by reducing these vested interests has to mobilise the small man in spite of his modest stake in any individual issue – a task that according to public choice theory should be attempted only by those determined to fail. Mrs Thatcher was compelled to attempt this task of political aggregation.

This has to be understood to make sense of what followed. Some of Mrs Thatcher's closest advisers, not to speak of many critics both sympathetic and hostile, were frustrated by her frequent failures to make large, logically coherent reforms of the many areas she tackled in some degree; by the absence of any grand master-design; and by some positively counter-productive deviations from the logical path of reform. The truth is that as a political entrepreneur with finely honed instincts for her trade she probably couldn't do otherwise.

Her chosen method has been the 'step-by-step' approach, whereby problems were picked off in order of urgency and solubility, while others were prepared for future full attention with minor measures, often experimental in nature. So in her first two terms we have seen three major campaigns: the defeat of inflation, the curbing of union power, and privatisation, *in that order*.

In 1979–82 the fight against inflation dominated all else; monetarism and the Public Sector Borrowing Requirement reached their apogee in political debate, and economic expertise about them flourished in unlikely parts of the *Guardian* and the *Daily Telegraph* alike. During this phase, taxes were even raised in the notorious 1981 budget to establish anti-inflationary credibility; this measure badly worsened the supply-side and incentives but it did succeed in its objective. Given that public expenditure proved resistant to further cuts after the easy ones on capital account, it had to be done. In our recent econometric reconstruction of this period, Kent Matthews and I concluded[2] that this tax rise brought inflation expectations down decisively, much in line with Sir Alan Walters' assessment[3] that it was a turning-point in establishing financial confidence.

The medium term financial strategy was designed to create credibility for a four-year programme of *gradual* reductions in money supply growth and in the P.S.B.R. as a fraction of national income. By announcing long-term targets that it would therefore find embarrassing to miss, the government, so the idea went, was committing itself, like Odysseus binding himself to the mast before passing the Sirens; hence markets would expect the targets to *be* met, and reflation would cease to be seen as a relevant option.

Events turned out differently. The government tried very hard to meet its targets; but the markets never really believed they would – and have not fully done so until quite recently, perhaps as recently as 1986. The reasons in retrospect are not difficult to locate in the political economy of making such targets stick when powerful vested interests, including senior Tories, did not want them to.

This failure of credibility increased the *costliness* of counter-inflation policy. Matthews and I estimated the cumulative cost in unemployment by 1984 at one million, because policy was systematically tighter than expected.

At the same time, the *gradualness* of policy was converted to *de facto* shock tactics because of the error in choosing £M3 as the target variable for money.* Because of banking deregulation £M3 turned out to be a misleading indicator. It overshot its target badly, the government tried to claw it back, and in the process delivered a very sharp monetary squeeze in 1980 and 1981: M0, the only remaining reliable indicator, fell from 13 per cent to nearly zero growth in just over two years. Inflation, of course, fell very sharply as a result.

It is rather like a general who announces he will crush the enemy with the gradual pressure of an infantry attack. The enemy does not believe he will attack at all. He does, but his commands are misinterpreted and activate the tanks and heavy shelling. The effects are devastating: the battle is won, but the casualties are high. How much

---

* M3 is a very broad definition of money which includes high interest-bearing deposits; £M0 is the narrow definition, consisting of cash in the hands of the public, and cash held by the banks at the Bank of England.

better if we could rewrite it: he threatens the tanks, the enemy believes the threat and, when the tanks duly appear, surrenders – a victory with no casualties.

But I hasten to add that the analogy is also correct in suggesting that gradualism was unlikely to succeed, just as an infantry attack would be too feeble against a stubborn enemy; also that the move to shock tactics (the tanks of our analogy) while initiated by a mistake was then deliberately followed through in what amounted to a tactical revision for good reasons. Matthews and I judged that inflation expectations would have declined too slowly under gradualism to impress the electorate with counter-inflationary results, while nevertheless the long series of negative fiscal and monetary shocks so precipitated would have raised unemployment significantly; all this when unemployment was rising anyway. That judgement is a political one, but it seems secure; Mrs Thatcher and her Chancellor were embattled in their pursuit of 'monetarist' policies, and failure to bring inflation down decisively while unemployment was rising powerfully would surely have given unanswerable strength to their critics. It follows that gradualism was unsound as a strategy from a political viewpoint whatever its merits in the laboratory, and that its revision on the ground into shock tactics was necessary.

So the inflation battle, like so many battles in history, did not go according to plan, and the plan itself could have been improved. But it was won, and paved the way for the next campaign – against union power.

The union measure of Mr James Prior in 1980 had been a toe-in-the-water affair, which caused union leaders little loss of sleep. But, weakened by recession in their manufacturing heartland, they were unable to resist the two major Acts brought in by Mr Tebbit; these dramatically removed their immunities from common law tort action for damages, except for 'primary' strikes sanctioned by a majority in secret ballot.

Allocating responsibility for the reduction in unions' powers between the recession, the firmer policing of pickets as in the coal strike of 1983–4, and these Acts is difficult; all were essential in the change. But it is clear that the Tebbit Acts achieved *permanent* change where the other events alone would have had a merely temporary effect; their importance lay in facilitating the introduction of these Acts, which altered the relative financial costs of strikes to firms and unions.

Matthews and I attributed much of the sharp growth in productivity since 1979 (roughly quadrupled in manufacturing and doubled in the economy as a whole from the miserable 1 per cent or so p.a. during the 1973-9 business cycle) to the decline in union power. Working practices have been transformed in the majority of industries, particularly but not only in manufacturing. While overmanning has been all but eliminated in manufacturing such as steel, cars, glass and chemicals, service industries such as newspapers, cleaning and, increasingly, financial services are also slimming down. The new service industries, such as computer software and bio-technology, are in any case not easily unionised, and so not held back in the application of new techniques.

This brings us naturally to the last major campaign of the first two terms: privatisation. Though initially this was just a side-show, the sale of council houses was one of those political products that sold so well that it begged for a follow-up: in political terms share ownership was the natural sequel. When so much in the shop-window is austere, like inflation-fighting, or confrontational, like union law, there is a particular need for softer-edged merchandise with sure appeal. This privatisation provided, in a way well explained by Cento Veljanovski.[4]

The main successes from a purely economic viewpoint have to date been in the commercial disciplining of large public sector money-losers like British Airways, British Steel, and British Coal, and the freeing of management from political interference in already promising public firms like Jaguar and Amersham. It is natural to credit privatisation with these effects even on the not-yet-privatised, as their managements either aimed for or feared entry to the private sector with much the same result. The gain has been in substituting shareholder for government monitoring of management, with improved managerial clarity of objectives, incentives and performance;

surely this too contributed to the productivity surge, even if it cannot be quantified in a macro model.

What there has not been to date is any increase in competition, and so consumer power to discipline price and quality. Competition has either been judged to be adequate (British Airways, Jaguar, for example) or been replaced by regulation (British Telecom and British Gas most obviously). The reason is political: the power of managements to make or break this sensitive new political product. Mrs Thatcher chose to keep the managements on her side and go for the immediate gains in improved managerial performance we have noted. The problem is that once these gains have been made progress is slow or even backwards, as has been illustrated by Gas and Telecom. Regulation, however able in the short term (as exemplified by Professor Bryan Carsberg at Oftel) is no long term substitute for consumer power as has been well attested by experience in the U.S.A.[5]

But there is no reason to write off this aspect now. The B.T. duopoly comes up for review in 1990 and technology will make possible a sideways move to greater competition from cable, satellite and other modes of message transfer. The C.E.G.B. is to be privatised around then also, which will allow the injection of a new competitive regime across energy. Managements will and are already fighting these developments, but the boot is now much more on the government's foot, with privatisation a settled programme.

I have reviewed the three major set-piece campaigns of the first two terms. But around these there has been much other activity, either unclear mopping up, in military parlance, or preparations for future campaigns.

Deregulation in the private sector, decontrol and contracting-out have been the natural accompaniment to privatisation. Though privatisation has had the limelight, real additional competition has been achieved by all this; for example in buses, long- and short-distance, in the stock exchange, in local authority operations, and in capital markets with the abolition of exchange controls.

The productivity miracle is surely also partly owed to this. So it must be too to the decline in marginal tax rates on the average earner (down from 49 per cent in 1979 to 45% today – after the 1988 Budget and allowing for V.A.T. and national insurance charges on both employers and employees), on the top earner (from 83 per cent to 40 per cent), and on the corporation (down from 52 per cent to 35 per cent).

But while we have examined the activity devoted to fighting inflation, and raising productivity via the supply-side programme on unions, privatisation, deregulation and tax cuts, we have said nothing about unemployment. A stable financial order and greater efficiency is all to the good, but an efficient *economy* must also utilise *all* its human resources properly. It is in this field of unemployment that Mrs Thatcher has been slowest to engage battle, indulging in much preparation and experimentation before taking the field proper.

Analysis available to her early on indicated that the problem of unemployment was one of incentives: getting people to take the jobs that were or could become available rather than those no longer available that they were used to and preferred, usually using out-moded skills but then commanding better pay than these alternatives.

Matthews and I calculated that by 1980 the *equilibrium* unemployment rate (towards which actual unemployment was naturally tending) was already 3.1 million. This is a measure of the incentives problem Mrs Thatcher had to deal with. Our analysis therefore suggests that the sharp rise of about 2 million in unemployment from 1979 to 1983 can be fully accounted for by the elimination of overmanning, as the actual unemployment 'caught up with' this equilibrium rate; in other words, had Mrs Thatcher's government done *nothing* and no other shock had occurred, unemployment would have risen this much anyway.

Of course, both policy and other shocks did occur which had effects in both directions. But the point is that if inflationary and interventionist 'fixes' were to be ruled out by other policy objectives, there could only be one way to cure this unemployment: that of reforming labour market incentives. Under such reform, the unemployed would opt for lower paid jobs outside union protection while union powers to hold up their members' wages above market-clearing rates would be curbed, so that by these twin pressures wages would fall across both union and non-union sectors, creating new jobs.

The problem was political. To create such incentives meant tampering with the benefit system, or expensive tax reform, or curbing union powers to push for wage increases in excess of productivity increases. Benefits were widely felt to protect those in genuine need. Expensive tax subsidies like the basic income guarantee were ruled out by cost and also would make incentives worse for ordinary workers. And union members on whom Mrs Thatcher relied for votes would not welcome wage curbs, much as they had supported productivity gains.

The search has been on for a viable political approach to this problem. It has been spearheaded by the Treasury looking at tax reforms, the Department of Health and Social Security pursuing benefit reform, and the Department of Employment investigating job-creation methods. Along the way numerous useful changes have been made: Mr Fowler's reforms of the state earnings related pension scheme and the poverty trap, the cuts in tax rates and restructuring of national insurance charges, and the corporate tax reforms that have massively swollen tax revenues in an impressive supply-side experiment. But until quite recently a coherent strategy for unemployment had not emerged.

That has now changed because of the success of the Restart programme initiated by Lord Young. It is no coincidence that unemployment began its steady fall in August 1986, one month after Restart went national. Backed by the ultimate sanction of benefit withdrawal for those failing the work test enshrined in the original Beveridge laws, Restart produced a large 'melt factor' as numbers withdrew from the register rather than come to interview. Some have said this represents a fiddling of the figures. Surely the truth is rather that the figures have been shown to be phoney, swollen by those either not wanting a job on reasonable terms or actually doing a job while claiming. This is not really a surprise, because the labour force survey had been saying for three years that around a million claimants either had work or were not genuinely seeking it.

If a problem is defined by a statistic, then a legitimate part of its solution is the refinement of the statistic. But Restart has done more than this. While offering positive help to the unemployed, it also defined their obligations in return for social support. This was a beginning in tackling the incentives problem, because in principle at least now a job had to be taken if available on pain of benefit loss. It therefore limited benefit, while not denying it to any in genuine need; incentives were tackled without shocking ordinary people's caring instincts. Thus more people are now taking places on the community programme and the training schemes available. The rate of place-ment by Restart in jobs or training places is also around 5 per cent, which, though still depressingly low, is an improvement for the long-term unemployed who previously were apparently stuck in this state.

Restart is now being built upon, basically by increasing the element of compulsion. The below-eighteens *must* now take a Y.T.S. place or go off benefit. The morality of this is unassailable, since anyone receiving state help should presumably in return contribute whatever little they can. This principle will no doubt be extended to older workers in time, in the manner of U.S. workfare, and the Swedish or Swiss benefit systems. Meanwhile it seems likely that the Chancellor intends quite sweeping personal tax reforms that will take large numbers in time out of the poverty trap.

The strategy is being completed on the union wage side by the new union bill now going through Parliament. This attenuates to virtual disappearance the remaining immunities, since unions will be stripped of the power to discipline those *members* who cross picket lines. Firms will be able to break even wage strikes by engaging disaffected union workers to help supervise non-union untrained ones. Under this new barrage it is possible that unions will cease to be monopoly agents and revert to their common law role of friendly societies providing insurance, legal assistance and communication channels with managers.

Other elements of the incentives problem are being tackled in the new 'inner cities' bills now also before Parliament. Rent deregulation will lower the cost for a migrant worker of rented accommodation in the south-east, and so facilitate mobility of unskilled unemployed from north to south. The rate reforms will push business from congested regions to unemployment black spots, both by the unified business rate and because the poll tax will limit the local domestic tax burden on incoming managers and skilled workers in these black spots. Education reform – if it is built upon boldly – offers the eventual prospect of higher productivity in these places' labour forces; because benefits are low relative to skilled wages, this improves incentives and job prospects.

What I have just described is the fourth campaign getting into gear as we go into this third term, its focus being on unemployment generally and particularly in our inner cities. This brings our account up to date. But what of the future?

When this latest wave of legislation is in place, whatever its adventures in the House of Lords, a stock-taking will reveal areas still in need of reform. There is the N.H.S., an anomaly in a largely privatised ex-public sector. Education will be seen to be patchily touched, and the rest of an impatient electorate will ask how their supposed new freedom of choice can be exercised. We will still have large regulated private monopolies failing to deliver satisfaction. Even if the Chancellor has done all that I expect he will, there will still be excessively high top rates of tax, the confiscatory inheritance tax, and numerous privileged savings outlets featherbedding sleepy institutions. Mrs Thatcher's reform seam is far from exhausted; indeed it is obvious that, though much improved, the British economy could by merely catching up with the best overseas practice raise productivity sharply again. Some of that gain is already in the pipeline; but the rest is dependent on completing the process of reform.

Looking back on this process, it can be seen that it does conform to a path towards the vision I sketched earlier. Money is being returned to consumers to allow them greater choice; producers are generally being exposed to greater competition and, where competition is still lacking, to greater monitoring pressure. The poor *are* being protected – as the statistics clearly show, the share of the bottom 20 per cent of households in income after tax and all benefits including health and education has remained basically unchanged between 1979 and 1985, the latest year available – but less through universal provision, and more through selective help. I described such a strategy in a paper in the spring of 1984 when policy was somewhat in the doldrums after the 1983 election on a thin manifesto. I argued that through the better utilisation of resources that would result, the public finances would find themselves with increasing surpluses, so allowing the transformation to accelerate. Utopian as it seemed to many at the time, that strategy has gradually been implemented and has been paying off in those terms, as the latest P.S.B.R. figures manifestly demonstrate. It is likely that the strategy will continue towards completion.

Could it have been done better? With the benefit of hindsight, it would be surprising if it could not. One obvious area is unemployment. I earlier suggested that one million was added cumulatively to unemployment by 1984 by the anti-inflation programme actually pursued from 1979. I have since calculated that inflation would have been more cheaply cured by shock tactics – as suggested by Hayek, for example – in 1979-80, rather than by the gradualism attempted.[6] Such analysis as there was of breaking inflationary expectations favoured shock tactics (Sargent, 1986); and this tactic was, as we have seen, finally adopted on the ground. Yet it was not as fashionable in 1979 as gradualism.

Furthermore, Lord Young's idea of Restart was actually suggested long before – by Ralph Howell in 1981[7] and by me in the context of a full analysis of the incentives problem in 1983.[8] American experiments with workfare were extant then, and the Swedish system was known about. There was an unconscionable delay in launching such ideas in a suitably British form.

These were two mistakes which could each have cost the programme its life. The reasons for them are surely in the time-lag between ideas and their acceptability in practice, whether to politicians or public opinion. Gradualism had been long in the public domain through the persuasive advocacy of Milton Friedman; the idea of shock tactics had not. It took the pressure of events to introduce them. Similarly with workfare/Restart: it was a new idea, as was the notion that unemployment could be substantially due to incentive problems. It took crucial time for this idea to hit the ground as strategy.

One could nitpick one's way through many *details* of the strategy, too. But that, to come back to my beginning, would be rather to miss the basic point about this whole operation.

Mrs Thatcher's reform odyssey has been, to repeat, a discovery process by a political entrepreneur of genius. And, like Odysseus, Mrs Thatcher has had hair-raising adventures, made many mistakes, and enjoyed both good and bad fortune; the fact is she is still afloat with a following wind. No one can tell whom, how or whether she will reach the shores of her Schumpeterian vision. But the omens are, I believe, favourable.

SIX

On Market Economies

FRANK HAHN

I am no friend of Thatcherism, but I shall, as far as I am able, attempt to distinguish those parts of Thatcherism which offend my values from those which offend my intellect. Only this last will concern me here. But there is, for the economist at least, a serious difficulty. Judging from her occasional pronouncements, Mrs Thatcher holds economics in contempt. For instance, she has boasted that she is not guided by 'mere economic theory'. Whatever guides her therefore it is not systematic thought on economic matters. For these reasons the economics of Thatcherism must be largely gathered from what her more grammatical subordinates, like Nigel Lawson and Alan Walters, and her admirers, like Patrick Minford, have claimed it to be. We cannot on certain crucial matters simply work backwards from the Government's actions to Thatcherite beliefs, because these actions have not been consistent. It is hard to deduce unique motives from actions anyway. For instance, high unemployment may not have been an unfortunate by-product of anti-inflationary policies but rather part and parcel of a purely political design. Of course we cannot ignore the policies altogether as evidence, but I shall be mainly concerned with such pronouncements from the Thatcherite Government and from its advisors which are economically literate enough to constitute claims about the economic world.

Let us start at the beginning, that is to say with Adam Smith. His intellectual achievement (which ranks amongst the highest in any subject) was the development of the proposition that an economy of self-seeking greedy agents need be neither chaotic nor have consequences which are against the 'common good'. It is a sad fact of contemporary politics almost everywhere that neither the Right nor the Left understand what this proposition means, nor are they aware of the quite outstanding work, particularly of the last fifty years, which has given the proposition sufficient precision to allow it to be discussed. The fact that there are also economists on both sides of the political divide who show no signs of comprehension is perhaps best understood under the heading of *trahison des clercs*.

Let me from now on call Adam Smith's economy the 'market economy'. We can show that on certain crucial assumptions such an economy need be neither chaotic nor against the common good, just as Smith claimed. No serious economist has argued that, as a result, market economies must be orderly and beneficial. The Smith claim is, in the first instance, a claim of logical possibility, not of practical necessity. *The Wealth of Nations* itself and the vast amount of subsequent work make this abundantly clear. In order to avoid the habitual slovenliness of the arguments concerning market economies I propose to summarise what economists can in fact demonstrate to be a logical possibility.

Consider an economy of very many agents, strictly a continuum, who all 'know what they want' and 'know how to get it'. In short, consider an economy of a large number of economically rational agents. Suppose that these agents can make binding contracts not only for the exchange of goods available today, but also for goods which will be available in the future. They can also make binding conditional contracts of the sort that says I shall deliver five bales of wheat in 1995 if the weather is fine, and nothing otherwise. That is, agents can insure each other. There are no public goods, and no externalities. Assume further that all production is under constant returns to scale. With these assumptions one can demonstrate the following results:

(A) There is an allocation of present, future and contingent goods amongst all the agents which has the property that no agent and no group of agents can attain an allocation which he or all members of the group prefer. In particular it is impossible for any one agent to be given an allocation which that agent prefers without at least one other agent having to be satisfied with a less preferred allocation. (The allocation is Pareto-efficient.)

(B) If all agents dealt in anonymous markets, that is if they all did the best for themselves at given prices of all goods (including prices for the future, and future contingent delivery of goods), then there would exist such prices at which agents would, in clearing markets, get exactly the allocation described in (A).

I realise that this is both abstract and not easy to take in on first reading. But I fear that it is neither easier nor indeed more laudable to engage in economic debate without knowledge than it is to discuss medicine or physics in ignorance. In any case it is the abstractness of these propositions, together with their postulates, to which attention needs to be drawn.

When one compares the abstract with real market economies, one is struck by the fact that the latter have far too few markets. Take some examples. In actual market economies it is not possible in general to have contracts for the future delivery of labour – slavery is not permitted. Keynes in *The General Theory* recognised that this absence of forward labour markets was an essential datum for his theory. Consider next births and deaths. Future generations can contract with the living only indirectly through the latter's benevolence, and in any case must rely on the accurate assessment of their desires and circumstances. Thus, for instance, if they could, future generations might well bid against developers who are now pulling down fine buildings or indeed bid for exhaustible resources. Firms in modern market economies cannot sell their outputs for delivery at distant future dates. It is not possible for them or their shareholders to – for example – insure profits against loss from the future action of some foreign government.

This lack of markets will, as the examples illustrate, make it impossible to demonstrate that actual market economies are Pareto-efficient. There are insufficiently numerous markets because markets are costly and because agents have different access to information. If you want to borrow (i.e. sell forward), the lender will not know your future circumstances as well as you do, nor is he able to know your future actions. For that reason he may require collateral or not be willing to lend to you at all. In other words, the assumption that future contingent contracts can be enforced requires objective knowledge of the contingency on the part of someone, and very often that is not available.

The lack of markets will be discussed further later. But first I propose to look, however briefly, at some other difficulties. The propositions (A) and (B) required there to be very many agents, so as to avoid any one agent having market power. An agent has such power if other agents in dealing with him have no equally good alternative possibility for their transactions. It is only in such economies that firms cannot influence the price at which they sell their output or the prices at which they can buy their inputs. It is for this reason also that constant returns to scale were postulated. I think one can see with the naked eye that these are not good assumptions to make in the world we inhabit. If they are not made, then once again the propositions cannot be established.

The last (of many more difficulties) to which I want to draw attention is the assumption that there are no public goods. A public good, like a television transmission, or information, has the property that any one agent's consumption of that good does not diminish the amount of it available to other agents. As an example, take scientific research. The successful researcher cannot, in a private market, benefit from his success: any purchaser can sell it again, and it is easy to show that its market price must be zero. That is why we have patents which, of course, have no business in a pure market economy. This is a simple point but not one firmly in the Thatcherite canon. There is also the related matter of externalities. These arise when the action of one agent, such as smoking, directly affects another agent. Mr Coase has argued that with sufficiently rich property rights – say to clean air – private negotiations between smoker and non-smoker could restore Pareto-efficiency. But we do not have such rich rights. Another famous example of an externality arises from a common resource like a fishery. The more fish you catch, the more costly and difficult is it for me to catch fish. This externality has led to the regulation of fisheries – in other words, to direct interference with the market economy.

Beside these well-known externalities there are, in practice, others which are less well understood but which are of central importance.

Let us agree that in actual economies there are missing markets. Agents who cannot trade forward, contingently or otherwise, in certain goods, must when making decisions form expectations of spot prices which will rule in the future. Suppose that the prices which must be forecast are those which will clear all markets at future dates. For present purposes we look at the simplest case which arises when all forecasts are correct. But now a very interesting possibility arises: there may be many correct forecasts – indeed recent work has shown that in general there will be many, so that market clearing and perfect foresight do not suffice to determine the path of the economy through time.

Here is a striking example. Suppose that we can all observe sunspots which are known to have no 'real' effects on anything like production or well-being. Suppose further that we all forecast future market clearing prices on the basis of observed sunspots. It can be shown that there may then exist a 'sunspot equilibrium'. That is, there will be a path of the economy dependent on the occurrence of sunspots, and on that path markets will clear at each date and no agent will revise his expectations of the future. Notice now that if you realise that sunspots have no 'real' effects you will still do best to base your forecast and actions on sunspots as long as you know that everyone else does so. There is here an 'externality of beliefs' as well as an externality of actions. In game theory we call this a 'Nash equilibrium': the action which is best for any one agent depends on the actions taken by the other agents. When there is a finite number of agents this externality can lead to outcomes which are worse for every agent than some other, co-ordinated, outcome which they could reach.

When there are 'missing markets' therefore, two things happen. Firstly there are many possible paths which an economy can take. Secondly there may be, amongst these paths, 'bootstrap' paths or 'bootstrap equilibria'. That is, the paths are what they are not because the world is what it is, but because beliefs about the world are what they are. Keynes saw this quite clearly and it has taken us fifty years to see that he was right.

This now has taken me back to Thatcherism and to a particular kind of damage which it has inflicted. Consider a situation in which there are constant returns and also unemployed labour. For present purposes I can assume that the latter are indifferent between working at the going real wage and receiving the dole. (Of course I, unlike perhaps Patrick Minford, do not take this to be descriptively accurate.) Suppose now the Government gave every citizen a gift of money proportional to that citizen's money holding. There are at least two possible consequences. All money prices and money wages will be higher in the same proportion in which each citizen's money stock is higher. Call this the 'inflation' consequence. Alternatively prices and wages can remain constant and output and employment are both higher in the same proportion as the money stock is higher. Call this the 'Keynesian' consequence. Which of the two has a chance of occurring will depend on beliefs: on the theories of the economy which agents hold. If they believe that every change in the stock of money will be tracked by money prices – in other words, if they have Thatcherite beliefs – then they will be self-fulfilling. The same goes for Keynesian beliefs. Thatcherism, by successfully promoting Thatcherite beliefs, has made government policies that much less likely to succeed. It has thereby reduced the influence which we collectively can exert on our economic destinies. Indeed, in the early days of Thatcherism the value of some monetary aggregate or other became the sunspot for a sunspot equilibrium.

To sum up the story so far: even if it is granted that the invisible hand ensures an orderly economy, it is only under quite unrealistic assumptions that we can suppose that the outcome is bound to be satisfactory in the sense of at least Pareto-efficient. The market economy leaves much scope for collective attempts to improve on its outcome. That is true not only at the micro-level (for instance, the public subsidy of research) but also at the macro-level (for instance, guiding the economy to a preferred equilibrium). Note that I am not comparing a market economy with a command economy. Behind this conclusion paradoxically stands the observation that a market economy has too few markets – indeed it is bound to have too few markets. To this one then needs to add the simple fact that there are areas of increasing returns and that there are many markets characterised by competition between the few rather than the anonymous many.

Now as I have already noted, Thatcherism has produced no coherent economic arguments. Such sub-arguments as there are – particularly in macro-economics – are based on a misunderstanding of textbook theory which I have just examined. That it is pretty incoherent can be deduced from the following contradictory arguments which will be familiar. It is maintained that Keynesian policies, especially those involving an increase in the quantity of money, can only result in inflation. The policies will have no real effects. Yet at the same time we are told that inflation is the greatest evil. In sophisticated monetarist circles the first statement is accepted while the second is toned down to what are called 'shoe-leather' effects of inflation, namely those costs which arise when people, in times of inflation, economise on money balances and have to keep running to the bank. Milton Friedman would add to this 'taxation outside the law' – that is, the evil of government acquiring resources by the expedient of the printing press. From what I have already said you will see that it is hard to take these arguments seriously. In a halfway realistic theory of the market economy, monetary policy can have 'real effects' and inflation can also have real effects beyond shoe-leather effects. In both cases the equilibrium path of the economy may be different from what it would otherwise have been, and that because there are many possible equilibrium paths.

But while Thatcherism is short on economics, it is stronger on what I propose to call 'Political Economy'. That is, while many of its policies, particularly those of the 'There Is No Alternative' variety, have been based on a slovenly appeal to textbook market economics, the heart of Thatcherism is elsewhere. It is in a vision of society in which economic arrangements are only a part of the whole. Indeed it is here in the company of left-wing thought, which is also based on a comprehensive vision, and incidentally equally incapable of getting the economics straight.

The political economy of Thatcherism seems to be a mixture of Schumpeter and Hayek. It is important to emphasise that both these scholars need to be taken seriously.

Hayek made a connection between the institution of a market economy and citizens' liberty. I confess that the more I think about his arguments here and the more I look at the evidence, the more convincing the Hayekian view becomes. But this today is not my main brief. The second element of Hayek's argument, however, turns on the dispersal of information amongst agents. A carpenter knows more about carpentry and the manager of a steel plant knows more about steel production than could any planner. A market economy in a certain sense 'aggregates' this private information. In particular, prices not only provide signals for the allocation of resources, they also provide signals from the informed to the uninformed. This property of a market economy has only recently received expert attention and Hayek undoubtedly was the pioneer. He is surely right in arguing that these considerations cast a baleful light on a project of comprehensive economic planning at 'the centre'.

But Hayek gave up too soon. An alternative to comprehensive social planning might be the conscious creation of a much better market economy than that provided by a capitalist society. This indeed was the claim of market socialists like Lange and Lerner. Let the means of production be owned collectively but instruct managers etc. to act as they are supposed to act in the textbook. To do so, the centre can attempt inter-temporal co-ordination by guiding the expectations of managers. That is, indeed, what was fairly success-fully done in France through 'indicative planning', and what still seems to be happening in one way or another in Japan. Whether it is possible in this way to have one's cake and eat it is too large a question to tackle now. But certainly there is nothing in the Hayekian argument to nullify the view that on some important matters in-formation at the centre is better than that available to any one agent. Nor does his argument affect what I have said concerning public goods and externalities. In other words, there is nothing here to suggest that governments cannot improve the working of a market economy. The information argument does not logically entail the cry of 'the less government the better', nor do I believe that this is deducible from the liberty argument. What *is* deducible is almost certainly the view that we cannot now devise a non-market system which ensures as much liberty and as much material well-being as does a market system which to some extent is influenced by government.

But that now leads us to Schumpeter. His view, put forth in two very fine books, was that the market competition which really matters is what some people call dynamic competition. It is competition through innovation and the associated birth and death of firms. Such competition has a hero: the far-sighted risk-taking entrepreneur. You will recognise him also as a hero of Thatcherism. On this view, possible misallocation of resources – Pareto-inefficiency – at any one time is of secondary importance to our well-being. What does matter is the vision and energy of the entrepreneur-hero. This however does not come 'for free'. The hero must have his reward to look forward to else he will not play his role. The rewards are the high profits which are temporarily available to him because he is first in the field with his innovation. Tax these profits highly in pursuit of egalitarian aims and, to mix the metaphor, you kill the goose that lays the golden egg. In short, the cost of egalitarian policies will be stagnation.

Thatcherism has enlarged the scope of this argument to include the somewhat less heroic ambition of 'self-improvement'. People will not work hard, learn new skills and seek better jobs without reward. The really potent motivating forces are private and not social. Few are willing to undertake an arduous and possibly unpleasant task 'for the good of society' but may do so for their own, or their family's, good. Once again the conclusion is that the cost of egalitarianism is high.

The vision of Thatcherism clearly embraces both these Hayekian and Schumpeterian strands. That the vision may have elements which correspond to reality cannot, I think, be denied. But like all visions, this one must be treated with the circumspection which comes from careful thought and evidence.

The first point to make is that it is by no means the case that the importance of 'dynamic competition' quite overshadows that of the allocative role which I have discussed. To take just a single example, the Schumpeterian entrepreneur requires finance. Now this entrepreneur is in a peculiarly bad position to get it because he claims to have information which the run of the mill person does not have. This is just the situation which I have argued will make it difficult to have a futures market, in this case to borrow on given terms. The pure Schumpeterian entrepreneur has no collateral – his capital is his superior knowledge of available market possibilities. So if we leave it 'to the market' we may kill the hero, just as we would by taxing his gains. To be fair, the Government seems to have an inkling of this, as is evidenced by some recent proposals of Lord Young. But these proposals *are* a recognition of market failure, and of the importance of such failure for dynamic competition.

But there are, of course, other examples. Schumpeterian innovation is intimately tied to the problem of monopoly. The 'first in the field' will be the first and so have some monopoly power. Schumpeter believed that this power would soon be eroded by imitators. But there is no guarantee of this. There are available all sorts of devices to delay the erosion of profits by imitation. Equally seriously, there are incentives to existing firms to buy and bury innovation. This is what happened in the case of the fluorescent bulb. Indeed if there are already in existence large firms with some market power, then the Schumpeterian entrepreneur can be given a hard time. Once again, then, the vision requires market interference: for instance the criminalisation of restrictive practices.

That these are serious considerations will be obvious from the experience of other economies. For instance, there are Latin American countries with low taxation of high incomes – taxation which itself can often be avoided – which are hardly exemplars of Schumpeterian innovative bustle or of Hayekian liberty. Evidently one needs to distinguish between necessary and sufficient conditions.

But are they in fact necessary? Or rather, in what sense are they necessary? Keynes argued that people, insofar as they are motivated by rewards, are motivated by relative not absolute rewards. In a sense he must be right. To claim 'I am rich' in, say, Pakistan must have a different meaning of absolute wealth than, say, in America. When I claim to have a 'good' job it must be a claim about this particular job amongst the set of jobs open to me. In any event, Keynes argued that we could elicit the efforts of the Schumpeterian hero and of the Thatcherite private person bent on self-improvement by much smaller absolute disparities in rewards. The hero should earn more than the average and there should be a ladder for the self-improver, but there is no evidence that these income steps need to be far apart.

Such research of an empirical kind as there is seems to support Keynes. Insofar as we judge our wellbeing by relative income, it does not seem to be true that making larger and larger steps has appreciable incentive effects. But in any case there is evidently more to the incentive story than income. Sir Ralph Halpern certainly seems to enjoy his high income, and it may well be a spur to effort. But it is equally clear that he enjoys the rewards of reputation and of power. So it is with most of us. The very reason why we may respond to the stimulus of relativities is that our self-esteem is gratified, and that can probably be achieved as well by a gentle upward movement in the income scale as by a jump.

I admit that this is as speculative as the contrary Thatcherite view. But unless we have better empirical knowledge here I would argue that the path charted by Thatcherism, that of large and growing inequalities, requires much more certain knowledge of the benefits of such inequalities than we now have. I would want these benefits not only to be substantial but also pretty certain. The example of Sweden suggests that this demonstration will not be easy.

On the other hand, Thatcherism has a defence here. If incentives do indeed depend on relative and not absolute income, then we certainly have a case of externalities. The question now is: in what distribution of income is one's relative position of importance? At present one must agree that it is not true that only the position in the British income distribution matters to British citizens. For many occupations, American and some European comparisons with British rewards are clearly relevant. This means, for instance, that tax rates abroad have an influence on British decisions. Certainly valuable people may emigrate. But even if they do not, the richer rewards abroad may depress incentives. It is, of course, not easy to decide what weight to give to this argument, but it will surely deserve some weight.

The Hayek–Schumpeter element in Thatcherism, unlike the economic textbook element, is harder to dismiss on simple grounds of logical incoherence. Its implementation, as I have argued, certainly requires market interference, but it is possible that policies designed with that element in view will have some success. But if they do, they will also be accompanied by a growth in the uncertainty of economic life. The vision of the bustling entrepreneur is also one of continuous change, of the birth and death of firms and of new kinds of jobs and redundancies in old ones. To some extent citizens will lose some control of their lives and, as I have repeatedly argued, there may be no way in which individuals can insure themselves. This aspect of a market economy Schumpeter called the cost of progress. What I want to stress is that there is no obvious way in which the individual citizen can choose how much to trade in security for progress.

Indeed this is a paradox for Thatcherism. Its political economy message is libertarian; give as much choice to the individual as possible. But clubbing together for mutual insurance is just as much a matter of personal choice as money spent on holidays. Thatcherism restricts some of our most important areas of choice; we may be able to choose how to spend money we have earned, but we are insufficiently able to choose a more certain steady income over an uncertain rising one. The latter choice can only be made collectively, but that does not mean that there is no individual choice.

It is now time to return to the less heady questions of economics. I propose briefly to consider a number of special topics in order to show that it is not particularly useful to contrast a market economy with a fully controlled one, and that there are grounds for the view that governments have an important role in making market economies 'work'.

My first topic is the labour market. This market is not at all like, say, an auction market for fish, although certain economists find it hard to allow themselves this disturbing observation. The literature on this subject is very large. Certainly in this country we must reckon with unions. Workers are not homogeneous goods like herrings. The quality of a worker is not accurately known when hired, his quality may improve by employment which gives firm-specific skills, and his supply of effort etc. may have to be monitored and fed with special inducements. Workers may have a sense of identity as a group or class and the unemployed may be unwilling to undercut the employed, or unable to do so because of credible threats. All these considerations lead me and others to the view that it is unsafe to suppose that 'the labour market always clears'. That is, it is unsafe to suppose that every worker who so wishes can obtain work at a wage of another more or less identical worker. This does not mean necessarily that the worker is unemployed. The skilled engineer may be sweeping floors. What it does mean is that we cannot simply assume that there is an efficient allocation of labour between jobs or between work and leisure, or that there are automatic market forces which will correct such an inefficiency. This, in more contemporary parlance, is the view espoused by Keynes.

Although some time ago politicians claimed that 'we are all Keynesians now', they now consider that he is dead and buried. It is not my purpose to argue a Keynesian case but rather to take note of the specious arguments of those who have assured present politicians, and Thatcherites in particular, that they can forget all about Keynes' problems.

The argument, somewhat surprisingly, is sustained by the simple expedient of making the clearing of the labour market into an axiom. In other words, it is not to be discussed. Here is this procedure in action: it is argued that there is no trade-off between inflation and unemployment. Hence, for instance, it is useless for governments to try to increase the level of employment, say, by deficit finance, which is taken to be inflationary as a matter of course. This argument is based, fundamentally, on the hypothesis that either at present, or in the future, on the basis of automatic market forces, everyone willing to work will have found work at the appropriate real wage. On that basis the argument can sometimes be correct. But now there is also nothing to discuss, since Keynes was concerned to deny the hypothesis. It is a matter of simple fact that none of the proponents of these new dogmas has given any plausible justification of the hypothesis. Note also that if the hypothesis is correct, then *prima facie* there is no reason for the government to engage in a macro policy to increase employment. In the final analysis the answer against Keynes is that 'labour markets clear'. Ask why, and the honest Thatcherite reply would have to be 'because I have assumed it'.

This leads directly to my next point. A central question concerning market economies is whether they constitute a self-regulating mechanism. I was careful earlier on to answer only the question whether it is *possible* for a market economy to be coherent and in some sense beneficent. The answer was affirmative. But there we were concerned with the invisible hand at rest, not in motion. In other words, the answer to the question of possibility is not an answer to the question of whether coherence and beneficence can be attained by a process which is inherent in the market economy. I have to report that economists have only the faintest glimmering of what a correct answer should be. The Smithian view that markets will cause goods in excess demand to rise in price and goods in excess supply to fall in price, even if accepted, does not establish the convergence of such a process to those prices which are consistent with coherence – that is, overall market clearing.

Matters here are very complicated indeed. We already know that, with missing forward markets, agents must form expectations. We now have to ask the market mechanism to guide them to adopt expectations which will not be systematically falsified by events. Even in highly simplified settings studied by Margaret Bray, it is not provable that the market mechanism will induce the required learning process. In any case, very little is known about the latter.

It was Keynes who advised economists to abandon theories which suggested that market economies were violently unstable. His view was that the evidence was overwhelmingly against such a conclusion. Of course a great deal depends on what is meant by 'violently'. The experience of the last eight years in this country certainly suggests that the market is not 'violently' stable either. According to the theories of Thatcherites, Thatcherite deflationary policies should have led to lower money wages and prices, not to lower output and employment. True, they allow for some lags but not for those which we have seen. My main contention however is elsewhere: the major sin of Thatcherism is to hide our essential ignorance on these matters in strident certainties. Of course it hides it not only from others but from itself. The consequence is that actions which would be justified under certainty are grotesquely out of place given actual uncertainty. (The 'British miracle of 1987' is no counterargument, because Thatcherites have been pursuing non-Thatcherite policies.)

I can sum up this part quite simply. There is no agreed, or even fully formulated, body of knowledge concerning the behaviour of a market economy when it is not in the coherent state which we call equilibrium, or, nowadays, rational expectations equilibrium. Given this ignorance, Thatcherite reliance on the market to do the job it wants done can be a hope, but not a reasoned hope. In such circumstances, prudence and rationality dictate pragmatism and restraint rather than dogma.

The last topic I propose to touch on concerns public goods and the public provision of goods. The former I have already mentioned. It suffices to say that all economists are agreed that we cannot rely on the market to provide the right amount of such goods. Thatcherism defines public goods very narrowly, and has never comprehensibly pronounced on this matter. However, to take just one example, the proposal that, for instance, museums should charge admission fees suggests that it is not properly understood. Any first-year student will tell them that such charges are only beneficial when there is a danger of congestion, while the plan to finance museums in this way finds no support from clear thinking.

The public provision of goods is a more complex matter. Thatcherism in some instances has provided a good counterweight to policies which were motivated by other dogmas and sustained by a similar but opposite misunderstanding of market economies. There are indeed sound arguments against nationalised road transport, for instance. However, even where justification for withdrawing from the public provision of goods is available, withdrawal has not been accomplished in the light of a clear understanding of what markets can and cannot deliver. In many cases far too little has been done, and often badly done, to provide for regulation and competition. Thatcherism regards the public provision of goods as *prima facie* a worse option than the market alternative.

Consider the public provision of health services. We can easily construct a thought experiment in which the provision is private and where private insurance premiums instead of national insurance contributions are the consumer's vehicle of health insurance. This thought experiment has been carried out by Arrow. He notes that the quality of the 'good' being sold here cannot be judged by an ordinary consumer. So one quickly comes to the conclusion that (as now) doctors, nurses and hospitals would have to be licensed. This necessity will mean that entry into this industry will not quickly respond to exceptionally high rewards which it may earn. Profit-maximising hospitals and doctors will provide the most profitable mix of services. Hence illness which is expensive to treat, and which is strongly correlated with low-pay occupations, will not be treated. Nor is there a satisfactory market mechanism to ensure that the variety of treatments available is best in the sense that a different variety might not be preferred by all. There is also the following somewhat unpleasant aspect. People may not insure because they know that even so society will not leave serious illness untreated: a moral hazard problem. If society does leave them to suffer or die then the penalty seems to exceed the crime. Moral hazard leads to the view that in this world insurance should be compulsory, which brings us halfway back to where we now are. On the other hand, to ensure treatment we may have to subsidise the poor. Even then, income inequalities will be made more glaring and, one presumes, less acceptable by unequal health treatment. We may only mildly envy the rich man in his castle, but we are apt to hate the rich man whose life is less at risk and whose suffering is more attended to than that of the poor man.

There are many other considerations. Insurance companies also face moral hazard (the insured takes less care) as well as adverse selection: at any premium those most at risk of ill health are likely to take out insurance in greater numbers and thus raise the actuarial risk of the company. It will for these reasons not be the case that, equity apart, the insurance menu offered will provide optimum insurance. Compulsory insurance by the state avoids the problem.

There is of course much more to be said. But I hope that this may suffice to show the difficulties with the pure private case. As I have argued so often already, actual problems are not solved by a blanket appeal to a mystical market. The same applies to an appeal to mystical collective action. It is very likely that in this case a mixture of both market and government can be justified. The Thatcher Government is moving in this direction, but Thatcherism is not.

However, the example serves to highlight a matter of great importance. When we earlier considered Pareto-efficiency, we were quite agnostic about the distribution of welfare amongst the citizens of an economy. I have also argued that the Schumpeterian element in Thatcherism makes it inimical to egalitarianism. The health service and many other publicly provided services are, amongst other things, devices to limit the moral costs of inequality, and probably the political cost as well. Thatcherism has been too single-mindedly and, as I have argued, often incoherently focussed on efficiency, and the related aim of growth. But ultimately we are interested in the welfare of people – and that is not adequately represented by G.N.P. and certainly not without noting its distribution. The blindness of Thatcherism on these matters, together with its simple-minded textbook economics, may yet be its downfall.

Let me conclude with some final remarks.

Thatcherism as represented by Mrs Thatcher herself is intellectually without interest. It consists of homilies on the virtues of hard work and ambition and on providing the carrot and the stick to elicit those virtues. Her macro-economic views are so incoherent as to make them undiscussable. For instance she habitually confuses finance – 'where is the money to come from?' – with resources. But her lack of intellectual power in these matters does not, of course, detract from her ability to inspire others to make an attempt to turn Mrs Thatcher into Thatcherism. It is with these latter that I have been concerned.

I have argued that these others have misused and misunderstood the models of market economies, whether derived from Adam Smith or from Schumpeter. There *are* great virtues in well-functioning markets and one cannot deny that Thatcherism, by leaning against an earlier prevailing wind, has done some good. But it is the coarseness with which Thatcherism conceives of market economies that is one of its prime and dangerous failings. This is most glaring in what it has claimed about the macro-economy and in its failure to grasp the special case of public goods. However on the former the Thatcher Government (if not the high priests of Thatcherism) seems to have changed its mind. For instance, we no longer hear any of the nonsense about the money supply and, in recent years, the Chancellor has treated capital receipts from privatisation as income and thereby moved in the direction of a Keynesian policy by stealth. On public goods their attitude, for instance, towards education and research shows their incomprehension.

The Government has been accused of 'wasting North Sea Oil' on a consumer spree. Thatcherism, in my view correctly, points to the growth of foreign assets. Their economics here seem sound. What is unsound is their unwillingness to use the latitude which this gives us with the balance of trade to follow more expansionist policies at home. Again, Thatcherism's preoccupation with the quality composition of the labour force is sound. What is unsound is its unwillingness to recommend a serious and large effort to improve matters here. And so it goes on: conclusions are reached before thinking has been completed or sometimes even started.

My last remark is on a subject which I have so far banished from consideration. The values of Thatcherism share with its economics a coarse simple-mindedness. Accepting the Schumpeterian model would not inhibit a civilised mind from pondering the trade-off between inequality and growth. It would be inclined to treat great and growing inequalities as a cost to be set against Schumpeterian benefits. Not so Thatcherism. Accepting that we need more people with industrial skill would not lead morally grammatical thought to the conclusion that society needs no other kinds of skills. One can go on in this vein for a long time. The simplistic economics when combined with grotesquely lop-sided values makes Thatcherism a very unpleasant 'ism' indeed. One cannot begin to accept it, even if one is willing to grant that Mrs Thatcher has done *some* good in the world.

SEVEN

The Emergence of the New Right

KENNETH MINOGUE

Among the many aspects of that curious composite called the 'New Right', the one to which least attention has so far been given is the repudiation of collective guilt. The reason, perhaps, is that this kind of guilt is so pervasive a feature of the contemporary world that it has almost ceased to be a distinguishable phenomenon of our moral life. Consider, for example, the collective involvements which can induce guilt in the average Briton. One of them is Britain's imperial past, a dominance over the non-European world often said to have damaged the inhabitants of our former colonies. Another is Britain's involvement in the slave trade up until the early nineteenth century, an involvement which to some extent animates the guilt of the white British population about contemporary race relations. The memory of the industrial revolution in Britain conjures up visions of its cost to the local working population in terms of child labour and the poverty of factory workers. And there are forms of moral sensibility which would regard Britain's warlike past and present possession of nuclear weaponry as a transgression for which we ought to atone.

Britain, of course, is not alone in experiencing this sensibility, and the argument I shall present about Britain could be formulated in terms of any other Western country, or of Western civilisation itself. In all cases, we find a form of moral sensibility highly susceptible to self-vilification. It is a sensibility whose range has been increasing ever since the early nineteenth century, when it began to develop. Collective transgressions multiply as new doctrines emerge, and are then projected backwards to embrace long stretches of national history. Thus the appearance of radical feminism has led to the discovery of many previously unknown episodes in the history of 'what men have done to women'. Here then is a highly moralistic sensibility which is fuelled by indignation and encourages the discovery of more and more sins to be atoned for by abstract classes of people.

This sensibility, I am suggesting, dominates a great deal of our public life. It supplies, for example, the rhetoric in terms of which we discuss most social issues. It generates a conception of modern Britain as a tangle of inherited injustices; some kind of reparation for them becomes a central part of the political agenda. And entrenched behind this sensibility will be found a significant group of the intellectual population of the country, for whom this sensibility is nothing less than decency, civilisation and justice itself. We may thus explain some of the hostile passions which the New Right has provoked as a recognition that nothing less than this entire sensibility is implicitly under attack. Indeed, the attack is not always merely implicit. Early on in her career as leader of the Conservative Party, Mrs Thatcher rejected something she called 'bourgeois guilt' and defined it as 'that sense of guilt and self-criticism that affects those, not only the very rich, who cling to a relatively comfortable life while feeling a troublesome pang of conscience because there are others less well off.'[1] In attacking the bureaucratic egalitarianism which had dominated British politics since 1945, Mrs Thatcher was offering a kind of psychic liberation to the middling prosperous centre of British life whose thinking about their place in the world had come to be bedevilled by a sense of being accountable for situations for which they had, as individuals, no responsibility at all. Here then is a theme implicit in contemporary political discussion, and our first task in understanding it must be to clarify the rhetoric of collective guilt.

My own reflections on this subject can be dated precisely from the moment when, on a radio talkback programme, a caller explained that he had felt guilt for Britain when watching the television news the previous evening. Horrifying scenes of Ethiopian famine had been juxtaposed with the abundance of a state banquet at Buckingham Palace. It is easy to see why he should have felt great compassion for the starving people of Ethiopia, but why, precisely, guilt? Neither he nor the banqueteers at the Palace were in any way responsible for the famine. No doubt Britain as a state could give assistance, and in fact it did. But why guilt?

Guilt can be nothing else but the violation of a rule. We are guilty only when we have done what we ought not to have done, or left undone something necessary. It is, however, all too possible to experience painful sensations of guilt without having done wrong, while many an evil-doer leads the sunniest of lives. The commonest form of modern guilt arises when we feel responsibility for great evils in the world without having any direct involvement in them, and certainly no real possibility of mitigating them. The reason is that the mind of modern man – by contrast with the simpler, custom-guided people at other places and times – is a vast tangle of rules, beliefs and sensibilities, and we constantly trip over them. It is hard to sustain the logical coherence of this tangle, and the beliefs we pick up in one area often start worming their way into another. Thus the common rule of manners among Europeans that one should treat other people as equals may carelessly turn into the belief that no one ought to be superior in conditions of life to anyone else. This is how the rich Western tourist with cameras dangling from his neck begins to feel not only sympathy but also guilt and embarrassment in the presence of the Third World beggar. From this common response, it is but a short step to the conviction that the plight of Third World countries is not the poverty of some of their inhabitants or the corruption of their rulers, but that it is simply an inequality of condition among the inhabitants. To the vulgar mind, a visible relationship easily becomes a causal one, and few things are more visible than the contrast between the rich around the swimming pool and the hovels of the shanty towns down the road. This visible relation has suggested to many a hasty observer not merely the (arguable) moral precept that the rich ought to give more of their goods to the poor, but the (highly implausible) causal hypothesis that it is the wealth of the rich which actually causes the sufferings of the poor. Once this idea begins fermenting in the mind of the average British *bourgeois*, the outcome is a sense of discomfort whose actual logic is largely inaccessible without an unusual capacity for intellectual rigour.

This kind of subliminal guilt can lead well-meaning people to feel a debilitating sense of responsibility for conditions they cannot possibly influence. Such mishaps in our moral psychology not only frequently occur, but are actively encouraged by the romantic idea that this kind of spectral guilt is the mark of a refined and cultivated sensibility. This was the real spectre haunting Europe in 1848, when Marx and Engels brought out the *Communist Manifesto*: the well-heeled bourgeoisie was becoming increasingly uneasy about the conditions of the poor. This unease has determined the entire cast of our culture in a way that the Mandarins of China and the Brahmins of India would have found quite incomprehensible. We have not only learned to live with this vague but persistent form of suffering; we have actually come to congratulate ourselves on experiencing it. It might well seem, of course, that all of this was merely the reinvention of the idea of original sin, but while such a Christian doctrine is no doubt part of the origin of the pathology I am considering, the sense of collective guilt is quite a different thing. Original sin is really a relaxing doctrine, since there is no way on earth that we can avoid it. Its secularised descendent of collective social and political guilt, however, is an agenda for political action to create an impossibly just world. We find ourselves on a moral treadmill, without hope of escape, even by paying reparation and making symbolic gestures which seldom have much affect upon real problems. The consequence is that, as Thomas Sowell, one of the more notable students of this phenomenon, has put it, 'political decisions about the future are made as if they were moral decisions about the past.'[2] The imperfections of the human condition itself cease to be something to be endured and turn impossibly into a problem to be solved.

It is not even possible to avoid this guilt by the device of leading an individually exemplary life. In Marxism, and in all the ideological variants which have imitated it, the evils of the world (and in many cases, the world is thought to be actually *constituted* of evils) are believed to result not from the free and culpable actions of individual evil-doers, but from the workings of an oppressive system. The sufferings of the poor, for example, result not from the greed of individual entrepreneurs but from the logic of profit, just as the sufferings of women are implicit in the logic of patriarchy rather than the brutishness of individual men. As with the doctrine of original sin, so structural determination might seem to release the individual from his predicament. Yet structural explanations never push their logic quite that far. While all are structurally determined by, say, capitalism, some are more structurally determined than others, and the imagined beneficiaries of the alleged system (the middle classes, men, whites etc.) find themselves even more indelibly marked by guilt. Responsibility for injustices – and more and more of them keep being discovered – extends continually further.

The spread of this miasma is, of course, by no means the end of the story. The rhetoric of guilt is the dominant idiom of contemporary politics, but it does offer to the sensitive modern citizen the option of playing the prodigal son game. He may choose to repudiate the supposedly guilty natural identity of his class, race or gender as if it were merely an episode of prodigality, and embrace justice as the fundamental commitment from which he had been briefly separated by the contingencies of his natural origin. The bourgeois may join the class struggle, the Briton repudiate the Falklands war, the white liberal attack the structural racialism of his community, and so on. Such a prodigal, like Jane Fonda at Hanoi, enjoys a dramatic access of virtue only possible to those who live within this particular ethical nexus and choose to exploit it. Such conduct is characteristically the virtue of an elite; they shine all the brighter in contrast with their mulish fellows, sunken in allegedly unreflective allegiances to the country and creed to which they were born. It is important to see such a saving remnant in the theological terminology of the prodigal son, because in recent decades much of the weight of a disoriented church has been thrown behind this secularised version of salvation.

Modern political discussion thus presupposes a logic of historic injustices pressing heavily upon the present generation. To be British is to inherit the guilt of one's nation, and can only be dealt with by repudiation of the allegiances to which one was born. Guilt is thus the mechanism by which people are released from their inherited obligations and mobilised to serve guiltless universals, such as peace, the United Nations, the environment, ecumenism and so on. The promise is harmony and rationality, but since these universals are themselves embodied in quarrelsome movements, the actual consequence is often but a new kind of conflict.

To sum up: the notion of collective guilt involves a return to the primitive belief in communal responsibility for misdemeanours. This belief was dissolved by Christianity and the Enlightenment, and it is on the basis of these standards that we judge apartheid in South Africa, where race rather than individual merit determines treatment. Yet guilt makes us prone to accept these collective judgements on ourselves.

Is guilt merely a feature of the *rhetoric* in which we conduct our public debates? On the contrary, it comes increasingly down to hard cash. What we are dealing with, in fact, is a shake-down.

The culture of guilt depends upon the discovery of more and more 'historic injustices' perpetrated upon classes of peoples whose descendants now stand before us with their hands out. In these terms, Marxism is a doctrine asserting the guilt of the bourgeoisie for what they have done to the working class. This guilt can only be expiated by joining the revolutionary movement, but it can at least be mitigated by giving things to the workers, and on one plausible view this is a significant part of the dynamics of the welfare state. As with many other such arguments from guilt, this particular one has a realistic partnering argument which explains such redistribution as prudently conserving social peace. Now Marxism is a typical product of the intellectual market place, whose ruling principle is imitation. Just as film producers try to cash in on the formula of a successful blockbuster, so intellectuals imitate arguments that deliver the goods. Europeans have generally passed on their ideas to the intellectuals who grew up in the Third World; these newly-hatched thinkers soon picked up the rules of the game and began to claim benefits from a West they had learned to revile as 'imperialist'. Feminists discovered that women could similarly be construed as the victims of an oppressive system, and began to advance claims for positive steps to be taken to grant them, as a matter of reparation, benefits which a modern civilisation has generated by skill and hard work. As such guilt-based liberations flourished, they spread into every corner of society. Homosexuals, racial minorities, the disabled, and many others hastened to set themselves up as separate tribes, each with its own history, value system and grievances, all claiming victim status. What this amounted to was a re-tribalisation of modern society, but the term actually preferred in the culture of guilt was 'community'. This is a sinister misuse of the term, for it suggests that communities are constituted in terms of some abstract homogeneity (as in talk about 'the homosexual community'), whereas the essence of a community is precisely that it is not a thing circumscribed in this way. Communities contain people of many types. In this area, however, the guilt culture borrowed its ideas from nationalism, and each abstract tribe sought, for example, to set up its own canon of great figures (thus exhibitions of women painters, anthologies of black poets) and its own claim to a guaranteed place in the cultural sun.

Guilt, then, constitutes a familiar element in the culture of our time, one whose roots go back to the last century, but which has only exploded in the last few decades. So far as Britain is concerned, it has found a special institutional base in local government, and in professional education. What, we may ask, is its point? The simplest way of explaining it is by invoking the basic distinction between politics and the economy. Wealth is created by the risky and arduous business of working to make things which can be exchanged in a market. It takes energy, application and self-discipline, and it is often slow and boring, especially for those whose work consists of constantly applying the same few skills. Many people get impatient and turn to easier ways of acquiring goods, such as crime, which is quick and often rather interesting. But in modern societies, a new option has developed in the form of pseudo-politics: the protest industry. A tribe can be constructed by a group of intellectuals who work out some sort of historic identity for it. Victim status is asserted, and reparation demanded for the oppressions of past and present. Just as the Third World has shaken down the West for vast quantities of money in the last few decades, so new tribes of victims have, on the home front, increasingly been demanding subsidies, jobs, preferential rules of advancement, immunities from various sorts of industrial discipline and many other benefits. There is thus a direct relationship between the culture of guilt and the viability of a large and thriving intellectual and bureaucratic interest in Great Britain.

The technical name for these tribes is 'minorities', and there are plenty of them. Women, for example, are said to constitute 51 per cent of the population. Again, the working class is a very slippery object, and by some measures has shrunken pitifully, but more than half the population must be working class according to widespread intuitions. Racial minorities are measured in millions, and while the art of tribalisation normally consists in distinguishing oneself as a minority from others, in the racial case many minorities of very different complexion have, for the purposes of the guilt culture, been aggregated together as 'black'. The unemployed and the homeless are a lively subject of interest. Homosexuals have claimed the status of historic victimisation since the 1960s and produce figures claiming to be 10 per cent of the population, as do the disabled. No doubt there is a good deal of overlap, but it does not require a statistician to discover that the oppressed class of the population, for whom there are many clamorous spokespersons, must constitute rather over 80 per cent of the entire British population.

Now one only needs to assemble together claims and arguments usually only encountered separately to see that we are dealing with a fantasy world. Everybody recognises this except a thin band of professional intellectuals whose jobs or self-esteem have become identified with the fantasy. Marx and his followers tried to dress up the working classes in the uniform of the 'proletariat', but the secret has long been out that most of the working class are too busy getting on with their own lives to bother being mobilised in a communist crusade. Most women, similarly, have better things to do than involve themselves in the pseudo-representation of feminist pseudo-politics. Gay Lib is for a minority of activists, and many blacks are highly resistant to the demagogy of racial constituencies. But the lack of actual popular support for the mutually contradictory demands of the clamorous spokes-persons of these tribes matters less than the fact that they make good copy. Newspapers need personalities, quotes and opinions, which are here in generous supply. Like everybody else in a modern society, those in the grievance industry are responding to an opportunity, and it is an opportunity created by the culture of guilt.

It is this culture, so pervasive that we take it as much for granted as the air we breathe, which determines the effectiveness of the dominant rhetoric of our time, found at every level from the United

Nations assembly to the local council chamber. It is an underdog rhetoric, demanding reparation from the rich and the powerful, and worth vast sums of money. Yet it is often confessedly hypocritical. At the United Nations, those who excoriate the West in public will often explain to their Western colleagues that what they say is strictly for home consumption. Machiavelli was clear on the point that in politics, evils must be attributed to necessity, benefits to the government. In terms of underdog rhetoric as it applies to international relations, evils come from the West, benefits from international co-operation. Thus when Kenneth Kaunda spoke recently about the problems of A.I.D.S. which, ravaging parts of Africa, had come to touch the President of Zambia's own family, he appealed for something called 'the international community' to tackle the problem effectively. Every time famine breaks out, appeals are similarly made to this same community for food. But who is the international community? Hardly Asia and Africa, from which for the most part, the appeals come. Not South America, sunk in debt. Nor the Communist world, which has great trouble even feeding itself. The international community is evidently the guilt-stricken West, including those pharmaceutical laboratories who, when not receiving appeals for help, are being snarled at as exploitative multinationals.

It is clear that the effects of this rhetoric of the underdog must seem, to people whose moral sense is quite different from ours, like a kind of mystifying benevolence, a cargo cult in which goods are showered down from heaven just so long as the beneficiaries indulge in rituals of complaint and stamp their feet unpleasantly enough. It is a familiar observation of psychologists that asymmetry in gift-giving produces psychological tensions.[3] Just such tensions have appeared in the West's relations with the Third World, and they occur wherever such transfers develop momentum. Perhaps the best analogy is with the husband who, in an unusual fit of thoughtfulness, brings home a bunch of flowers for his wife – and is thrown out of the house because she *knows* he would only bring gifts if he had done something to be ashamed of. Similarly, in the rhetoric of guilt, it is the very reparation itself which comes to confirm the reality of guilt.

Many people have, of course, long been restive about the pervasive effects of guilt upon our public discussion, but the assumption was so impregnably moralistic that it was difficult to attack without seeming to be brutal and uncivilised. For a long time, critics such as Peter Bauer (who focussed his attention on the issue of Western aid to the Third World) could be shrugged aside.[4] What really burst the bubble was the energy crisis of the early 1970s. As a result, the redistributive bureaucracies operating within the welfare state became increasingly burdensome. One of the early moves of the Reagan presidency in the United States was to send Jean Kirkpatrick to the United Nations, where she was able to introduce a bracing realism – at least by local standards – into the patter of that unreal institution. More recently, the withdrawal of both Britain and America from u.n.e.s.c.o., a body entirely dedicated to diffusing the plethora of Western guilt, has been another step in repudiating these illusions. But it is Mrs Thatcher who has become emblematic of the new realism which has entered contemporary politics.

It is significant that the Joan of Arc who has raised the siege of the vigorous and active elements of Britain and the West should have been both a woman, and one of no particular social eminence. Advantaged in this way (if we may parody the rhetoric of guilt) she was well placed to repudiate the ideological parasitism to which the Heaths and Macmillans had proved so fatally prone. Disinclined to play the feminist game, she was impervious to its being played against her. Indeed, the feminist dislike of Mrs Thatcher is the thread of Ariadne which allows us to understand a great deal about these murky but forceful currents of thought in British politics. On the face of it, she ought to be a feminist heroine. What a role model with which to shatter the male political clubland! Feminists take no pleasure in her, however, and the reason is, I think, that feminism has very little to do with women. It is, rather, an infatuation with a communal form of life which, being unconvincing to voters in liberal democracies, hops about from one natural class or another in search of a base, latching upon workers, or women, or racial minorities, or any other notional tribe which, not being articulate in its own right, can be spoken for without too much implausibility. Feminism is to women as Bolshevism is to Russia: an alien parasite trying to dominate forms of life with their own inherent vitality.

It is, then, precisely the fact that she is a woman which dramatises this central feature of the New Right: its repudiation of the culture of guilt. Most other exponents of this movement in its broadest sense – from David Lange in New Zealand to Deng Shao Ping in China – have focussed upon liberating productive enterprise from the weight of bureaucracy, regulation and heavy taxation. Mrs Thatcher has a wider resonance because she is emblematic of these deeper currents of the New Right. It would thus be misleading to interpret her success in purely economic terms. It is clear that many of her supporters will be found among the rich and vigorous, including many prospering in the working class, while her most passionate opponents are to be found among the beneficiaries of redistribution. But the fact is that she has considerable support even among those who might be expected to regard her with dislike, including even the unemployed. And the reason can best be seen if one considers the Falklands war.

It would be difficult to exaggerate the features of a situation which could induce in British political judgement a more paralysing sense of guilt. The conflict concerned islands of no direct value to Britain itself and left over from an imperial past. The Argentine population was united in a passionate conviction of its right to the islands and – as was clear with Hitler in the 1930s – nothing more arouses the self-doubt of the liberal conscience than the passionate certainty of an opponent. Further, in the wings was waiting one of those delusively universal organisations specifically designed to release nations from the dilemmas of their particularism: the United Nations. Except for the vile character of the Argentine regime itself, nothing could have been artificially contrived that was more certain to make the British weary and hesitant about defending themselves against what was indisputably an act of military aggression. And it did indeed take a Mrs Thatcher to set on foot the campaign to repel the invaders and restore the islands to British control. It has been common ground ever since that no feasible ruler of Britain at the time, except Mrs Thatcher, would have had the will to face the immense risks of the enterprise. The guilty would rather lose everything than face up to the risks of a cause in which they could so easily find reasons for disbelief.

Britain, like the other democracies of the West, has been hobbled in recent decades by a powerful public conviction that there must be no resort to force except on morally impeccable issues. Few such issues exist. What Mrs Thatcher has denied, and here she is a representative figure of the New Right, is that a state must be impeccable before it can resort to force in defence of its interests. No such 'clean hands' doctrine inhibits non-Western states. Here again we have a case in which the arguments of the New Right were at last given practical force by the movement of events. Just as it was the increasingly intolerable costs of the welfare state which led in some degree to a rejection of the rhetoric of guilt about national matters, so the spread of terrorism and aggression against Western interests during the period of detente in the 1970s allowed the realism of the New Right to come into its own.

The New Right is thus a return to an older realism which had been obscured in recent generations by an entire culture of guilt. The terms of public discussion had come to be dominated by the clamour of victimisation and demands for reparation. In simple terms, a debate had developed between two views of what politicians ought to do, and the general issues had been complicated by diverse and powerful interests on both sides. The Falklands war was one of those rare events in which the elements of the debate appeared almost uncluttered by ambiguity. The political culture of guilt had to be challenged across the entire spectrum of its preoccupations. It necessarily responded by denouncing the British recapture of the islands in the strongest terms. What was the ground of its reaction?

The line taken was to identify paralysis and the concessive character of the policies of guilt with nothing less than morality itself, while the vigorous action of the British government was taken to be the response of savage natural emotions. A typically hostile reading of the significance of the Falklands war runs as follows: 'There has been a frightening upsurge of a kind of atavistic, tribal chauvinism.' This is the playwright David Edgar. His use of the word 'frightening' is the standard claim within the political culture of guilt to a higher moral sensibility, while the 'atavistic' conveys the idea that military self-defence was an act of civilisational regression. David Edgar's development of this theme may carry our understanding of the terms of the grand debate even further. He writes that the 'aggressive chauvinism of Thatcherite culture is a function of the reassertion of masculinity and the anti-feminist backlash.' Clearly this is the kind of remark a woman can laugh off in a way that a male Prime Minister might not. The remark is interesting also as exhibiting the holistic character of the rhetoric of guilt: everything is packaged together under the rubric of 'Thatcherite culture', as if in a state ruled by Mrs Thatcher no one could read Kafka or listen to Harrison Birtwhistle – as if, in fact, a liberal democratic state were no different from a Marxist one in which there would indeed be a correct line on culture. In the next sentence, the actual events of the war (the decision-making of Mrs Thatcher, John Nott and the many other partici-pants) are described with unintentional humour as 'a pressing crisis of masculinity'. This is so bold an affirmation that Mr Edgar seeks for support in a remark he attributes to Julie Burchill, quoted (somewhat incredibly) as writing that 'Men are at bay: they are getting nastier and nastier as women get stronger, and they have not finished yet.' One might think this remark hard to cap, but Mr Edgar has a valiant try. Referring to a gunman who had run amok in Hungerford in mid-1987, just before Mr Edgar was composing his thoughts, Edgar concludes that this was 'an assertion that Michael Ryan with his privately-made privately-hired videos, and his privately bought and legally sold armoury, was about to prove.'[5]

Here, *en clair* as it were, is the basic response to the New Right's rejection of the culture of guilt. It is, of course, a pretty extreme case, but it is all the more revealing for that. The commonest point made is simply that Thatcherism is the apotheosis of greed. David Edgar may again be quoted in another place expressing the standard view:

> The achievement of both Reaganism and Thatcherism has been to weld together the instincts of individual greed and collective self-righteousness into a coherent model of the world, in which the rhetoric of freedom can co-exist with the reassertion of virtue. Put crudely, the new authoritarianism allows people to

vote in their own narrow self-interest, but yet to feel good about doing so.[6]

The crucial point here is that people have been enabled, in rejecting the political culture of guilt, to 'feel good' without paying their tribute to the necessary causes. They have refused to pay the psychological tax which the exponents of guilt had successfully imposed upon the middle classes.

From this point of view, the culture of guilt is an instrument for controlling the behaviour of citizens and voters. Yet it is character- istic of its exponents to ignore this element of psychic coercion and emphasise, rather, their permissiveness on such issues of individual behaviour as abortion and contraception, which are here confusingly called 'social' issues. On this basis, the New Right is charged with the inconsistency of being economically permissive and socially 'authoritarian'. The evidence cited ranges from Conservative measures to control the sale of 'video nasties' to 'Victoria Gillick's success in securing a judgement in 1984 that it is illegal for doctors to prescribe contraception for children under sixteen without parental consent'.[7] These instances are often associated with the moral enthusiasm of American evangelists so as to present an account of the New Right as being contradictory at heart. Mrs Thatcher has indeed affirmed her belief in traditional values and seeks to sustain the family against the atomistic tendencies of social life in the permissive era. Against this, it is important to recognise that no political position need be consistent in terms of a single abstract principle. In fact, social stability is a condition of economic dynamism.

In responding to the New Right, the political culture of guilt has thus raised the stakes and claimed for itself the very crown of morality and civilisation. This is a typical ideological move, for it tries to force us to construe its opponents as the victims of their own narrow prejudices and passions. On this point, we may merely say briskly that to identify the Conservative Party under Mrs Thatcher with the abstract passion of greed is a category mistake which could only be made by very simple people. To say such a thing is to assert that a very large part of the population of the country, containing many individuals of evident good sense and humanity, need no longer be taken seriously, and that there is only one right opinion. Such political dogmatism is unmistakably a form of irrationalism, which leads directly to totalitarian domination. A much milder form of the same sort of category mistake is made by churchmen when they preach that a vote for a socialist or welfarist party *is* an act of charity. It must surely be common ground among all who seriously take part in public life that these opinions cannot be sustained, and that they result from the dogmatic error of trying to establish that a political tendency is identical with morality itself.

This does not, however, dispose of the issue, because what I have called 'the culture of guilt' need not be the property of any particular political party. There are undoubtedly many people who hold the belief that a refined moral sensibility must be one in which the individual is painfully aware of his responsibilities for the condition of the world, and in which, as a consequence, he must take up a political position on a great range of issues.

Even those who recognise that the collective guilt we often feel is illusory may still believe that human beings preoccupied in this way will be more civilised than those who have been released from its burdens. Only guilt, some would argue, restrains those selfish passions which impel men towards chaos and self-destruction. That guilt sustains virtue is certainly the pronouncement of popular Freudianism, and in twentieth-century drama nothing is more likely to be the climax of a play than the realisation by the characters that the circle of guilt spreads far more widely than anyone had yet recognised: in fact, we are *all* guilty. Such a recognition is often the closest modern characters get to personal transcendence. If we fail to recognise the guilt in which we are entangled, runs the doctrine, we can only remain imprisoned within the prejudices and passions to which we were born.

The consequence of this doctrine is that political issues become moralised, and this happens in proportion to the distance between us and the issue. With local issues which affect us directly, we commonly take a broad and complex view, but when we take up positions about events in distant countries we enjoy the luxury of being immune to the consequences of any policy we recommend. The

Vietnam war can be treated in terms of the effect of Agent Orange on man and beast, and we are not troubled by the collapse of South Vietnam into a despotism, nor by the deaths of thousands of boat people. The complexities of South African politics reduce to a moral judgement about apartheid. The average liberal intellectual is left with no room for manoeuvre, because indifference would break the basic rule that we must be involved in the fate of our suffering human fellows. The modern citizen is thus denied even the luxury of neutrality. But it is by the same token that he is licensed to be indifferent to the actual consequences of the position he takes up. He must thus be guilty if he does not repudiate the regime of the Shah of Iran as a Western ally, but is absolved from guilt about the actions of the Ayatollah, whose rule his protests may have helped to bring about.

It will be evident from these remarks that the culture of guilt cannot be taken seriously as a genuinely moral response to the world, for it deals in abstractions and partiality. To the question of whether we can be moral if we do not constantly feel responsibility for the great evils of the world, the answer is certainly that we can. Indeed, it is only by rejecting the moral surrogacy of collective guilt that we can be properly moral at all.

The reason is that to be moral, we must be able to see the world straight. The guilt-ridden live in a fundamentally self-enclosed world from which they find it hard to escape because everything turns into the drama of their own redemption. Such a drama casts others in some such abstract role as victimhood, and the protagonists become preoccupied with resentments which may exist only in their own imagination. Like selfish parents who make up for a deficiency of love by a shower of gifts, they ease their guilt by mechanical reparation. Mistaking their own moral imaginings for reality itself, they give attention not to the real ills of the world, but only to those evils which can be slotted into the drama. In the early 1970s, for example, when the liberal conscience of the West was in deep contortions over the Vietnam war, the Hutu of Ruanda were engaged in the massacre of an estimated 100,000 Tutsi. Sometimes this was a matter of taking children out of classrooms and smashing their skulls with sledgehammers. The *bien pensants* of Britain and the

West took not the slightest interest in these events, and since no one can doubt that they were horrifying, one must look for the reason in the fact that inter-tribal African massacres cannot be plugged in to the psychic system of guilt, indignation and reparation. Quite apart from the remarkable perceptual distortions of the Western response to international events (a blindness to some extent orchestrated, of course, by left-wing activism) there remains the fact that much of what is done supposedly to benefit people construed as victims actively damages the beneficiaries themselves. The history of aid to the Third World, no less than that of attempts at positive discrimination within liberal democratic societies, strongly suggests that people who manage to acquire benefits by exploiting an abstract status as victims of oppression are demeaned and corrupted by it.

The political culture of guilt contains, then, hidden absurdities. To fall into the idea that we in Britain are responsible for such distant events as the famine in Ethiopia is covertly to entertain the assumption that we are omnipotent. Reality in our relations with other people depends, however, on recognising how very little influence we can have over them. Within the culture of guilt, however, those who make reparation are persistently looking for appropriate responses from those they choose to benefit. Such responses are very frequently not forthcoming. In both international and national dramas of this kind, the well-meaning British exponent of social justice begins by trying to alleviate oppression, and ends by facing a charge of moral domination. And not entirely without reason.

It is this entire culture of guilt which the New Right has repudiated, and Mrs Thatcher's political style reflects it clearly. She insists upon treating people as rational and responsible rather than as candidates for special favours. She has recognised that the idea of 'consensus' has been corrupted into an instrument for obscuring economic and other realities. When, towards the end of the great coal strike of 1984, a guilt-driven chorus led by churchmen appealed to her to make some sort of symbolic compromise with the National Union of Mineworkers, she was entirely unmoved. That great struggle had been a classic case of reactionary sentimentalism being used to lever limitless economic benefits from the state. Then and now, the political culture of guilt invokes a familiar rhetoric: caring, compassion and consensus, the three fudging Cs. Those who reject these shibboleths are castigated as greedy and hard-hearted. To dispense with this political syrup without falling into genuine ruthlessness has become the central moral dimension of British politics at the end of the twentieth century. The issue has now emerged, but the discussion of it is still hampered by the melodramatic simplicities of earlier times.

EIGHT

The Continuing Relevance of Socialism

BRIAN BARRY

What is socialism? In proposing a definition, I want to steer between two common notions. One is that 'socialism' is simply a word to be applied nowadays to relatively egalitarian liberals. The other is that socialism is a kind of religion, which hopes for a transformation of human nature and rests on a series of predictions about historical events. Such a view is supported, for example by *Pears Cyclopaedia* (1967) where, in the 'Ideas and Beliefs' section, 'socialism' is followed by 'Southcottism' – the belief in the predictions of Joanna Southcott – and 'spiritualism'.

The conception of socialism that I intend to put forward does not depend in any way on beliefs about the course of history, and does not require a transformation of human nature. To approach it we can follow the course that J. L. Austin often recommended, namely, that when asking for the meaning of a word we should start by looking at its opposites. In the case of 'socialism' the two pairings that immediately come to mind are 'socialism versus capitalism' and 'socialism versus individualism'.

What can we learn from the opposition of socialism to capitalism and individualism? I think that both contrasts fit together with the following definition of socialism: 'A socialist society is one in which the citizens of that society are able, by acting together, to control the major features of the society and, in particular, to overcome the undesirable consequences of individual actions.' Thus conceived, socialism is, above all, a theory of citizenship: it is concerned with empowering citizens to act collectively in pursuit of the interests and ideals that they share with one another and that can be realised only by collective action.

Let me briefly follow through the relations between socialism as I have just defined it and the two contrasting terms, capitalism and individualism. The most prominent contemporary defenders of capitalism, Milton Friedman and F. A. Hayek, constantly claim that its primary virtue is its automatism. Thus Friedman, in his well-known essay 'Capitalism and Freedom', argued that in a capitalist society nobody exercises any power – not even the managers of massive corporations – because all actors are so tightly constrained by the discipline of the market that on any given occasion only one course is open to them. Those who do anything different disappear from the system as a result of bankruptcy. And in his book *The Mirage of Social Justice*, Hayek argues that, precisely because the distribution of income does not arise from any central decision-making process but from millions of independent decisions, the concept of social justice is inapplicable to market outcomes.

Whether we look for our historical antecedents to Marxism or to Fabianism, we are safe in saying, I think, that the core of socialism has always been the rejection of claims such as those of Friedman and Hayek. Where Friedman sees the market as a realm of freedom because nobody has any power, the socialist sees it as a realm of necessity precisely for the same reason. The transformation from a society ruled by the tyranny of the market to one of freedom requires collective control over the economy. Similarly, the socialist turns Hayek's argument on its head. It is precisely because the market is incompatible with the introduction of considerations of distributive justice that it cannot be accepted as the arbiter of income distribution.

As I am presenting it, the core of socialism in its economic aspect is the constraint and modification of the market to accommodate the interests of people as workers, consumers and citizens. The citizens of any society are quite naturally and rightly concerned with large accumulations of power in private hands, and it is a consequence of such a concern that socialism is opposed to private ownership of the means of production. I am sympathetic to the idea of workers' self-management, but what must be emphasised is that no reorganisation of ownership (including ownership by the workers in a firm) can overcome the inadequacies of the market that I shall sketch in a moment. If so-called 'market socialism' denies this, then it is a contradiction in terms.

I've been talking up to now about socialism versus capitalism. What about socialism versus individualism? Individualism is best seen, both historically and analytically, as the generalisation of the case for capitalism to non-economic matters. It is no accident, I suggest, that the notion of the hidden hand originated in the heyday of deism. According to the deistic picture of the universe, God, having arranged things to operate according to universal laws, did not intervene any further in his creation. What appeared to be imperfections were merely the unavoidable by-products of the best possible set of general laws. The parallel with the standard rationale of the market could scarcely be clearer. Hayek particularly, who has often said that he finds himself most at home intellectually in the late eighteenth century, is identified strongly with the ideologically-loaded concept of the 'rule of law'. According to this, states must operate by general laws only and not intervene in the workings of the economy in order to bring about specific outcomes. And, like Leibnitz, Hayek assures us that, even if the results sometimes appear unfortunate in individual cases, all is for the best in the best of all possible worlds so long as we have the best set of general laws.

Individualism, I suggest, is simply what you get if you take the optimistic analysis of the market and extend it beyond economics to the whole of social life. The market paradigm says that, given the right framework of general rules (enforcement of property rights and contracts, maintenance of competition, etc.), pursuit of individual self-interest is transmuted into social good. Individualism – epitomised, for example, in Mill's *On Liberty* – takes this structure of thought and makes it the basis for a whole theory of society. So-called libertarianism, represented by, for example Ayn Rand, Murray Rothbard and their disciple, Robert Nozick, is simply individualism that has run amok. Indeed libertarianism has been well defined as the form taken by liberalism as common sense asymptotically approaches zero.

What marks liberal individualists of all kinds is a distaste, amounting in some cases to detestation, of politics. The wheeling and dealing, the messy compromises that are inseparable from politics, are anathema to them. To them, the worst thing you can say about some area – education, say, or public transport – is that it has become 'politicised'. It might be naively supposed that, in what is supposed to be a democracy, subjecting important areas of public policy to political scrutiny and control would be thought of as a good thing. But no – according to the tenets of individualism, once the general rules have been laid down, people are free to act individually, but not collectively.

Some observers claim to have found something paradoxical in the fact that the Thatcher regime combines liberal individualist rhetoric with authoritarian action. But there is no paradox at all. The two are in fact simply opposite sides of the same coin. Even under the most repressive conditions – in Soweto or the Gaza Strip and the West Bank, for example – people seek to act collectively in order to improve things for themselves, and it requires an enormous exercise of brutal power to fragment these efforts at organisation and to force people to pursue their interests individually. Things are no different here: left to themselves, people will inevitably tend to pursue their interests through collective action – in trade unions, tenants' associations, community organisations and local government, for example. Only the pretty ruthless exercise of central power can defeat these tendencies: hence the common association between individualism and authoritarianism, well exemplified in the fact that the countries held up as models by the free-marketeers are, without exception, authoritarian regimes.

It was, at one time, fashionable to suggest that socialism should be defined as the pursuit of equality. There is, however, nothing distinctively socialist about equality: there can be (and are) egalitarian anarchists and egalitarian liberals as well as egalitarian socialists. Socialism thus has no monopoly on egalitarianism; but more than that, there is nothing in socialism itself that commits one to equality. The central demand of socialism is that outcomes – and this obviously includes the distribution of income – should fall under collective control. But this leaves open what the distribution of income ought to be. Some socialists believe that those who contribute more to society through their work should get more; others believe that the ability to contribute more arises from good fortune and does not constitute a valid claim to finish up with more. The ultimate resolution of this issue depends, I think, on a satisfactory solution to the problem of free will, and I don't think this can be expected soon. (It's significant that the fallen angels in *Paradise Lost* pitched on this as a topic as being good for a few million years of debate.) Anyway, pending the cracking of the problem of free will, socialists can, I suggest, legitimately disagree about equality.

The idea has been put about that socialism is bound to be unattractive to most people because it demands too much in the way of sacrifice. In fact the paradigm of socialism is the prisoner's dilemma, where what is most in the interest of each prisoner individually – to confess – is contrary to the interests of both of them together. Examples abound in real life: if we all try to drive our cars at once, the roads become so congested that none of us can get anywhere; if we all have garden bonfires whenever we wish, none of us can hang out the washing or sit outside in comfort; and so on. The remarkable ideological success of Thatcherism is to identify the selfish, antisocial choice with self-interest, so that the choice in favour of the interests which we share collectively is treated as a piece of self-sacrifice. Obviously, if socialism is to succeed this ideological obfuscation has to be removed; but it is important to recognise that the task is one of education rather than one of mass conversion to altruism.

To any socialist, the operations of the market provide an unending source of illustrations for the thesis that the aggregate results of the pursuit of private interest may well be collectively damaging. The pollution created by firms in the course of profit-maximisation is a hackneyed but none the less central example. I can see no incompatibility between the politics of red and green; on the contrary, socialism seems to me to provide the essential intellectual framework for environmental concerns. It is, of course, true that one of the most arrogant, obstructive and unconscionable polluters in Britain is the Central Electricity Generating Board. But all that shows is the inappropriateness of this kind of public corporation as a socialist instrument.

Pollution by producers is a form of market failure, in that there is no way in which the market can incorporate into its calculations the economic costs, aesthetic damage, and threats to health and life itself created by pollution. Acting through the instrumentality of the state, citizens must step in to curb the pursuit of profit – and let me emphasise that this is equally true whether the producers are privately owned firms, public corporations charged with acting commercially, or workers' co-operatives.

The evil is generated by the logic of the market mechanism itself. To the degree that it works in the way postulated by the elementary textbooks, that is to say to the degree that it is genuinely competitive, it forces firms on pain of bankruptcy to do whatever is legal (or, more precisely, whatever is cost-effective, taking into account the probability and cost of conviction) in the pursuit of profit – however injurious this may be to the labour force, to those living in the neighbourhood, or indeed to the purchasers of their products.

There are more subtle forms of market failure, which again illustrate the way in which uncoordinated individual decisions may add up to outcomes that are not desired. There is no way in which a market can register the willingness to pay for having a service available. Many of us attach a good deal of importance to having public telephones disseminated over the country in case we are stranded and need them, yet it may well be that a large number of these do not get enough use to 'pay for themselves'. Acting according to a commercial criterion here would be failing to provide people with what they want and are willing to pay for. A fanatical marketeer could, presumably, suggest that everyone should adopt a telephone kiosk in some remote village and drive out periodically to it with a sackful of coins to make long telephone calls to Australia. It requires no great intelligence to see what is wrong with this proposal.

There are also, of course, distributive arguments in favour of retaining a dense network of public telephones, and the same mix of collective benefit and distributive considerations can be invoked in many other areas, of which public transport is probably the most important: here again, the value of public transport is not adequately measured by the fares that are collected, because its very existence has a value.

In these examples, the market can be shown to fail even in its own terms: it does not manage to come up with the goods that we want in our capacity as consumers. But the market can also fail in ways that take us beyond the limited perspective of consumerism. If I want to see some beautiful stretch of coastline protected for ever against development, or the ancient quarter of some city saved from demolition, it may indeed be because I want to preserve the option of going and looking at it myself some day. But it need not be. I may simply think that it is good and right for the country to be one in which natural beauty and artefacts of historical interest or aesthetic value are preserved.

Another very significant illustration of the potential clash between market forces and the wishes we have as citizens is this. In very many countries, and sometimes localities within countries, people feel an intense sense of discomfort if more than a certain proportion of the real estate and productive capacity fall into the hands of non-nationals. As individuals they may be quite willing to sell to the highest bidder, but as citizens they may at the same time vote to put a cap on foreign acquisitions. The socialist principle is that what people want as citizens should prevail.

The distribution of income and wealth in a society can be analysed with the same apparatus. According to the by now notorious argument of Robert Nozick, if a large number of people voluntarily pay, say, fifty pence to watch some star performer, they can obviously have no valid objection to whatever distribution of income arises from it, even if the result of this set of transactions and innumerable other sets of transactions like it is to create a grossly unequal distribution. The argument, if such it can be called, is obviously a variant on Locke's suggestion that by 'consenting to the use of money' people consent to whatever distribution of income and wealth comes about. You might as well say that every time we turn on a light we consent to nuclear reactors and acid rain, or that by not between us putting some arbitrary amount of money per year into a public call box somewhere on the Yorkshire moors, we consent to its being carted away.

All that can be deduced here is that a lot of people, taking independent decisions, preferred paying fifty pence to missing the star performer. We cannot say that they approved of the resulting distribution of income, because that was not a choice on offer. The distribution of income is an aggregate outcome, and can be chosen only by a collective decision. We have already seen how we may choose collectively to modify the outcomes we would bring about individually – preventing profitable development that we would pay for as consumers, or barring sales to foreigners that would pay us as individual sellers. And so here too we may for a whole variety of reasons – distribution of power, concern for the quality of social relationships, as well as considerations of equality – wish to change by collective action the outcome of a mass of individual decisions.

Let us simplify the analysis by contrasting two ideal types of educational system. In one, children are allocated to schools so that each school will be representative of the social class and ethnic mix of the district – the area of the local authority, for example. In the other, parents either have educational vouchers which can be used at any school or have the right to apply for their children's admission to any school in the appropriate age range run by the local authority. The schools in turn can select children from among the applicants.

Let us look at the operation of the second system. The result of all the decisions by parents and schools will be some pattern of allocation which nobody chose and perhaps nobody wants. Typically, it will be one in which there is a pecking order of schools. Even if all the schools in an area have equally good facilities and equally good teachers, all that is needed to create a hierarchy is a preference by parents for schools with more rather than fewer children of high academic attainment, and selection by schools among applications on the basis of academic attainment.

From a consumer point of view, this may be a quite unattractive outcome. If there are five schools and everyone wants to get into one of them, four-fifths of the parents are going to be disappointed. Freedom of choice is really no more than freedom to apply: the only school that can be chosen unconditionally is the one at the bottom of the heap – precisely because few choose it. There is no way in which it can be shown *a priori* that parents or children will be more satisfied on average with such a system of so-called parental choice than with one in which each child is allocated to a school whose composition is similar to that of the others in the area.

Suppose, however, that parents were happy enough to have their children educated in schools that were relatively homogeneous with respect to social class and ethnicity. The system of parental choice could then count as a success from the consumer point of view. But we then have to ask how it should be regarded from the point of view of the citizens – those with children currently in the school system and those without. I think the answer is that it should be looked on with misgivings. We live in a society where racial and ethnic tensions have already given rise to large-scale riots, and where the frustration and resentment of losers leads to vandalism and violence. Does it makes sense to perpetuate the divisions of class and ethnic group in the schools? If we leave the composition of the schools to parental choice that is what we shall be doing, even though the choice will not be made explicitly.

The relevance of socialism is here, as in my other examples, to insist that an outcome is not saved from critical assessment by its origin in individual choices. The overall result of a lot of choices made by parents and schools has to be compared with what can be achieved by allocating children to schools with the object of creating a microcosm of the area in each school, and then trying, by precept and practice, to encourage equal respect and understanding among children of different backgrounds.

Miracles are not to be expected from schools: they cannot themselves compensate for everything else that is wrong in a society. But what must be emphasised is that, whether by default or by explicit action, every society chooses either to perpetuate and intensify its divisions in its schools, or to make some effort to overcome them.

The core of socialism, as I have presented it, is that people should act collectively through central and local government to attain ends that cannot be achieved by individual effort. Collective action for shared ends can, of course, be undertaken by people outside the framework of government. Trade unions are an excellent example: though not in themselves socialist, because they pursue a partial interest, they provide a model of socialism in action. Hence their importance in the history of socialism.

The trade union model of collective self-help is also of great significance for social welfare policy, because trade unions all over

Europe in the course of the nineteenth century developed schemes of insurance as a natural extension of their other activities in pursuit of the collective benefit of their members.

In most Continental European countries (the Scandinavian ones taking the lead) these mutual benefit societies were first subsidised and rationalised by the state and then finally more or less completely absorbed in schemes of universal social insurance. The usual way in which these schemes operate is that both contributions and benefits are roughly proportional to income, subject to some minimum level of benefit. There is, therefore, not a great deal of transfer between income strata, with the implication that those with higher incomes have no self-interested reason to resist a generous level of provision. The question people in each stratum are invited to ask themselves is what level of benefits they want to pay for; and the answer has turned out to be 'a lot'. It is a commonplace that, in the last forty years, the scale of transfer payments in Western Europe, outside this country, has grown phenomenally, so that costs run at around a fifth of the national income in most countries.

Meanwhile, the British experience has been strikingly different from that of the rest of Western Europe. Starting in the immediate post-war period with one of the best-funded systems, Britain has by now slipped below most of the others in the proportion of the gross national product that goes on income maintenance. Why is this? One possible explanation is that in the same period Britain has slipped from having the highest income per head to having one of the lowest, and, therefore, cannot 'afford' as much as the others. But why should relative poverty produce a lower *proportional* expenditure? One might think that, if anything, insurance would be relatively more important the less well off people are.

We should I think look for an answer at the attitude of mind that thinks in terms of 'what the country can afford' instead of 'what coverage people want to pay for'. Abstracting from their variations, let us say that the Continental systems exhibit the 'insurance model'. How then shall we describe the underlying ethos of the British system, as it has developed over the course of this century? I suggest that it should be called the 'needs model'. By this I understand the following guiding idea: that payments should be made only to those who are in need, and should be set at a level sufficient to get them above some defined poverty level.

I shall not stop to belabour all the differences between a pure insurance model and a pure need model, but it is, I hope, evident that they are opposed at every turn. The most striking contrast between them is that the needs model entails means-testing for all benefits, whereas the insurance model in its pure form has no room for means-testing at all. Thus, under the insurance model people who are sick or unemployed will automatically receive (say) three-quarters of their previous income, while under a needs model they may receive nothing if they have too much money in the bank or a continuing source of family income. From the insurance point of view, this is as bad as an insurance company's refusing to compensate for a burglary on the grounds that the policy-holder can perfectly well afford to replace the stolen items out of his or her own pocket. Conversely, from the needs point of view, paying out a lot of money to someone who is already well off is a 'waste' of resources that could be better 'targeted' on the 'needy'.

Life never makes things completely easy for the makers of models. Although the bulk of the money disbursed within the Continental systems falls under the insurance model, each country also has some kind of means-tested assistance for people who fall between the cracks. Conversely, the British system is some way from exemplifying the needs model exclusively. Formally, the system is one of social insurance with flat-rate benefits. There are, however, two observations to be made. The first is that flat-rate benefits, the legacy of the wartime Beveridge report, violate the insurance concept, which is one of income replacement. A flat-rate scheme is like a system of fire insurance in which every houseowner gets just enough to rebuild a minimal house whatever the size of the one that has been burned down. It is clear that, in spite of its insurance trappings, a flat-rate system is best seen as a way of meeting needs – something that Beveridge himself acknowledged.

The second point to make is that, in any case, Beveridge's flat-rate benefits have never been set at a level above the official poverty line. The result has been that at no time since the war have there been fewer than millions of people on means-tested supplementary benefits. If the insurance-related benefits have to be topped up in this way, it seems fair to say that the system as a whole conforms primarily to the needs model.

As a further support for this view of the matter, I can adduce the fact that the surviving elements of the insurance model are seen as anomalies. Why, it is asked recurrently by some wiseacre, should 'we' be paying good money to people who don't need it? The solution, which is constantly being independently discovered, is a negative income tax which would put all benefits on a means-tested basis. (The change in name to negative taxation is thought for some reason to solve all the existing problems of means-tested benefits.)

On the face of it, the needs model is rather attractive: those who can afford it give, and those who need it receive. It is noteworthy that, with almost no exceptions, Anglophone philosophers who have written about the foundations of the 'welfare state' have seen the task as one of defending the claims of need. The needs model is Good Samaritanism writ large, and indeed arguments in favour of it often start by appealing to cases when one person can save another from some situation of dire need. The basis of Good Samaritanism is that the aid is given without any expectation of return. The Samaritan may, of course, hope that somebody will do the same for him if the occasion ever arises, but there is no link between his present altruistic act and what may or may not happen to him in some like contingency in future.

I expect that what I have just said will already have reminded some readers of Richard Titmuss's argument in *The Gift Relationship*. In that book, voluntary blood donation, an act of unconditional altruism, was advanced as a paradigm for social policy generally. Now blood donation is significantly different from other areas of collective provision precisely in that it is voluntary: no supporter of a general scheme of transfer payments is going to suggest that the wherewithal should come from voluntary contributions. The relevance of blood donation is, however, taken to be this. Blood donation may be taken as an expression of social solidarity, which we may understand as the generalisation of Good Samaritanism. And social policy might then be seen as an expression of social solidarity too, here understood as universal and compulsory

Good Samaritanism. Concretely, this would entail that those who can afford it vote to pay taxes to support those in need out of a sense of empathy.

Both Titmuss and his fellow L.S.E. professor, T. H. Marshall, argued that the moral basis of the post-war welfare state was laid in the experience of the Second World War, and in particular the sense of common vulnerability and interdependence generated by the blitz. Granting all this, the obvious problem was, as Marshall pointed out, that, as the wartime conditions of deprivation were relaxed, the spirit of wartime solidarity melted away too.

What happens when a system founded on an assumption of a high level of social solidarity has to exist in a society where that assumption has failed to be true? The answer is, I suggest, what has actually happened in this country over the past forty years. That disasters, natural or man-made, stimulate social solidarity is one of the best-documented findings in social science. But what is equally well-established is that after things return to normal, solidarity gradually diminishes. I simply do not think that our society could be transformed by acceptable means into one displaying solidarity of an intensity sufficient to support a generously-funded system of welfare benefits.

Where does this leave us? Fortunately, it leaves us still in a good position. The insurance model is, I wish to say, the implementation of the socialist principle with regard to social security. Insurance by its very nature requires a lot of people to get together, and the best insurance occurs when everyone is in it, with the power of the fisc as the ultimate underwriter. The reasons for state insurance are as strong now as they were when the mutual benefit societies were absorbed on the continent of Europe. Unemployment, for example, has never been satisfactorily insured against in the private market. And it is inevitable that private sickness pay insurance – like medical insurance – will charge higher premiums to those who are poorer health risks, or even refuse to insure them altogether. (We can see this phenomenon at work in the distasteful but entirely logical efforts of insurance companies to exclude from life insurance coverage those whom they regard as being at risk from A.I.D.S.).

What I have just said should bring out an important point about social insurance. It is not the object of social insurance simply to ape the workings of private insurance, but to provide coverage for everybody without discriminating against bad risks. This is one of the ways in which social insurance is better than private insurance. The point of insurance is to provide protection against misfortunes, but no private scheme will provide protection against the misfortune of being a bad risk in the first place. Social insurance can and does.

Now it is, of course, true that, as a result of this, some very fortunate people would be better off in a hypothetical private market than under a social insurance scheme – though we should not forget the very high overheads of private insurance, which are inherent in the attempt to keep out poor prospects. It is often suggested that, because of this, social insurance is not really insurance at all. The suggestion is obtuse in presupposing that private insurance is the only kind of insurance. Social insurance is a different and better kind of insurance because it is, as the cliché has it, 'from the cradle to the grave' (or, more briefly, 'from womb to tomb'), and membership in it is not voluntary.

Because membership is compulsory, there is no necessity to treat bad risks less well than good ones. Moreover, those who are severely disabled from birth, so that they have no prospects of ever earning enough to pay insurance contributions, can be included by a simple and obvious extension of the insurance idea, namely, that, of all the things we would wish to insure against if we could, being severely disabled at birth must surely head the list.

It is apparent that social insurance calls upon a certain degree of solidarity in that, for example, people of voting age know whether or not they are severely disabled, and the great majority are not. It is, however, in the nature of all public goods that some people get more out of them than others, and the disproportion between contribution and expected benefit is probably less for a system of social insurance than for almost any other public good. And I think that, if once people see the logic of social insurance, they should be able to see that it would be an anomaly to discriminate against or exclude the bad or hopeless risks.

The fundamental argument for socialism, as I hope I have illustrated in my various examples, is simply that it is the only way of satisfying a lot of important desires. Of course, the antithesis of socialism – capitalism or individualism – gives us some of what we want. But it forces all aspirations into the one narrow channel of making and spending money. There is nothing about socialism that is incompatible with making and spending money, but, as I have tried to show, the object of socialism is to provide us with options in our capacity as citizens as well as in our capacity as individual consumers.

Acting through the market, we can do nothing to change a grotesquely unjust distribution of income, to create an adequate system of income-maintenance, to prevent industries from polluting and farmers from destroying the countryside, or to provide ourselves with properly-funded public services of all kinds. Only in our capacity as citizens can we, acting collectively through local and national governments, bring about the outcomes that we want.

But do we really want them? I think it must be conceded that it is possible to create a society in which the response to market failure is not a swing to socialism, but an exacerbation of individual efforts to stay ahead by making and spending yet more money. Does the public health service have long waiting lists and inadequate facilities? Buy private insurance. Has public transport broken down? Buy a car for each member of the family above driving age. Has the countryside been built over or the footpaths eradicated? Buy some elaborate exercise machinery and work out at home. Is air pollution intolerable? Buy an air-filtering unit and stay indoors. Is what comes out of the tap foul to the taste and chock-full of carcinogens? Buy bottled water. And so on. We know it can all happen because it has: I have been doing little more than describing Southern California.

Now it is worth noticing two things about the private substitutes that I have described. The first is that in the aggregate they are probably much more expensive than would be the implementation of the appropriate public policy. The second is that they are extremely poor replacements for the missing outcomes of good public policy. Nevertheless, it is plain that the members of a society can become so alienated from one another, so mistrustful of any form of collective action, that they prefer to go it alone.

Let's not feel too sorry for the inhabitants of Southern California. Most of them have enough money to carry out the project of extreme privatisation in style – and anyway there's all that sunshine. What is much less of a joke is the prospect of the same thing in a country with a third of the income and even less than a third of the sunshine.

Can it happen here? The object of the present government is undoubtedly to create the conditions for its happening. By systematically reducing the quality of public services of all kinds, it hopes to turn people away from them and encourage them to seek solutions individually. There is, it seems to me, no guarantee that this strategy will fail. As I said before, I do not regard socialism as having any built-in prophecies. Perhaps, however perverse it may be, most people will get locked into pursuing private solutions to public deficiencies. But I hope not because this would entail all of us living more limited and impoverished lives.

NINE

The Paradoxes of Thatcherism

DAVID MARQUAND

It is plainly impossible to discuss the paradoxes of Thatcherism without offering a definition of Thatcherism; and the more I contemplate the phenomenon, the more protean and elusive I find it. I will therefore begin in a rather tedious fashion by explaining how I do not intend to proceed. I do not intend to look, except in passing and by way of illustration, at the policies actually followed by the Thatcher governments. It would be all too easy to point to paradoxes here. A rather striking paradox which occurs to me is that one of Mrs Thatcher's greatest triumphs as Prime Minister, namely the victory in the Falklands war, might not have been achieved if the government had carried out the cuts in naval expenditure which it had thought of making before the war. That paradox reflects the inherent tension between the assertion of national pride, which is one element in Thatcherism, and the assertion of very strict control over public expenditure, which is another element. An even greater paradox, perhaps, is that the government has not, in fact, cut the proportion of the gross domestic product going to public expenditure. Indeed, by the end of the second term of the Thatcher government it was very slightly higher than it was when the government came into office.

All this, however, seems to me to be small beer. Democratic government, in a complicated mass society, managed through enormously complex bureaucracies, is bound to display paradoxes of this kind – particularly when the society concerned has been undisturbed by war or revolution for a long time. A very obvious, if rather worn, metaphor for modern government is that of the oil tanker which continues along its existing course by simple force of inertia, almost irrespective of what the captain on the bridge is trying to do. Any government, no matter what its political colour, coming into power in 1979, would have inherited a vast backlog of commitments and expectations from the previous forty years; no government would have found these easy to change. Judged by the outputs of the system, moreover, it is at least arguable that the most important break in the continuity of post-war economic policy took place in 1976, not in 1979. The first monetarist Chancellor of the Exchequer since the war, apart from the brief interlude of Peter Thorneycroft, was Denis Healey, not Geoffrey Howe. The government that did most to screw down the rate of wage increases to restore private sector profitability was that of Harold Wilson and Jim Callaghan. By the same token, it is also arguable that if the Labour Party had won the 1979 election, one of the most important features of the Thatcher era – the upsurge in the exchange rate which took place in 1981, and the sharp fall in manufacturing exports which followed – would have taken place under a Labour government instead of under the Conservatives. So the fact that even after nine years in power the Thatcher government has not jettisoned all the legacies of the post-war consensus is not very surprising or very interesting.

If Thatcherism is not the policies of the Thatcher governments, what is it? Any definition will be arbitrary, and my definition is no doubt open to challenge. As I see it there are four dimensions to Thatcherism. In the first place, Thatcherism is a sort of British Gaullism: 'sort of' because it differs from French Gaullism in a number of ways, some of which I shall mention in a moment. Like Gaullism, however, it was born out of a growing sense of despair, reflecting the experience of a generation of apparent national decline. That sense of despair was often focussed on the economic sphere, because relative economic decline was the most obvious aspect of national decline. It was not, however, the only aspect. Political decline, though less obvious, was in some ways even more important. As in Fourth Republic France, moreover, a generation of political decline seemed to many to have led to a crisis of governability and of legitimacy – not, of course, anything like as severe as that which brought President de Gaulle to the Elysée, but nevertheless a crisis of governability more severe than anything experienced by the British political class since the First World War.

Therein lies the similarity between British Thatcherism and French Gaullism. Now for the contrast. Both of them may be seen as attempts to challenge, to halt, if possible to reverse the processes of decline, and to do so by reasserting national traditions, behind which lie deep reservoirs of popular support. But, of course, the Gaullists sought to reassert French national traditions, whereas the Thatcherites have reasserted British ones. And there is a very important difference between the two. For de Gaulle, the national tradition which had to be reasserted was the tradition of the active Colbertian state – a tradition which goes back through three hundred years of French history. With that was combined an attempt – at the least a rhetorical attempt, but for most of the time, more than just a rhetorical attempt – to assert French leadership of Europe against the perceived hegemony of the 'Anglo-Saxons' in the Western world. These were French traditions; and the policies springing from them corresponded with deeply-held French attitudes. In Mrs Thatcher's case, the equivalent set of national traditions is altogether different. Hers – and her country's – are the traditions of economic liberalism, of the minimal state as opposed to the active Colbertian state. In the foreign sphere, they are the traditions of glorious isolation, of little Englandism, combined in practice with a very strong commitment to close ties with the United States, and to an Atlanticist foreign policy.

That leads on to the second aspect of Thatcherism which seems to me to be of interest: its economic liberalism. In part, no doubt, a broadly neo-liberal approach to economic policy is a matter of necessity rather than of choice. I suggested just now that no matter which party had been in power between 1980 and 1982, it would have been impossible to stop the upward movement in the exchange rate of the pound sterling, given the fact that it was now a petro-currency, and that it was therefore subject to fluctuations which had nothing to with the competitiveness of British exports, and everything to do with basically political decisions by the oil-producing states. That is only one example of the ways in which any medium-sized nation state in the modern world is vulnerable to economic forces beyond its frontiers. To that extent, all British governments are bound to be at least partially neo-liberal in practice. In a sense, there is nothing else to be: they cannot insulate themselves against the effects of policy decisions taken (or, in some cases, not taken) elsewhere. However, the Thatcherites have not been neo-liberal solely by *force majeure*. They have been so by conviction as well.

The central elements in their neo-liberalism are familiar, and it is not necessary to spend much time on them. The first is a rejection of Keynesian macro-economic management. This springs, of course, from the belief that such macro-economic management is inherently inflationary, at least in the long run; that the attempt deliberately to maintain what the 1944 White Paper on employment policy famously called 'a high and stable level of employment' is, in the long run, doomed; that if governments try to follow such a course, all they will do, in the long run, is to produce even higher unemployment, as well as debauching the currency, raising the level of inflation and so distorting the whole process of resource allocation. Secondly, and equally obviously, the neo-liberal project involves an attack on the whole idea of micro-economic intervention by public authorities. It rejects the whole idea of 'planning', and it also rejects the notion of 'tripartism', the quasi-corporatism of the 1960s, and the 1970s. It does all this in the belief that only the market can allocate resources efficiently; that if government intervenes to change the outputs which market allocation would have produced, in the interests of some goal of national success in the long run, it is bound to make mistakes; and that in consequence the economy will, in the end, function less efficiently than it would have done without government intervention. Government can only back losers; it cannot back winners.

Those are very obvious elements. There are one or two others that seem to me slightly less obvious, but more interesting, and in some ways more important. Implicit in the neo-liberal diagnosis of Britain's economic failures in the 1960s and 1970s was a political theory; and that political theory was in some ways more interesting than the economic one. In essence, the political theory ran as follows: Keynesians and planners both held, and held on respectable classical economic grounds, that it might at times be right for public authorities to correct market failure. In practice, however, government failure is more likely than market failure. Even if there is a theoretical case for government intervention to correct the failures of the market on purely economic grounds, it would be wiser not to intervene because government itself is prone to failure, and to failure of a more destructive kind. Government is prone to failure for two reasons, both inescapable in a modern mass democracy. In the first place, the processes of electoral competition in a modern mass democracy are themselves inherently inflationary. The vote market is not like other markets because the consumer (i.e. the voter) operates with no budget constraint. It makes sense for the consumer in the vote market to buy the most expensive products (i.e. policies). It also makes sense for the salesmen in the vote market (i.e. the politicians) to sell the most expensive products because they know that they will sell better than cheap ones. Thus, the whole process is inflationary in two ways: in the obvious sense that, in order to pay for the excessive expenditures on which governments are bound to embark in these circumstances, they will debauch the currency and expand the money supply; and in a moral sense, because the voters themselves will be under constant pressure to make ever more exaggerated demands.

The second reason why government failure is inherently likely, and inherently dangerous, is that within the complex, bureaucratic apparatus of the modern state there is a built-in pressure for bureaucratic empire-building. The way in which bureaucrats maximise what is, for them, the equivalent of profit is to maximise their bureaus. They therefore exert an irresistible pressure for expanding government on the politicians who are nominally, but only nominally, in control of them. Linked with all this, moreover, is a moral argument for the free market. It is only in the free, competitive market that men and women can realise themselves and their aspirations without interference from others. In the political market place their preferences are distorted and corrupted. In the real market, the economic market, they are themselves, acting for themselves, choosing for themselves, and responsible for their own actions in a sense which is not, and cannot be, true of the political market. So for moral reasons, as well as for practical reasons, government should leave the market to its own devices.

That is, I hope, a fair summary of the main elements of what might be called the neo-liberal strand in Thatcherism. But there is a quite different strand running alongside it, which has very little to do with economic liberalism and which, in some respects at any rate, is at odds or in contention with it. Within Thatcherism there is a strong element of traditional Toryism, as well as of economic liberalism. Thatcherism also stresses patriotism, pride in being British, the need to re-assert British traditions. Victorian values, and the rhetoric of Victorian values, are clearly central to it. It stresses the virtues of authority, of hierarchy, of discipline, of order: in a nutshell, the military virtues. And of those virtues, liberalism, even economic liberalism, is inherently subversive.

Finally, there is a fourth strand in Thatcherism, which it is equally important to try to understand, but which is, at the same time, extremely nebulous and difficult to grasp. In a sense which has not been true of previous peacetime Prime Ministers, at any rate in recent times, Mrs Thatcher's political style is both populist and charismatic. (Again there is an obvious parallel with De Gaulle.) She is, of course, leader of the Conservative Party and head of the government; as such, she commands a formidable battery of institutional power. But in a sense – or, at any rate, to an extent – which has not been true of any of her recent predecessors, her authority is independent of the institutions over which she presides. In Thatcherism, as in Gaullism, the leader embodies the popular will; the leader knows instinctively what the populace feel and want; her heart beats in time with the people's hearts. And because her heart beats in time with the people's hearts, because she knows that and because they know it too, she can appeal over the heads of the supposed representatives of the people (including her own ministers) to the people themselves.

Hence arises one of the most fascinating features of Thatcherism in practice: the Prime Minister's extraordinary capacity to, so to speak, run against herself, or rather to run against her government. The implications are worth exploring. Modern government is, among other things, an exercise in frustration, in disappointment. No government carries out all its promises, or does what it said it would do; no government succeeds completely, and all governments upset and offend the governed. By the same token, all democratic electorates are disappointed in their governments, resent their failures and feel aggrieved by the gap between promise and performance. Yet by an extraordinary feat of political legerdemain, these inevitable resentments and grievances have, under the Thatcher governments, been mobilised by the head of the government in her own cause. One reason, no doubt, is the economic liberalism which I discussed a moment ago. Standing, as she does, for limited government, it is not altogether illogical for Mrs Thatcher to pray in aid any examples of government failure, even if they occurred during her own term of office. But I do not believe that that is the whole story, or even a very substantial part of it. Much more significant is Mrs Thatcher's sense that she embodies the real will of the people, as opposed to the apparent will of their representatives who may from time to time speak on their behalf; and that, by virtue of this, she stands above and beyond the government of which she is the head.

It is not difficult to see why all this should possess popular appeal. Two aspects of that appeal are worth looking at here. The first is cultural. Thatcherism, it seems to me, is at one and the same time a revenge for, and a paradoxical continuation of, the cultural revolution of the 1960s, of the so-called permissive society. The element of revenge is plain enough: 'Go back, you flower people, back where you came from, wash your hair, get dressed properly, get to work on time and stop all this whingeing and moaning.' That side of Thatcherism is very obvious; and the reasons why it appeals are obvious too. Plain people were shocked by the mixture of sexual indulgence, cultural nihilism and half-baked Marxism which constituted the radical *chic* of the Sixties; and, still more perhaps, by the defeatist me-tooism with which guilt-ridden elites – educational, cultural and sometimes even political – so often greeted the manifestations of that *chic*. The element of continuity is more complicated. The cultural revolution of the Sixties stressed self-fulfilment, and demanded instant gratification for the claims of the self. It emphasised the values of authenticity, of direct experience, of free choice, of all that was implied by the fashionable solipsism, 'doing your own thing'. Emotionally, indeed even intellectually, those values are first cousins to the values of market liberalism. In market liberalism, after all, the consumer is king, driven solely by the desire to maximise pleasure and minimise pain. In a strange, paradoxical way, Thatcherism can therefore appeal both to the inheritors of the Sixties, to yesterday's hippies who are now today's yuppies, and to the defenders of traditional values who yearn retrospectively for a chance to beat the hippies over the head.

The second aspect of its appeal is related to the first, but can best be described as social. In a way which has been true of no previous Conservative politician, indeed of few British politicians of any party, the Thatcherites have managed to tap the resentment of raw, uncouth, socially and psychologically insecure new elites, or rather would-be new elites, against old and established elites, rather as Joe McCarthy did in the United States in the early Fifties. As Julian Critchley once pointed out, Mrs Thatcher was swept to the leadership of her party by a 'peasants' revolt'. Now the peasants are in control. But they are not ordinary peasants; they are *kulaks*, upwardly mobile, economically successful, and desperate to buy the status to which they think their success entitles them. Like so many similar groups in previous periods of history, they have discovered that status is not for sale – or not, at any rate, at the price most of them can afford. The old mandarinate is still there, still looking down on them; and the more they bustle and push, the more the mandarins despise them. Norman Tebbit reaches the Cabinet, but in the eyes of the mandarinate he is still the Cockney airline pilot. Mrs Thatcher reaches Number Ten Downing Street, but Oxford refuses her an honorary degree. Not surprisingly, the peasants react with a mixture of envy and contempt. Thatcherism is the vehicle of their envy: the doctrine of the tough, hard, no-nonsense new men, the thrusting boosters as my son calls them, who see standing in their way an old, tired, defeated yet still privileged Establishment, which still possesses an uncanny ability to inspire unease among those who wish to displace it.

Allied to that resentment, moreover, is a resentment which goes very deep in the provinces, and which seems to me to have gone deeper in recent years, against the metropolitan cliques which are seen to be running the country, and particularly its cultural media. That resentment too is grist to Thatcherism's mill. The Thatcherites' patent loathing of the B.B.C., and their equally patent wish to humble it, has, of course, an expedient side. If the B.B.C. can be intimidated into behaving as the government wishes, the government will find it that much easier to achieve its purposes. But there is more to it than expediency. The B.B.C. is (or at least was, in the days before Mrs Thatcher came to power) pre-eminently mandarin, as much a bastion of the toffee-nosed south-eastern establishment as Oxford and Cambridge, the Foreign Office or the Athenaeum. Norman Tebbit's speeches and Brian Walden's *Sunday Times* columns provide ample examples of the resentments to which all this gives rise.

Hence, I suspect, the paradoxes which most need examination. The first and most obvious of these paradoxes – but not, for that reason, the least interesting – has received a good deal of comment from a number of standpoints. Andrew Gamble put it well when he pointed out, soon after Mrs Thatcher came to power, that the Thatcherite free economy would have to go hand in hand with a strong state: that taking the state off the backs of the people, to use Thatcherite rhetoric, entails a stronger, and in some respects, a more intrusive state than we knew before. Examples are legion. The Education Bill is only the most recent, though perhaps the most vivid. Another is the attack which central government has launched against local government, and which seems to have destroyed what James Bulpitt once called the 'dual polity'. This last is, of course, one of the most striking features of the last few years, as the community tax, the abolition of the metropolitan counties and the changes in housing policy all show.

The logic of the paradox is, however, more interesting and more deserving of attention than these examples. There are two aspects to it. The whole neo-liberal project is paradoxical in the first place. At the end of his three-volume masterpiece, *Law, Legislation and Liberty*, F. A. Hayek points out that a market order can flourish only if the values appropriate to it prevail; and that in late twentieth-century societies those values are in retreat. The values appropriate to a market economy, he writes,

> were inevitably learned by all the members of a population consisting chiefly of independent farmers, artisans and apprentices who shared the daily experiences of their masters. They held an ethos that esteemed the prudent man, the good husbandman and provider who looked after the future of his family and his business by building up capital, guided less by

the desire to consume much than by the wish to be regarded as successful by his fellows . . .

At present, however, an ever-increasing part of the population of the Western world grow up as members of large organisations and thus as strangers to those rules of the market which have made the great society possible. To them, the market economy is largely incomprehensible; they have never practised the rules on which it rests and its results seem to them irrational and immoral.[1]

The implication is clear. The market order, in which free men maximise their interests, will not produce the best results for society as a whole unless one has the sort of men who can in fact be trusted to behave in a way that the market order requires. People living in a society which has been corrupted by large organisations and state hand-outs will not freely and spontaneously behave in the kind of way that the market order requires. Nor will they start behaving in new ways by someone telling them that it is in their interests to do so, because it was an essential part of neo-liberal diagnosis of the evils of the 1960s and 1970s that, catastrophic as were the results for society of the industrial behaviour prevalent at that time, that behaviour was completely rational from the individual point of view, given the existing set of social arrangements. Therefore it is not enough simply to preach market liberalism in order to get people to behave more sensibly. One has to carry through a profound cultural change. Implicit in what Hayek says is that a neo-liberal government which really did wish to return to a market order would be forced to engage in an enterprise of social engineering at least as heroic and intrusive as anything attempted by the social engineers of the 1960s and 1970s.

Let me give an example. There is not much doubt that the explosion in welfare spending, both absolutely and as a proportion of G.D.P., which took place in the 1960s in all developed societies, did so, at least in part, because women were beginning to rebel against traditional attitudes to the family and to their role in the family, and because it was therefore becoming necessary for the state to pay people to perform the caring services which women had previously performed for nothing. If that is so, it is no longer simply an interesting aberration that many neo-liberals wish to reassert 'Victorian values', and to bring women back into the home where they will once again perform these caring services without payment. It is an essential part of the economic programme, one of the aims of which is to contain the ever-mounting cost of social welfare.

Thus, the paradox of the strong, intrusive state and the free economy is built in to the neo-liberal project itself. But that paradox, of course, is greatly exacerbated by the Gaullist element in Thatcherism, which I mentioned earlier: by the Thatcherites' belief that they must take traditional elites and the traditional establishment by the scruffs of their necks, and force national recovery onto our sadly battered economy. Martin Wiener's now famous book, *English Culture and the Decline of the Industrial Spirit*,[2] was not Thatcherite in intention, but whether intentionally or not it encapsulated one of the most important aspects of Thatcherism – the belief that Britain's economic decline, which it was part of the Thatcherite project to reverse, was due to the aristocratic embrace of the old establishment and the old elites, which had snuffed out the entrepreneurial spirit of the hard-driving Victorian manufacturers who made Britain great in the nineteenth century. On these assumptions, Sir Keith Joseph's 'enterprise culture' could be achieved only by a very complicated exercise in social engineering. Hence the Education Bill which is now going through Parliament, among other measures.

That leads on to a second and more fundamental paradox. It is the paradox of, or perhaps the tension between, the Gaullist side of Thatcherism, for which the object of the whole exercise is to reverse a century of national decline, and the neo-liberal view of the world market and of the proper attitude of a national government towards the world market. Logically, a neo-liberal must be for free trade and against neo-mercantilism in any of its various forms. The state cannot know better than the market. Therefore, adjustment by any national economy to the changes which take place in the world market must be market-led.

The traditional doctrine of international trade says, in effect, that free trade benefits everybody. It benefits not only the strong, but the weak as well, because everybody benefits by producing those goods in which they have a comparative advantage, and by importing those in which they have a comparative disadvantage. The trouble with this theory is that it is static, not dynamic. It is a very good theory for people who are already well-equipped for the market, as Britain was in the middle of the nineteenth century. It is not such a good theory for those who need to equip themselves for the market. This, of course, is why it was not accepted by Imperial Germany in the nineteenth century, and why it has not been accepted by Japan, the prime example of an entrepreneurial state in modern times. That fact presents no problems for a French Gaullist. Colbertian national development, by and through a strong, interventionist state is part of the tradition to which French Gaullists appeal. It does, however, pose a very difficult problem for British Gaullists. Their national traditions point in exactly the opposite direction. Britain's national tradition is that of those who could afford free trade, in whose interests it was that the whole of the world should accept the free-trade doctrine, and who could enjoy the benefits of what one American historian has called an informal 'free-trade empire'.[3] But in the days when that tradition took shape Britain was the leader. At a time when, by definition, Britain is no longer the leader, when she is suffering the consequences of one hundred years of relative decline, matters are much more complicated. Today, the national traditions to which Thatcherism appeals point not towards a renewal of Britain's old economic supremacy, but towards subordination to stronger economies and multinational firms. It is too early to tell how this paradox will be resolved, but there are intriguing signs that the Mark II Thatcherism of the middle and late Eighties may be different in this respect from Mark I Thatcherism, and that covertly, without making a great song and dance about it, Mark II Thatcherism is becoming more like French Gaullism and less like its own early incarnation than one might imagine. In other words, the Thatcher government may, in fact, be moving nervously and gingerly towards becoming a kind of developmental state, on the Gaullist or Japanese pattern, watering down its neo-liberal view of the world market in the process.

The last paradox I want to explore is cultural in character. I believe that it goes to the heart of the Conservative Party, and of the emotional bases of that party. It follows from what I have been saying that Thatcherism is both revolutionary and counter-revolutionary; that it appeals to new aspirations, and at the same time reasserts old values; that it promises both freedom and order, choice and discipline. The last paradox I want to discuss springs from this. The best way to approach it is by means of one of my favourite political quotations. It is from Edmund Burke, who wrote that 'To be attached to the sub-division, to love the little platoon we belong to in society, is the first principle (the germ as it were) of public affections.' That attitude, it seems to me, is pretty close to the heart of at least one very important element in the British Tory tradition. What Burke was saying was that the greater society, the wider society, is a mosaic of smaller collectivities; and that it is in these smaller collectivities that civility is learnt. Between the state and the citizen there lies, and there ought to lie, a mass of intermediate institutions which protect the individual from arbitrary power, much as the ozone layer protects the earth from cosmic radiation.

Traditionally it is radicals, the Left, who have been suspicious of these intermediate institutions. Not all radicals, of course; in twentieth-century Britain, one very important set of intermediate institutions, namely the trade unions, have been part of the labour movement and have provided an important part of the Labour Party's power base. That, however, has been a bit of an embarrassment to the Left, at any rate to the doctrinaire socialist Left. And in terms of thought, even if not in terms of action, the Left has tended to assume that intermediate institutions, if not corrupt, have at any rate an inherent propensity for corruption. Mancur Olson's famous book, *The Rise and Decline of Nations*,[4] attributing economic decline to the operations of selfish and non-encompassing intermediate institutions, pursuing their own narrow interests without reference to the general interest, is firmly in the tradition of American radicalism, and close to one element in the tradition of British radicalism. But the Tory tradition in this country has always seen such institutions as nurseries of civility and bastions of freedom, needing to be nurtured and protected, and to be interfered with, if at all, only with great caution and a certain degree of humility. That is why the Tory party in Britain, unlike right-wing parties in many other countries, found it extraordinarily easy to come to terms with the rise of organised labour, and partially to incorporate the rising labour movement into the political order after the First World War. Moreover, some of these intermediate institutions, at any rate, are inextricably bound up with the Tory culture, which has sustained the Tory party for so many decades and even centuries. Yet partly because of its radical populist element, and partly because of its patriotic, Anglo-Gaullist element, Thatcherism has launched a sustained and powerful attack on a whole range of important inter-mediate institutions – not just on the B.B.C., on the trade unions and on local authorities, but also on the universities, including the ancient universities of Oxford and Cambridge, and even, it sometimes seems, on the Church of England.

What happens to Tory culture if that attack continues and succeeds? The other day I had the privilege of talking to a rather senior high Tory who said he thought the battle between wets and drys in the Cabinet was now over. There were no wets; the wets had been smashed to pieces. Everybody accepted the dry economic diagnosis; and everyone agreed with the dry economic cure. But, he went on, there is a very acute tension within the government even so. The real line of cleavage within the government is between those who want to sell off every cathedral close to Tescos in the name of the free market, and those who want to preserve them in the name of being British, or at least of being English: between those who believe in economic liberalism without qualification, and those who wish to erect barriers to market forces, not in the name of wet compassion but in the name of continuity, community and nation. Which will come out on top? There is no way of telling, of course, but I have a suspicion that it will be the traditional Tories, not the hard, radical Thatcherite ones.

TEN

A Sociologist's View of Thatcherism

A. H. HALSEY

I shall argue in this essay that neither socialism nor individualism can be written out of the political culture of Britain. I shall look for the roots of current controversy in past political debate and sociological theory, take a view of the question of whether economic liberalism can create a good society, and end with some remarks on our tendency to exaggerate the productive and neglect the reproductive problem of the Western European countries. Calm reflection shows up both Mrs Thatcher's rhetorical resolve to drive socialism from the public agenda and hard-Left demagoguery about the overthrow of capitalism by class revolution to be the quintessential stuff of sensationalism. It is in the nature of the media to follow fashion and to substitute ephemeral fancy for sober fact. The image of Mrs Thatcher is to politics what the scantily-clad lady portrayed in the daily tabloid is to domesticity – the promise will always outstrip the performance.

It is true that Mrs Thatcher affirms that there are no societies, only individuals and families. But Mrs Thatcher is no social philosopher. It is true, too, that the 1988 budget and the revised regulations for social security signal the intention of our present government to turn its back on fiscal strategies towards greater social equality, and instead to seek common wealth through individual enterprise. But welfare states are not to be demolished easily. They are the historical outcome of adaptation to the industrial mode of production, and they have their vested interests in all classes and at all points on the political spectrum.

The first myth to be dispelled is that there is anything new here for the newspapers. Even the serious press misleads us all with demands

for 'the big idea' with which to confront Thatcherism. If Mr Hugo
Young looks for it at party conferences he should not be surprised to
find only gibberish. It is no different at either Labour or Tory
conferences. The more interesting, if less newsworthy, truth is that
the debate is ancient. Mrs Thatcher is no more modern than Harriet
Martineau. The arguments are fundamentally the same as those
which surrounded the 1834 Poor Law. Thomas Malthus, Alex de
Tocqueville, Karl Marx, the Chartists and the political economists of
laissez faire are still alive and well. The ideas are the same; only the
circumstances change. Romance and reality are both essential to
successful political movements: but so far we have been witnessing
no more than small practical steps beneath large programmatic
statements towards realigning the balance between individualism
and socialism.

Now, as in the nineteenth century, the central battle is between
economic liberalism and democratic socialism. The battle, fought in
the transition to classical industrialism, is being refought in a new
transformation of technological capacity and an equally awesome
potential for the political control of people. Individualism is a naive
politics, even anti-politics. Socialism is a politics with the difficult
task of enlightening naivety through appreciation that the welfare of
a nation is much more than the sum of individual fortunes in the
market place.

Britain has a long history of attempts to reconcile the state and society
along these lines. It was the wave of individualism manifested in
triumphant capitalist enterprise, and not Marxist socialism, which
brought us near to revolution in the nineteenth century. The resur-
gence of economic liberalism and not the recrudescence of the
Militant Tendency is what threatens the social order at the end of the
twentieth century.

In British sociological tradition the problem of social order was
formulated by Hobbes in the seventeenth century. Hobbes distinguished between the state of nature and the state of civil society. As
every schoolgirl knows the pre-social state of the human species was
described by Hobbes as 'nasty, brutish and short'. It was a situation
in which 'every man's hand was turned against every other man's

hand': there was a fractionalised, individualised conflict, wasting human energy with respect to the distribution of the bounty of nature by force or fraud. Hobbes's 'if so' story was that, at a moment of temporary consultative truth, a social contract was proposed whereby all would follow a set of rules of allocation, raising the level of welfare of the whole society by lowering the waste of distributional conflict. Hobbes's own interpretation of the problem took the form of creating a leviathan, or supreme political authority. More generally the subsequent history of the debate has bequeathed us two interpretative traditions – the liberal and the Marxist.

Marx's brilliant insight, accepting Hobbes's view of the state of nature, was the theory that transition to the state of civil society in fact involved not the elimination of conflict but its incorporation into the structure of society itself as class conflict over the means of production. Thus we can modify the *Communist Manifesto* of 1848 to read not the history of all hitherto existing societies, but that the history of all hitherto existing civil societies is a history of class conflict. That insight has been a powerful analytical tool for the understanding of classical industrial society. It made sense of Manchester, Leeds and Liverpool – described as capitalist factories with dormitory annexes downwind – as the centres for the development of new class consciousness among exploited workers, which might lead through industrial and political organisation to the overthrow of the capitalist regime by revolution.

The liberal interpretation of the Hobbesian problem is different. The key is not the ultimate elimination of conflict by ineluctable historical forces leading to class revolution. Instead the answer lies in socialisation – the encouragement of common moral sentiments leading to co-operation and peaceful competition through the attachments of individuals to family, neighbourhood, community, and country. The pathway to a social utopia lay through the creation of economic, social and political arrangements which would develop an internalised commitment to moral beliefs, maximising enlightened self-interest and minimising external force.

Of course liberalism as well as Marxism has its historicist versions including, in the British tradition, the Whig theory of history. I would accept neither, but would instead emphasise that out of the debate we can conceive of the good society as one which comes not from any necessitous history, materialist or idealist, but one which, albeit heavily conditioned by historical and material forces, is essentially dependent on the moral character of the individuals who make up society.

This view, which I would want to label ethical socialism, is, I believe, our best hope for a civilised future. Economic liberal doctrines have at their centre the conception of an autonomous, rational, calculating individual, and only at their margins the conception of a collective tradition of respect and care for other people. The ethical socialist tradition in Britain has cherished the idea of the collective good, and at the same time resisted the Marxist interpretation which drives morals out of politics, or rather defers them until the final success of proletarian revolution takes us out of the kingdom of necessity into the kingdom of freedom.

Ethical socialism is a distinctive variant of democratic socialism. As my colleague Norman Dennis and I have defined it, it

> abhors idleness and is suspicious of intellectuals. It gives socialism a marked bias towards individual autonomy and an anti-historicist slant. It distrusts the bureaucratic state. It is aware of the enemies and false friends of freedom on the Left as well as on the Right, and is implacably opposed to totalitarianism from either of these directions. It gives egalitarianism a pronounced emphasis on the importance of respect and dignity rather than material equality. It gives fraternity a no less distinctive sense of history, love of country, dislike of violence, and above all faith in the good sense of ordinary people. Accordingly it favours parliamentary government while seeking also to extend the democratic principle to participatory citizenship in all spheres of public and especially industrial life.[1]

This tradition, which can be traced to Thomas More in the sixteenth century, has had to resist challenges from the (Marxist) Left and the (economic liberal) Right at all stages of transition in the British economy. Thomas More's *Utopia* is a protest, in ethical socialist terms, against the Tudor version of privatisation and warmongering. The conscience of Christendom was his formulation of the good sense of ordinary people.

Thus the ethical socialist tradition steers a moral and political course between the amoralisms of the Left and the Right. It is said that if anyone mentioned morals in politics Marx would roar with laughter, while Trotsky dismissed Ramsay MacDonald's Labourite doctrines as 'a prosaic rehash of the Sermon on the Mount'. And the fashionable Right has always interpreted politics as the provision of means not the determination of ends. The good society is one that facilitates individual pursuit of private ends. But ethical socialists have always believed that men and women are neither social puppets of historical forces nor rational angels. The good society is made by good people seeking the highest realisation of agreed human values, both ultimate and procedural. There is no mechanical solution or permanent state of social accord. The expression of the socialist conscience has to be sought anew in each generation and at every turning point of the collective life.

In all these transitions, including our own, a fundamental drama is being acted and re-enacted. How shall we care for the vulnerable, the defenceless, the unfortunate, the casualties among us? And in doing so, how shall we preserve order and prosperity? What values are at stake? Liberty, fraternity, equality? Do we seek individual or collective solutions? What is the proper role of the market and the state? These are age-old issues of moral ends and social means. We saw them in the adaptation of Britain from an agrarian to an industrial mode of production, which generated a debate about the poor law in terms which we are recapitulating now in the context of a new transformation to a yet more powerful and more vulnerable mode of production.

I am, in short, suggesting that it is not too fanciful to see Mrs Thatcher and her circle entering office in 1979 to enact a replay of the 1834 Poor Law Amendment Act. The material circumstances are different, in that there has been a huge leap forward of industrial productivity in the century and a half between: but a Kondratieff wave of depression of prices and employment dominated the economy then as world-wide depression and deflation overshadows the economy now. The rhetoric and the ideological intention, the firm disbelief in the state welfare of either of our Elizabeths, indicate historical moments of uncanny similarity. Then, as now, a prosperous country is defined as threatened in its will to work, its rate of investment, and its support for innovation by what Tocqueville called 'legalised charity'.

There were two great playwrights of the historical drama we are considering – Tocqueville and Marx. Both still contend for our stage. Their parts are those of the contemporary Right and Left. But on one thing they agreed against common sense and folk wisdom. They recognised that prosperity increased pauperism, not the reverse. Of course, in the Marxist play the theme is that of the immiseration of an increasingly large class of proletarians on their historic path through class consciousness to revolution. Tocqueville feared social chaos rather than class uprising, but made no prediction. He did, however, graphically assert the positive correlation between the creation of industrial wealth and the vulnerable dependency of the industrial classes. In his 1835 *Memoir on Pauperism*, based on his travels in England in 1833, he wrote:

When one crosses the various countries of Europe, one is struck by a very extraordinary and apparently inexplicable sight.

The countries appearing to be most impoverished are those which in reality account for the fewest indigents, and among the peoples most admired for their opulence, one part of the population is obliged to rely on the gifts of the other in order to live.

Cross the English countryside and you will think yourself transported into the Eden of modern civilisation – magnificently maintained roads, clean new houses, well-fed cattle roaming rich meadows, strong and healthy farmers, more dazzling wealth than in any country of the world, the most refined and gracious standard of the basic amenities of life to be found anywhere. There is a pervasive concern for well-being and leisure, an impression of universal prosperity which seems part of the very air you breathe. At every step in England there is something to make the tourist's heart leap.

Now look more closely at the villages; examine the parish registers, and you will discover with indescribable astonishment that one-sixth of the inhabitants of this flourishing kingdom live at the expense of public charity. Now, if you turn to Spain or even more to Portugal, you will be struck by a very different sight. You will see at every step an ignorant and coarse population; ill-fed, ill-clothed, living in the midst of a half-uncultivated countryside and in miserable dwellings. In Portugal, however, the number of indigents is insignificant. M. de Villeneuve estimates that this kingdom contains one pauper for every twenty-five inhabitants. Previously, the celebrated geographer Balbi gave the figure as one indigent to every ninety-eight inhabitants.

Instead of comparing foreign countries among themselves, contrast the different parts of the same realm with each other, and you will arrive at an analogous result: you will see on the one hand the number of those living in comfort, and, on the other, the number of those who need public funds in order to live, growing proportionately . . .

Tocqueville distinguished two forms of charity. One is ancient, private, and individual. Epitomised by the Samaritan parable, it was made a divine virtue by the Christians. It remains the wellspring of altruism in society, the *sine qua non* of welfare. The other is hardly less ancient, though public and collective. All organised societies have made charity an institution. The Romans gave bread to the poor. Yet 'legalised charity', Tocqueville believed, ultimately corrodes the wealth of nations. The 1834 Poor Law, for all its harsh principle of less eligibility, still retained charity as a legal right rather than a moral duty: it would therefore prove no exception. We shall never know whether Tocqueville would have followed Malthus, who wanted to abolish rather than reform the poor laws, for he never redeemed his promise to expound a policy for dealing with pauperism. Perhaps we shall never know whether Thatcherite conservatism would ultimately abolish the Welfare State. All we do know is that Tocqueville believed that the 1834 Act would not work. Instead he turned his attention to the implications of democracy, and for that we may be grateful because, as it turned out, the reform of the franchise probably had more relevance for the future of charity – or, as we would now describe it, political redistribution – than any poor law reform.

I am suggesting, in short, that the 1832 rather than the 1834 play has more to tell us about our first question – the hypothesised crisis of the welfare state. Of course, it need hardly be said that with respect to the first or Samaritan form of welfare, there was, is, and always will be, a crisis. While there are births and marriages, deaths and crop failures, the need for help will always tend to outrun its spontaneous supply.

But such a commonplace about the balance of misfortune and generosity neither enlightens us nor matches the problem as put either by Tocqueville or his intellectual descendants among contemporary liberal-conservatives. The problem has to be set in terms of the second form of welfare – the governmental apparatus which is characteristically set up in a civilised society to regulate the giving of charity. Tocqueville saw England as the first and most conspicuous example of a modern society taking seriously the institution of legalised charity. Interestingly, he traces the problem historically, so as to connect the first to the second form of welfare. The crucial turning point was the Reformation. In Catholic agrarian Europe the charitable organisation and commitment of the church was adequate to supplement the relatively secure market and community conditions of the peasantry. Henry VIII's expropriation of monastic property and destruction of priestly welfare took away privately organised charity and exposed the state to demands which it, in Tocqueville's view, could never satisfactorily meet. The Elizabethan Poor Laws of 1601 were a landmark of essentially ineffective response. We might describe them now as the state apparatus of welfare for an agrarian society, and note their devolved form of administration. Congruent with the dominantly local character of labour markets, they charged parish overseers with both the Beveridge responsibility for income maintenance and the Keynesian function of public works for idle hands.

In retrospect we can see that both the Elizabethan and the 1834 Poor Laws were deficient not so much because of Tocqueville's or

Malthus's fears of the consequences of legalised charity as because of the widening and fluctuating character of markets and, eventually, the bureaucratic and fiscal problems of state welfare. Tocqueville was mistaken to suppose that state-run charity would destroy prosperity, just as orthodox Marxists were wrong to postulate immiseration leading to capitalist crisis.

Tocqueville was immensely more prescient concerning the implications of democracy, and in this sense the 1832 Act was more consequential for the development of welfare than the 1834 Act. For new forms of social insurance were gradually developed by nation states in adaptation to nineteenth-century industrialism. Whether of the Bismarckian Right or the Attlee Left, social policy became a central commitment of the state. The liberalism of Cobden and Bright became liberal exceptionalism, 'interfering' politically with the market distributions of income. Marxism in Western Europe became social democracy and non-revolutionary ameliorative labour movements. Conservatives and Socialists alike came to accept and to urge the state to serve the compromised interests of both capital and labour. Eventually a British Labour government came to full majority power in 1945, and declared itself the custodian of the welfare state: and thirty years of 'Butskell' consensus followed under alternating Conservative and Labour administrations. Even Marxists, or at least those of revisionist persuasion, came to see state welfare as serving the interests of both the great classes of industrial society. The capitalist class used the state as an instrument for the supply of the infrastructure of high productivity. The state supplied investment, particularly in road, rail, electricity, and other public services. The proletariat negotiated an increasing array of economic and social protections against accident, ill health, unemployment, and infirmity which the employing classes would concede in the interests of social order and a compliant work force. And the middle classes gained from both improved and subsidised opportunity and secure employment in the enlarged state bureaucracies. Democracy in the form of state welfarism gradually triumphed over the market. Economic growth sustained the viability of increasingly massive political redistribution. Citizenship guaranteed rights which mitigated the class inequalities of market exchanges.

Then came the cessation of boom in the mid-1970s. There was O.P.E.C. externally and the collapse of faith in Keynesian aggregate demand management internally. Economic growth faltered, unemployment began to rise, and the Phillips curve of trade-off between inflation and employment ceased to work. Tax revolts and critics of mammoth, impersonal, inefficient, and centralised bureaucracy became widespread. Government 'overload' and fiscal incapacity were diagnosed as the basis for a resurgent market liberalism. Mrs Thatcher, along with President Reagan in the U.S.A. and Mr Frazer in Australia, were voted into office to 'roll back the frontiers of the state'. This was the new 1834 play, but not stageable, I would argue, unless combined with the 1832 play. Such a synthesis provides a possible drama of considerable complexity.

The arguments, it must be noted, were paraded in sophisticated form among the politically educated in the 1880s and 1890s. They can be recapitulated by reference to the German sociologist Max Weber's dissection of types of social principle or social organisation. Among them he identified as of great empirical importance the principles of status and contract. An estate society works on ascriptive allocation to the social division of labour, while a contract society depends upon calculated negotiations between individuals and groups. In the year after Marx died Herbert Spencer published his *The Man Versus the State* (1884), taking up Sir Henry Maine's theme that there had been progress in human society from status to contract, away from the compulsory co-operation of status towards modern society in which there would be free co-operation of separate individuals. The caste society was prototypical of status organisation – a society which enabled the writing of obituaries at birth because occupations, spouses, place in the social hierarchy and every aspect of life chance was essentially determined by ascription. Modernity held out the promise of a new society in which people were rational, knew their own marginal advantages and preferences, bargained with one another and so produced the miracle that out of individualised, egotistical calculation would come the maximisation of the collective good. That, in essence, is the theory of economic liberalism. Its classic formulation is that of Frederick Von Hayek. The early part of the nineteenth century had seen the elaboration of *laissez faire* doctrines, with particular emphasis on the need to destroy the growth of a corrupt state. The state had to be seen as the enemy of the development of a society of integrated egotism with the market at its centre. Hayek understood, of course, that the development of an economic liberal society would always require a strong capitalist state. It is in fact no paradox that a Thatcherite intention to roll back the frontiers of the state can result in centralised power. Nor can it be sociologically surprising to find such regimes concerned with reducing intermediary centres of power in the process of reconstructing a society of free market bargaining. There is no mystery, on this view, as to why the local authorities and the trade unions are the *bêtes noires* of the present government.

Herbert Spencer was angry at the trend in British politics. He had always understood, and rightly, that Tories had stood for the status principle in the past, whereas Liberals wished to destroy inherited privilege and to substitute free contract. Yet the new liberals appeared to him to be reinventing the powerful state and believing it to be an essentially benign form of association.

The new liberalism was represented sociologically by L. T. Hobhouse, who took much of his assessment of the state of British society from the work of other sociologists, such as Charles Booth or Beatrice Potter, and from economists such as J. A. Hobson and Alfred Marshall. These social analysts took it to be true that the Marxist ideas of the 1840s had been tested in the natural laboratory of history and found wanting. Yet they themselves invented a bourgeois version of the old theory of surplus value, and they emphasised particularly the unfree character of free markets. Indeed they recognised that, just as there are no free lunches, there are no free markets. And they drew the conclusion that the state was the appropriate instrument for restoring the surplus to its rightful owners. The benign state could use the surplus, estimated at about 20 per cent of the national income, to provide high quality public services.

Among these services, as Alfred Marshall had argued in his famous 1873 lecture on the future of the working class, was a greatly expanded provision for education. The democratisation of the style of life of high-minded Cambridge dons was central to the conception of a new society. There was, in other words, a gentlemanly socialism involved. Individualism could be developed in the arms of socialism by democratising gentlemanly privilege, and the means were at hand. The state could use collective wealth to invest heavily in a programme of educational expansion, and so in turn change an economy of low wages and long hours of brutalising toil into a new economy of short hours and high wages based on technology. Educational expansion could produce both material prosperity and spiritual wealth.

Putting together the ideas of modern democracy, the benign state, the surplus and the collective good, the new liberals heralded a notion of society which could be bound together not by the economic liberal principle of contract, with its central institution of the market, but instead by citizenship. This conception – which evolved among the educated upper middle classes and was elaborated by T. H. Green and his successors, culminating in the analysis of the condition of England set out by R. H. Tawney in *The Acquisitive Society* and *Equality* – justified democratic socialism and the welfare state through the first three-quarters of the twentieth century. The citizenship principle contains the assumption of rational auton-omous individuals, but places them in a society in which people are educated to understand that their high quality of life is dependent on supporting a generous public provision. The ethical socialists among them would have expressed the thesis in Christian terms – that we are members one of another. In more secular language, the point would be put that we have the stark alternative of providing protection by privatised security, burglar alarms and private pension arrange-ments, abandoning the streets to a state of nature, or we can turn to the citizenship principle through which every individual carries an ethic of social responsibility and a determination to act against any infringement of the rights and dignities of others.

It is appropriate to note that these notions were partly carried by an imperial class, now disappearing, with ideas of public service and a willingness to combat established authority. That class gave the socialist movement the idea that gentlemanliness could be democra-tised, despite the sentimentalities and hypocrisies which could and did accompany it. The ethic was certainly independently generated out of the respectable working class, and gave the British Labour movement some of its distinctive qualities. A prototypic figure is Thomas Burt, the miners' leader, with his background in primitive methodism, who became the father of the House of Commons and was described by Earl Grey as the most perfect example of a gentleman that he had ever met – hating anything underhand, always truthful, always prepared to stand up for the right, afraid of no man but at the same time forbearing and gentle in his treatment of persons.

This ethic has been sadly attenuated in the post-war period. It is another and longer story, but the question has to be asked as to how far the failure of this ethic to be perpetuated in subsequent gener-ations can be explained by an impoverished conception, particularly in the Labour movement, of educational policy. The educational problem as a transmission of agreed social values integrating new national, ethnic and international communities is vastly more urgent and complex than it was when Durkheim laid out a crucial role for schools and school teachers in the French Third Republic. Kenneth Baker's reforms seem more likely to divide than to unite Britain at the end of the twentieth century.

Mrs Thatcher had ridden to power in 1979 on a national mood of disenchantment with the welfare state and rejection of the moralising politics expressed by R. H. Tawney. Legalised charity, it was held, had eventuated in the bureaucratised and soulless state apparatus, with all its inefficiencies and corruptions. The value of the market had been undervalued, the individualism of people had been sapped, the Poulsons and Dan Smiths had been allowed to practise state-protected rackets in Labour-dominated constituencies, there was over-manning in state industries and Britain had become the sick man of Europe.

Meanwhile the Labour Party had engaged in an exhausting internal struggle for dominance between its Marxist/Trotskyist elements and the idealism of the old Labour Party. By 1987 a dis-integrated Left faced the task of attempting to dislodge a Thatcher Government confidently expounding popular capitalism. A popular drama was staged on television as essentially a debate between economic liberalism and democratic socialism. Resuscitating Tawneyesque rhetoric, Neil Kinnock and the Labour leaders argued in the ethical socialist tradition that real strength was demonstrated in the care of weak, that the National Health Service was the impoverished emblem of a civilised society, and that a return to public investment was the path to economic prosperity and social peace. On the Conservative side it was argued that a successful nation, like a wise family, doesn't prosper by sharing out what it has but by giving the best shares to those capable of enterprise, who will in turn create wealth for the weaker members. Economic growth through the enterprise society, not equality in economic decline, was the best path to a desirable future.

There can be no doubt as to who won the debate. Forty per cent of the vote went to Mrs Thatcher, which was thirty per cent of all those entitled to vote. It was a minority, but a bigger minority than those who voted for the opposition voice. The Right was further encouraged in its ascendance over the Left.

On this view, the task for the Labour Party before 1991 is neither that of finally driving out the irrelevance of second-world communism nor that of inventing new arguments against the Thatcherite version of economic liberalism. It is instead to win again the intellectual arguments against basing society on the unregulated market which were so successfully expounded by the New Liberals a hundred years ago to make us 'all socialists now'.

Blighted communities and neglected manufacturing bases reaffirm the need for common wealth, and veil the fact that we have the means to be rich. By today's standards the first majority Labour government ruled a poverty-stricken country exhausted by world war. Wealth and welfare are partners. They both rose under Attlee's socialism, Macmillan's opportunity society and Butskell's consensus.

So the problem is to devise a socialism of prosperity. Here a second myth obstructs – that Labour support has been eroding because the classical working class is being consigned to history by the passing of coal and steam industrialism. The class structure is slowly changing: but Labour, as recent polls show, still has a potential majority. A fall of twenty percentage points in votes since the 1960s can only be attributed to the extent of about a quarter to changes in social structure. Three-quarters of it is due to political ineptitude and policy mistakes. Moreover the volatility of the electorate also reflects incipient weakness in Conservative as well as Labour Party politics despite the Westminster triumphs of Mrs Thatcher since 1979. The political argument is staged before an electorate more persuadable now than it was when Attlee swept into office in 1945.

The argument can be won for democratic socialism. Socialism can be a system of production which is both more efficient than market capitalism and more just in distributing wealth to all of the people who make up the nation. Democracy is also an ancient modernising idea which gives substance to freedom through a framework of collective decisions containing individual choices in the market place.

The Labour Party has to re-educate a majority to understand the nature of future prosperity. The model of a highly successful and wealthy country with high quality public services, low inflation, efficient education and training, and very low unemployment is there as an object lesson, for example in Sweden. The lesson has to be learned, as it has been by John Edmonds, that trade unions must be friends of the citizen as consumer and not only of the worker as producer. If a high quality of collective life means high taxation, Labour must remind us that Callaghan left office in a country twice as well off as Attlee's. The enlightenment of the comfortable is not just moral exhortation to give, but educated interest in giving less out of more to receive a still more secure abundance.

In the end it comes to a choice between Conservative prosperity for a majority shamed by a minority excluded from affluent citizenship, and the Labour alternative of an even more prosperous country in which all live in decent abundance and none suffer either guilt or resentment.

The politics of production are likely to remain at the centre of the debate. But I would end by questioning whether the analysis of society contained in modern Conservatism is not totally inappropriate to the problems of the twenty-first century. With respect to the advanced industrial societies of Western Europe, a powerful case can be made for the view that the problem is not one of production but of reproduction. Economic liberal policies aim at maximising economic growth. It has been an error of the democratic socialist movement to accept the debate in these terms. It is significant that Anthony Crosland in the 1950s, though noticing that prosperity was accompanied by dissatisfaction, nevertheless turned his attention to an answer to the question of why West Germany and Japan achieved higher rates of economic growth than did Britain.

It seems to me to be obvious, if unfashionable in some economic circles, that there is no reason to suppose that the bounty, not of nature but of society, that is enfolded in modern technologies could not realise the dreams beyond avarice of anyone who wants to be rich. The difficulty is that the development of our powers of production has been accompanied by an equally significant if less noticed weakening of the reproductive institutions. The new demographic regime of low fertility, low mortality and longevity is moving us into an unprecedented social era. The decline of traditional familial and kinship organisations in modern Europe is spectacular, as may be seen from the rising rates of divorce, separation, illegitimacy and attenuation of kinship ties. One aspect of the new social order is revealed by the ratio of working to retired people. This was about nine to one in the 1930s, and on present trends will, by the second decade of the twenty-first century, be nearer to two to one.

New opportunities for 'the third age' are opened by this prospect. But at the same time it should surely be noticed that the declining probability of surviving kin in an ageing population presents great challenges to the public provision of opportunities for a high quality of life. Much political and social invention will be needed to cope with the new dependencies of 'the fourth age'. Traditional kinship solutions are demographically impossible. The market is a solution which would only add to social polarisation. Public sector solutions need urgently to be developed along the lines of local imagination within a strong state framework.

In short, the politics of prosperity will have to be addressed increasingly to social rather than to economic engineering in order to meet the challenges that economic liberalism, as well as Labourite

socialism, were designed to face. Neither individualism nor socialism, as I have argued, can be written out of British culture. But the
future will require imaginative reconstruction of their balance.

ELEVEN

Changing Social Values under Mrs Thatcher

RALF DAHRENDORF

The story of Thatcherism starts in the 1970s – the decade, as it now seems, of the gathering crisis. In 1971, the United States gave notice to an international monetary system which had served the post-war world well, and there began a period of instability which is still with us. In 1972 the Club of Rome published its first report, *The Limits to Growth*, and doubts about the possibilities of growth persisted throughout the 1970s. In 1973 the first oil shock forced all advanced countries to enter into a phase of adjustment which many found it hard to cope with; it also produced a mountain of petro-dollars which led directly to the Third World debt crisis.

The important point, though, is the way in which the O.E.C.D. countries reacted to these shocks. Essentially they used the instruments of the 1960s, especially the late 1960s, to cope with the new problems of the 1970s, and as a result created stagflation, a combination of inflation, unemployment, and years of what a strange euphemism describes as 'negative growth'. The instruments used were those of big government. Some of the earliest adjustment processes in most advanced countries can be described as a bargain between governments and social groups, involving a redistribution through government of funds which seemed to be available but turned out not to be, in return for the co-operation by interest groups in the adjustment process.

This close, often organised, co-operation between government, trade unions, and employers' associations has been described by the word corporatism. Corporatism was inspired by the sense that the best way to deal with national problems is by getting everyone round a table, or into Number Ten Downing Street, and trying to hammer out some kind of agreement. It is hard to deny, in retrospect, that the combination of stagflation and corporatist decision-making led in quite a few O.E.C.D. countries to a sense that nothing was moving any more, that it had become exceedingly difficult to innovate, technically as well as socially. It was almost as if these rich, modern societies were moving towards a state of entropy.

All this was aggravated in Britain by the fact that this country had certain social characteristics which were specific, certainly in their mixture. Some years ago, when I produced a B.B.C. television series on Britain, I argued that every country has the strengths of its weaknesses and the weaknesses of its strengths. I said that the strengths of Britain – the sense of tradition, the autonomy of institutions, the sense of solidarity – were perhaps obstacles to the kind of economic dynamism more characteristic of those countries with less tradition, a much weaker sense of social solidarity and much less autonomy of social institutions. I shall return to this point, which has much to do with the value changes which we are experiencing in the 1980s.

What can happen when a society reaches such a state of immobility? Mancur Olson's book, *The Rise and Decline of Nations*, seems to say that once a country has reached this state, there is very little that can be done. But then he quotes Jefferson to the effect that 'every now and again the tree of freedom has to be fed with the blood of patriots.' He seems to hint that unless there is a war or revolution or some other bloody event, a country will remain stuck in a state of rigidity. Certainly he saw no real way out of the stagflation which was the subject of his book. Decades earlier Max Weber had had a vision of the modern world as 'an iron cage of bondage of bureaucracy', as a world in which initiative either by politicians or by the people was virtually impossible because of that air cushion of bureaucracy between them within which all initiatives were suffocated. When Weber described this iron cage of bondage he too asked himself what was the way out, and who could help in such a situation. It was in this context that he introduced into the language of political analysis that most unfortunate word, 'charisma'. He argued that unless charismatic leaders emerge who somehow manage to break out of the bureaucratic nightmare, societies are likely to end up in a state of entropy.

I point to these dramatic analyses simply to underline some of the difficulties characteristic of the late 1970s, and some of the questions underlying the new political trends which broke through this rigid system of corporatism and stagflation. In another context it would be interesting to discuss the role of the Greens as a reaction to the same situation: more generally the question of how far the breakout from corporatist stagnation can only be accomplished by social movements rather than by traditional political parties.

In Britain, the predicament I have been describing gave rise to Thatcherism. Thatcherism was not identical to the traditional Conservative Party which found itself a somewhat puzzled vehicle of a highly personal set of ideas and style of leadership. It acquiesced in this situation, partly because it found in Mrs Thatcher a leader who could deliver repeated electoral success. Moreover, the electorate which voted Conservative was increasingly different from the traditional Conservative electorate: for example, in 1987 the Conservatives for the first time captured a majority of the votes of the skilled working class. However, this is not the whole story. A point often underestimated is that British constitutional arrangements make it easier than in most other countries to get out of the straitjacket of stagflation. Once again, weaknesses from one point of view are a strength from another. The strong position of party leaders, the particularly strong position of a prime minister whose party has a parliamentary majority, the electoral system which enables minority parties to get majorities in Parliament, all combine to create circumstances under which changes can be introduced which are deeply significant, much more significant than is likely in other bureaucratic systems.

As an example, take the major difference between the British and the German political system in the budget process. Before a budget is announced in the House of Commons very few people know what is in it; even members of the Cabinet have only been informed that same day. After a budget has been announced, everybody acts as though it is already law. No one seems to bother about what Parliament may think, because it is assumed that a majority is there for whatever proposals the Chancellor has announced. When the German Minister of Finance introduces a budget in parliament he has already given about fifteen press conferences, and talked to the party faithful all over the country. What is in the budget has been extensively discussed. Few people are interested in the actual budget speech because it is followed by several months of parliamentary committee debate, lobby input, and discussions within and between the two houses of parliament.

This constitutional background helps one to understand why the British reaction to the crisis of the 1970s has diverged from that of the Continent. It is interesting that after many years in which Germany was regarded as a model of enterprise, many now regard Germany as the example to avoid and point to the specific blocking corporatism of the German system. Although Germany got through the first oil crisis rather well, since the second oil shock growth rates have been low, and unemployment very high indeed. If one takes into account the fact that Germany has conscription – which is going to be extended – and an apprenticeship system with vocational schools which keep a million youngsters out of the unemployment statistics, it could be argued that Germany has the highest unemployment rate in Europe. In Germany, in other words, the corporatist culture remains largely intact; whereas in Britain Mrs Thatcher has, in her nine years as Prime Minister, probably effected a deeper change in social values that any other democratic politician in the post-war period.

What are these changes? If one looks back to the values of the 1970s, one of the main ones had to do with the maintenance of prosperity for all. But it was a rather defensive notion, more to do with minimising loss that with maximising gain, of defending what there was rather than exploiting new frontiers. This was coupled with a strong sense of social responsibility; or, put differently, with the idea that it was the duty of the state to see to it than an overall sense of fairness was maintained. A further aspect of the value system of the 1970s was the belief that organisations which existed in society, whatever the specific interests which they represented, had to be recognised and drawn into consultation so that there should be a climate of consensus and co-operation. If there was an enemy in the

1970s it was usually an abstract enemy. Government was there to shield and shelter people from the terrible things which it could not influence, like the great oil price rises.

Among the attitudes introduced in the Thatcher era, and justly connected with her, is the notion that such passivity and defensiveness keep down initiative, and that the important thing is to encourage people to aspire to new personal wealth, to get rich quick, by means of government policies which reduce the burden of taxation and withdraw the embrace of what some have called the 'nanny state'. People must be encouraged to fend for themselves, not to rely on help from a system of redistribution. Mrs Thatcher has shown a distinct preference for a state which is much closer to some of the minimal-state ideas of modern contract theorists in the United States than to the all-embracing state of the 1970s.

This has led some to complain about a loss of fairness, of kindness, in everyday life, as well as a loss in quality, especially in the quality of services, sacrificed to a rather ruthless individualism and greed. The more important objection, however, is that this Thatcherite vision is based on an intellectual mistake: the belief that if economic growth is sufficiently sustained, it will in the end benefit all. In reality, there are two sets of social issues which make up the modern social conflict, one of which has to do with the range of choices which people have, the other with people's entitlements: what is available in the shops, and who is in a position to go into them and buy those things that are available there. Greater choice does not lead to greater access. What happens, and has happened before in history, is that entitlement barriers persist, or are created by a new burst of wealth creation, which are not easily, and certainly not automatically, crossed by an increase in G.N.P. This is a rather involved and abstract way of describing the new social divisions which have arisen in this country and elsewhere in the 1980s. In the United States the problem is persistent hard core poverty. In Britain and in Germany it is persistent hard core unemployment. Both have a lot to do with the values of the 1980s.

Another value of the 1970s was that all social groups have to be brought into a consensus. But Mrs Thatcher has said that 'There is no such thing as society; there are only individuals, and families.' I suspect that the word 'families' is an afterthought, more a concession to the Conservative Party than a fundamental element in the train of thought. For the traditional Conservative Party does believe in society. Douglas Hurd, the Home Secretary, recently talked about 'knitting society together', and even Mrs Thatcher, in her strange reference to St Francis of Assisi on the morrow of her 1979 election victory, talked of her mission to 'heal'. But this has not been the ethos of her government; and the reason I take the reference to families to be an afterthought is that it makes her statement contradictory. Once you admit families, you admit society, and the first half of the statement loses all meaning.

What are the implications of saying that there is no society, only individuals? Undoubtedly one of the problems bequeathed by the 1970s was that the word 'society' had become grossly overused. Many people had become too ready to discount the role of the individual and put in its place some undefined social entity. It is difficult to assess calmly what was right and what was wrong about the claim that individual crimes and transgressions are socially caused; but there was too much readiness to assume that it was not the individual perpetrator who was responsible but, in some strange sense, society. From this it seemed to follow that it was wrong to hold the individual responsible; the important thing was to change the social conditions in which the individual had grown up. The word 'society' here is being used in such a way as almost to make the individual as a moral being disappear behind an abstract smokescreen. But what happens if one goes all the way in the opposite direction? One loses all those qualities which make up society. Society is fundamentally a set of norms by which we live and which make lives between people predictable and therefore bearable. Built on these norms are institutions. In other words, the norms have themselves become something which is not just a short-term agreement, or a contract in the commercial sense, but an underlying network of institutions which sustains us all and which is the basis of secure life, and indeed of progress. What is lost by the claim that there is no such thing as society is the greatest achievement of human history, the civil society – the idea that societies accept the rule of law, and administer the law, in order to enable citizens to make use of the opportunities which have been created by all citizens together.

In a book I wrote thirty years ago called *Homo Sociologicus*, I described how our social lives take place in roles which we play, in normative contexts which we don't define for ourselves but which are given to us, which are a part of tradition. At the time I argued that this was fine for sociological analysis, but that it was a dreadful alienation of the true or real individual. And there are bits of my argument which encourage people to rebel against these norms and roles in the name of some abstract, non-social, individual. I now believe that I made a major mistake in not realising that progress can never consist in an attack on norms, roles, society *as such*, because that is a route which destroys the very instrument of civilisation, civil society, and thus the means of creating more opportunities for more people. Progress has to consist in the transformation of social norms, the attempt to use society to improve society. I go further today and say that morality is hard to conceive of without the presence of rules, norms, sanctions. To say there is no society but only individuals is fundamentally an amoral position. It puts individual interest in place of civic virtue, thus making it very hard to identify the sources of binding norms for all of us. It is the philosophy of social darwinism, in which the struggle for survival dominates life, and the survival of the fittest is the excuse for all other consequences of that particular struggle.

These thoughts are by no means entirely divorced from what has been happening. There are two ways of describing the policies of the Thatcher governments. On the one hand, these policies can be seen as so many attempts to dismantle obstacles to growth, innovation, initiative, and individual choice. The removal of these obstacles remains the chief subject matter of the government's speech-making and the explicit object of its legislation. In place of a tradition of solidarity, there is an insistence on competition between individuals. Traditional institutions are attacked in the interest of new opportunities for choice. One can readily think of a whole series of examples: the systematic reduction in the role of the trade unions, the privatisation programme, the recent statements about the future of the health service, and the whole attitude towards the professions.

However, one could also describe what has been happening as an insidious process of deinstitutionalisation. The current Education Bill is a good example. The opposition of the universities to Mr Baker's plans is partly to do with academic freedom; but the much more important part has to do with autonomy – with the autonomy of institutions which, in the British tradition, and in the absence of a written constitution, has been the central guarantee of freedom. If one puts in the place of an established University Grants Committee a flimsy University Funding Council with members selected by a system which ensures that they cannot take a continuing deep interest in the subject; if one removes, for certain purposes, the role of Chancellors or Visitors or other 'courts of appeal' open to lecturers and students; if one adds to this the many statements that the Secretary of State can, should, will make rulings and determine what is going to happen, the result is a much less institutional, more personalised, structure. We are assured, of course, of the benevolent intentions of government. But for freedom to survive, government benevolence is no better than government malevolence. Both are fundamentally arbitrary. The essence of freedom lies in institutional guarantees – in the fact that people are not dependent on whether a minister is well-meaning or not. The whole British system of local government, the civil service, the professions, the B.B.C. describes a set of institutions which are characterised by a peculiar, in many ways illogical, kind of autonomy, so that the process of deinstitutionalisation raises serious questions about the future of freedom in this country.

Moreover, once deinstitutionalisation has set in it is very difficult to get back to the old system, partly because it was so illogical. I am not sure that the Civil Service of 1988 is still the Civil Service of 1978, or can easily be turned back towards the non-partisan approach. I am not sure that one can easily reestablish the theoretically absurd but practically effective independence of the B.B.C., which was run by governors supposed not to be accountable to any organised group, once it has been through a period in which appointments have been made in order to push it in a particular political direction. The same is true of the Arts Council. There may well be a good case for reforming some of the professions. But one of their enormous strengths was that they were self-governing, and being self-governing made them reliable in ways in which professions directly subject to government regulation are not. This is one of the reasons why, on the Royal Commission on the Legal Services, I defended even the conceptual absurdity of the conveyancing monopoly of solicitors, given that it existed. In all these cases the mechanisms of self-government have been systematically weakened. I am not sure that the universities will readily recover from a period in which they have become adept at responding to, or even anticipating, signals from the government, with those opposed driven either into hiding, or to the United States, or to the expedient of writing an occasional letter to a newspaper editor and hearing their friends say to them 'What enormous courage!' What sort of society are we living in if it takes courage to write a letter to a newspaper criticising one's government?

It is often said that Mrs Thatcher's ideal is the United States. But this comparison is misleading. In the United States there are very clear socially sanctioned customs. The difference can be illustrated by the following story. A few years ago a prominent industrialist went to the Prime Minister with a proposal to set up a 'One Percent Club' of British industry, committed to making one per cent of profits available for charitable purposes. At that time, Mrs Thatcher's response was 'But how can you do that to the shareholders?' (I believe she has since changed her mind.) Her notion was that self-interest should govern the economic process, and that there was something wrong in taking profits away from the shareholders to give to charity. In the United States there is a long tradition of corporate giving which is, in most cases, not directly related to the interests of the companies concerned. There is now a 'Two Percent Club' which is very large, and people are talking about a 'Three Percent Club'. A company which failed to make donations of this order could not face its shareholders! America is an example of a civil society which does not seem to need much government because it is in so many ways self-governing. No one in America would say there was no society.

The balance of this argument is not simple. Three points can be made in conclusion. Firstly, the social and political condition of Britain in the late 1970s was untenable. There was a clear case for a dose of innovation, of entrepreneurship, of extended individual choice. Transforming a society from rigidity to flexibility required rough and, for many, painful measures. Countries which have not taken these measures are now paying, or are about to pay, a high price for their neglect. Germany is a case in point. In France there is the constitutional problem of 'cohabitation'. In Spain, the prime minister, Filippo Gonzales, has been one of the most courageous advocates of the need to open up rigid structures to competition, while maintaining social cohesion. In other words, a return to the good old days is both an illusion and a mistake.

Secondly, social darwinism as a set of values has curiously paradoxical consequences. One of them is a withdrawal of government from social responsibility, indeed the abandonment of certain groups and certain perceived needs. At the same time, it seems to imply a curious insistence that those in government – not government as an institution, but those who happen to be there – know best. The result is a strange combination of the withdrawal of institutional authority, coupled with a stream of highly personalised instructions telling people how to make use of the choices which have been opened up for them.

The third point I regard as the most important. The appearance of authoritarianism has a great deal to do with the absence of effective opposition. This is not simply an organisational problem for the parties of opposition. It is the result of a genuine ambivalence. There are two sets of potential opposition issues. One is concerned with the consequences of economic and social policies, and would therefore need to address the issue of entitlements: the need to reinforce entitlements after a period of extending choices, so that citizenship does not become an empty word. The other has to do with institutions. Those on the Left who object to the social consequences of Mrs Thatcher's policies often have their own doubts about institutions and may even have a sneaking sympathy for the deinstitutionalisation policies of the Thatcher government. Many in the Labour Party would – as Brian Sedgemore M.P. wrote in a letter to the *Independent* – 'like to see the professions shaken out of their apathy and shorn of their conservatism'. I have no particular illusions about the views of the Left about the autonomy of the universities: it was, after all,

Reginald Prentice who, as Labour's Minister of Education, recommended Oxford and Cambridge to sell their art treasures to stay afloat.

The point is that those who object to the social consequences of Thatcherism are not the natural defenders of institutional autonomy. Those on the other hand – chiefly the so-called Tory Wets – who object to this deinstitutionalisation may mind a divided nation, but will not actually fight politically for redistribution or for new entitlements. It is probably unrealistic to think of any viable political group which would at the same time defend institutions and take the need for citizenship rights seriously. It is therefore quite likely that the change in values discussed here will continue for some time to come. It is equally necessary that we do not cease to keep public debate on these issues going, and at least make an alternative intellectual case where there seems to be at present only one political case.

References

Introduction

1 For an exhaustive account of this movement from individualism to collectivism see W. H. Greenleaf, *The British Political Tradition*, Vols 1 and 2 (London, 1983).

2 E.g., F. A. Hayek, *The Road to Serfdom* (London, 1944); Robert Nozick, *Anarchy, State, and Utopia* (London, 1968); Milton and Rose Friedman, *Capitalism and Freedom* (London, 1962).

3 David Graham and Peter Clarke give a summary of this episode in *The New Enlightenment* (London, 1986) pp. 15-18, based on an unpublished account by R. M. Hartwell.

4 Daniel Bell, *The End of Ideology* (New York, 1962) p. 402.

5 The phrase is Peter Jenkins' in *Mrs Thatcher's Revolution* (London, 1987), p. 4.

6 Taken from Samuel Brittan, *The Treasury Under the Tories 1951-1964*, (London, 1964), p. 139.

7 David Marquand, *The Unprincipled Society* (London, 1988), especially chapters 1 and 2.

8 J. C. R. Dow, *The Management of the British Economy 1945-60* (Cambridge, 1970), p. 384.

9 T. W. Hutchison, *Economics and Economic Policy in Britain 1946-1966* (London, 1968), pp. 121-2.

10 See R. C. O. Matthews in Sir Alec Cairncross (ed.) *Britain's Economic Prospects Reconsidered* (London, 1971), p. 14.

11 Richard E. Caves and Associates, *Britain's Economic Prospects* (London, 1968), p. 17.

12 For a compendium of these structural problems as they were viewed at the time, see 'Suicide of a Nation?', *Encounter*, July 1963. *Encounter* devoted its whole issue to the matter.

13 Ian Gilmour, *The Body Politic* (London, 1969), p. 170.

14 Michael Shanks, *The Stagnant Society* (London, 1961), p. 68.
15 In Cairncross, *op. cit.*, p. 117.
16 Max Nicholson, *The System* (London, 1967), p. 491.
17 P. J. Sinclair, 'The Economy – A Study in Failure' in David McKie and Chris Cook (eds) *The Decade of Disillusion: British Politics in the Sixties* (London, 1972), p. 94.
18 John and Anne-Marie Hackett, *The British Economy: Problems and Prospects* (London, 1967), p. 31.
19 Michael Stewart, *The Jekyll and Hyde Years: Politics and Economic Policy since 1964* (London, 1977), p. 21.
20 Jenkins, *op. cit.*, p. 13.
21 Michel Crozier, *The Stalled Society* (London, 1970), pp. 1, 160.
22 Jenkins, *op. cit.*, p. 60.
23 See David Coates, *The Labour Party in Power 1974-1979* (London, 1980), Chapter 1.
24 Bernard Donoughue, *Prime Minister* (London, 1987).
25 Coates, *op. cit.*, pp. 5, 13.
26 *Ibid.*, p. 14.
27 Jenkins, *op. cit.*, p. 62.
28 See William Keegan, *Mrs Thatcher's Economic Experiment* (London, 1984), pp. 49-52.
29 See especially Anthony King 'The Problem of Overload' in Anthony King and others, *Why is Britain Becoming Harder to Govern?* (London, 1976) and Richard Rose and Guy Peters, *Can Government Go Bankrupt?* (London, 1979).
30 King, *op. cit.*, pp. 18-19.
31 S. Brittan, 'Can Democracy Manage an Economy?' in R. Skidelsky ed., *The End of the Keynesian Era* (London, 1977), p. 45.
32 S. Brittan, *The Economic Consequences of Democracy* (London, 1977), p. 248.
33 Peter Jay, 'How Inflation Threatens British Democracy with its Last Chance before Extinction', *The Times*, 1 July 1974.
34 John Campbell, *Contemporary Record*, autumn 1987, p. 3.
35 See the evidence of Milton Friedman, David Laidler and Patrick Minford to the House of Commons Treasury and Civil Service Committee, *Memoranda on Monetary Policy* (H.M.S.O. 1980), pp. 51, 61, 142.
36 C. F. Pratten, 'Mrs Thatcher's Economic Experiment', *Lloyd's Bank Review*, January 1982, p. 40.

References

Has the Electorate become Thatcherite?

1   Stuart Hall, 'The Great Moving Right Show', in Stuart Hall and Martin Jacques, eds, *The Politics of Thatcherism* (London, 1983), pp. 19-39 (originally published in *Marxism Today*, January 1979).

2   The classic exposition is in Anthony Downs, *An Economic Theory of Democracy* (New York, 1957), especially Chapters 7 and 8.

3   A useful and critical account of the speech is given in Peter Jenkins, *Mrs Thatcher's Revolution* (London, 1987), pp. 64-5.

4   C. Goodhart & R. Bhansali, 'Political Economy', *Political Studies*, 18, 1970, pp. 43-106.

5   Anthony Heath, Roger Jowell and John Curtice, *How Britain Votes* (Oxford, 1985), pp. 96-9.

6   Anthony Heath and Sarah-K McDonald, 'Social Change and the Future of the Left', *The Political Quarterly*, 88, 1987, pp. 364-77.

7   See Ivor Crewe, 'On the Death and Resurrection of Class Voting: Some Comments on *How Britain Votes*', *Political Studies*, 34, 1986, 620-38; and Anthony Heath, Roger Jowell and John Curtice, 'Trendless Fluctuation: a Reply to Crewe', *Political Studies*, 35, 1987, 256-77.

8   In the 1959 campaign the Conservatives' slogan was 'Life's Good under the Conservatives: Don't Let Labour Ruin It'.

9   The 1959 data are taken from Heath *et al. How Britain Votes*, p. 30. Note that the 1959 figures are adjusted to assume that Liberal candidates stood in every constituency in Great Britain.

10   Hall, *The Politics of Thatcherism*, p. 30.

11   Peregrine Worsthorne, 'Who Now Speaks for the People?', *Sunday Telegraph*, 12 June 1983.

12   According to the British Election Studies, the proportion in favour of restoring the death penalty fell from 75 per cent in 1979 to 63 per cent in 1983.

13   Ralph Harris and Arthur Seldon, *Welfare Without the State* (Hobart Paperback No. 26) (London, Institute of Economic Affairs, 1987), p. 21.

14   See *The Economist*, 25 May 1985, p. 22.

15   Jim Bulpitt, 'The Discipline of the New Democracy: Mrs Thatcher's Statecraft', *Political Studies*, 34, 1986, pp. 19-39.

Margaret Thatcher as a Political Leader

1   Some of the ground covered in this essay is also covered in Anthony King, 'Margaret Thatcher: The Style of a Prime Minister' in Anthony King, ed., *The British Prime Minister*, 2nd edn (London, 1985).

2 See David McKie, 'Thatcher Eyes New Milestone', *Guardian*, 30 December 1987.

3 Byrum E. Carter, *The Office of Prime Minister* (London, 1956).

4 The details can be worked out from David Butler and Gareth Butler, *British Political Facts 1900-1985* (London, 1986), pp. 70, 224–8. The only difficult cases are the two wartime changes of Prime Minister: Asquith to Lloyd George in 1916 and Chamberlain to Churchill in 1940. For the purposes of the figures used in the text, the first of these has been coded as constituting a change in the party in power, the second not; but the argument remains the same even if the two cases are treated as though they were alike.

5 Richard E. Neustadt, 'White House and Whitehall' in King, ed., *The British Prime Minister*, p. 168. Actually Neustadt was referring to American Presidents but in the course of likening them to Prime Ministers.

6 Niccolo Machiavelli, *The Prince*, translated by George Bull (Harmondsworth, 1961), pp. 96-7.

7 See Anthony King, 'The Rise of the Career Politician in Britain – and its Consequences', *British Journal of Political Science*, 11 (July 1981), 249-85.

8 Richard E. Neustadt, *Presidential Power: The Politics of Leadership from F.D.R. to Carter* (New York, 1980), p. 44.

9 *The Prince*, p. 96.

The Future of the Left

1 In J. Gould and W. M. Kolb, eds, *A Dictionary of the Social Sciences* (London, 1964), p. 383.

2 See my 'The Labour Left' in C. Cook and I. Taylor, eds, *The Labour Party: An Introduction to its History, Structure and Politics* (London, 1980), pp. 163-88.

3 See D. Carlton, *MacDonald versus Henderson: The Foreign Policy of the Second Labour Government* (London, 1970), p. 16.

4 A. Taylor, *The Trade Unions and the Labour Party* (London, 1987), p. 1.

5 *The Evolution of the Labour Party 1910-1924* (Oxford, 1974).

6 See P. Addison, *The Road to 1945: British Politics and the Second World War* (London, 1977), p. 17.

7 According to the 1899 T.U.C. decision that effectively launched the Labour Party: 'to ensure that working-class opinion should be represented in the House of Commons by men sympathetic with the aims

and demands of the Labour Movement, and whose candidatures are promoted by one or other of the organised movements'. Cited in K. Coates and T. Topham, *Trade Unions in Britain*, 3rd edn (London, 1988), p. 334.

8   M. Cole, ed., *Beatrice Webb: Diaries 1924-32* (London, 1949), p. 138.

9   'A new class of politics', *Guardian*, 15 June 1987.

10 P. Williams, *Hugh Gaitskell* (London, 1979), pp. 538-9.

11 E. Durbin, *New Jerusalems: The Labour Party and the Economics of Democratic Socialism* (London, 1985), p. 286.

12 A. Crosland, *The Future of Socialism* (London, 1956).

13 *Human Nature in Politics*, 2nd edn. (London, 1910), pp. 103-6.

14 See B. Pimlott, ed., *Fabian Essays and Socialist Thought* (London, 1984), pp. 6-7.

15 Michael Harrington, *The Next Left: the History of the Future* (London, 1987), pp. 147-8, 166.

Mrs Thatcher's Economic Reform Programme

1   Mancur Olson, *The Rise and Decline of Nations* (New Haven, 1982).

2   Kent Matthews and Patrick Minford, 'Mrs Thatcher's Economic Policies, 1979-87', *Economic Policy* (1987), p. 5.

3   Sir Alan Walters, *Britain's Economic Renaissance – Margaret Thatcher's Economic Reforms, 1979-84* (Oxford, 1985).

4   Cento Veljanovski, *Selling the State* (London, 1986).

5   George Yarrow, 'Privatisation, a Survey', *Economic Policy* (1985), p. 3.

6   Patrick Minford and Anupam Rastogi, 'A New Classical Policy Programme' in the forthcoming (1988) proceedings of the N.I.E.S.R. Conference on Demand Management.

7   Ralph Howell, 'Why Work? A Radical Solution', Conservative Political Centre (1981).

8   Patrick Minford with David Davies, Michael Peel and Alison Sprague, *Unemployment, Cause and Cure* (Oxford, 1983).

The Emergence of the New Right

1   'Let Our Children Grow Tall', Centre for Policy Studies, 1977, p. 4.

2   'Suicidal Morality' in *Pink and Brown People and Other Controversial Essays* (Hoover Institution, 1981), p. 50.

3   John Carroll, *Guilt: The Grey Eminence Behind Character, History and Culture* (London, 1985) p. 18.

4   See, as one example of his painstaking work, the essays in *Equality, the Third World and Economic Delusion (London, 1981)*.

5   'The Moral Dilemma', *Marxism Today*, October 1987, p. 23. Compare with this an alternative version of the same charge, which construes Mrs Thatcher as a disciple of Enoch Powell in his demagogic mode: 'The most important aspect of Thatcherism has not been economic theory, but populism: the instinctive assessing of public mood, and the enthusiastic exploitation of it. Since the Falklands war, the Prime Minister has shown a startling talent for discovering, anticipating, aggravating and even leading popular passion and prejudice' (Ben Pimlott, *The Times*, 9 February 1988). A prevailing socialist view is that democracy is the people saying the right thing, populism is what happens when they support the wrong thing.

6   'The Free and The Good' in *The Ideology of the New Right*, Ruth Levitas (ed.) (Oxford, 1986), p. 76.

7   Ruth Levitas in her introduction to *The Ideology of the New Right*, *op. cit.*, p. 5.

The Paradoxes of Thatcherism

1   F. A. Hayek, *Law, Legislation and Liberty*, Volume 3: *The Political Order of a Free People* (London, 1979), pp. 112-27.

2   Martin J. Wiener, *English Culture and the Decline of the Industrial Spirit* (Cambridge, 1981).

3   Bernard Semmel, *The Rise of Free Trade Imperialism: Classical Political Economy, the Empire of Free Trade and Imperialism* (Cambridge, 1970).

4   Mancur Olson, *The Rise and Decline of Nations* (New Haven, 1982).

A Sociologist's View of Thatcherism

1   N. Dennis and A. H. Halsey, *English Ethical Socialism: Thomas More to R. H. Tawney* (Oxford, 1988), p. 4 *ff.*

List of Contributors

BRIAN BARRY is Professor of Political Science at the London School of Economics, having previously been in the U.S.A. for ten years at the University of Chicago and California Institute of Technology. He is the author of *Political Argument, Sociologists, Economists and Democracy, The Liberal Theory of Justice* and *Theories of Justice*, Volume 1 of a three-volume *Treatise on Social Justice*. He is a Fellow of the British Academy and the American Academy of Arts and Sciences.

DAVID BUTLER has been a Fellow of Nuffield College, Oxford, since 1951 and has been associated with the Nuffield College studies of each General Election since 1945. He has also written widely about constitutional matters and about American, Australian and Indian politics.

IVOR CREWE is Professor of Government, University of Essex and co-editor of the *British Journal of Political Science*. He was Director of the S.S.R.C. Data Archive 1974–82 and co-Director of the British Election Study 1974–81. His recent books include *Decade of Dealignment* (with Bo Särlvik), *British Parliamentary Constituencies* (with Tony Fox), *Electoral Change in Western Democracies* (with David Denver) and *Political Communications: the General Election of 1983* (with Martin Harrop). He is currently completing a book on the rise and fall of the S.D.P.

RALF DAHRENDORF, Warden of St Antony's College, Oxford. Professor of Sociology in the University of Konstanz, Germany. Formerly Director of the London School of Economics (1974–1984) and Member of the Commission of the European Communities (1970–1974).

PROFESSOR F. H. HAHN, F.B.A., Professor of Economics in the University of Cambridge, Fellow of Churchill College, President of the Royal Economic Society, Foreign Member of the U.S. National Academy of Sciences.

PROFESSOR A. H. HALSEY, Director, Department of Social and Administrative Studies, Oxford University and Fellow of Nuffield College, Oxford.

ANTHONY KING is Professor of Government and Pro-Vice-Chancellor (Academic) at the University of Essex. He edited *The British Prime Minister* and is about to embark on a three-year study of the prime ministership as a political and governmental institution. He regularly comments on electoral and political matters for B.B.C. Television.

DAVID MARQUAND has been Professor of Contemporary History and Politics at the University of Salford since 1978. He is joint editor of the magazine *Political Quarterly*. He is the author of *Ramsay MacDonald, Parliament for Europe, Politics of Nostalgia, Taming Leviathan* and *European Elections and British Politics* (with David Butler).

PATRICK MINFORD is the Edward Gonner Professor of Applied Economics at the University of Liverpool. He is the author of *Unemployment: Cause and Cure*, a book which has been influential in the development of the present government's economic policies; also of other books and numerous articles on international macroeconomics.

KENNETH MINOGUE is Professor of Political Science at the London School of Economics. He has written *The Liberal Mind, Nationalism, The Concept of a University* and *Alien Powers: The Pure Theory of Ideology*, as well as a great deal both in academic and intellectual journals. In 1987 with Michael Biddis he edited *Thatcher: Personality and Politics*.

BEN PIMLOTT is Professor of Politics and Contemporary History at Birkbeck College, University of London. He is author of *Labour and the Left in the 1930s* and *Hugh Dalton*, which won the Whitbread Biography Award. He is the editor of *Fabian Essays and Socialist Thought, Trade Unions in British Politics* (with Chris Cook), and *The Media in British Politics* (with Jean Seaton). He has also edited the Dalton Diaries. He has been a political columnist for the *New Statesman* and *The Times*, and, currently, for the *Sunday Times*.

ROBERT SKIDELSKY is a Professor of International Studies at Warwick University. He has written *Politicians and the Slump, English Progressive Schools, Oswald Mosley* and *John Maynard Keynes*, vol. 1; and edited *The Age of Affluence* (with V. Bogdanov) and *The End of the Keynesian Era*.

Index

Abrams, Mark, 69
Amersham plc, 99
Arrow, 121
Asquith, Herbert Henry, 52, 53
Attlee, Clement, 41, 44, 55, 66–7,
    73, 81, 186, 187
Austin, J. L., 143

Baker, Kenneth, 185, 198
Baldwin, Stanley, 53, 70
Balfour, Arthur, 53
Barry, Brian, 23
Bauer, Peter, 134
B.B.C., *see* British Broadcasting
    Corporation
Bell, Daniel, 3
Benn, Anthony Wedgwood, 7, 68
Bevan, Aneurin, 70
Beveridge, William, 153
Bevin, Ernest, 58, 84
Biffen, John, 59
Booth, Charles, 183
Bray, Margaret, 120
British Airways, 99, 100
British Broadcasting Corporation,
    45, 67, 69, 76, 166–7, 172, 192,
    198
British Telecom, 100
Brittan, Samuel, 16
Brookings Report, 5

Brown, George, 6
Brown, Professor Phelps, 5
Buchanan, James, 15
Bulpitt, James, 45, 167
Burke, Edmund, 171
Burt, Thomas, 185
'Butskell' (Butler and Gaitskell),
    181, 186

Callaghan, James, 2, 12, 13, 17, 19,
    44, 53, 81, 88, 160, 187
Campbell, John, 18
Campbell-Bannerman, Sir Henry,
    53
Carlisle, Mark, 59
Carsberg, Professor Bryan, 100
Carter, Jimmy, U.S. President, 95
Central Electricity Generating
    Board (C.E.G.B.), 100, 147
Chamberlain, Neville, 53
Churchill, Winston, 26, 44, 53, 55,
    57, 67, 73
Coase, R. H., 110
Creighton, Bishop Mandell, 66
Crewe, Professor Ivor, 18, 21, 86–7
Cripps, Sir Stafford, 58
Critchley, Julian, 166
Crosland, Anthony, 188; *The
    Future of Socialism*, 90
Crossman, Richard, 68

Crozier, Michael, 10

Dahrendorf, Ralf, 22
Daily Mirror, 71
Daily Star, 71
Daily Telegraph, 68, 71, 96
Deng Shao Ping, 135
Dennis, Norman, 176
Desborough, John, 74
Disraeli, Benjamin, 31, 70
Donoughue, Bernard, 12
Douglas-Home, Sir Alec, 6, 26, 44, 53
Downs, Anthony, 15
Durbin, Professor Elizabeth: *New Jerusalems*, 90

Eden, Sir Anthony, 26, 44, 52, 53
Edgar, David, 136–7
Edmonds, John, 187
Erhard, Ludwig, 94

Falklands War, 135–7
Foot, Michael, 81
Fowler, Norman, 102
Frazer, Malcolm, 182
Friedman, Milton, 39, 105, 113, 144

Gaitskell, Hugh, 68, 81; *see also* 'Butskell'
Gamble, Andrew, 167
Gaulle, General Charles de, 26, 160–1, 163
Gaullists, 169–70
Gilmour, Sir Ian, 59
Gladstone, William Ewart, 35, 70
Gonzales, Filippo, 200
Government Failure, 4, 8, 14–17, 162–3

Green, T. H., 184
Guardian, 71, 96
Guilt-Culture, 125ff., 165

Hahn, Frank, 19–20
Hall, Stuart, 26, 32
Halpern, Sir Ralph, 117
Halsey, A. H., 22–3
Harrington, Michael: *The Next Left: The History of the Future*, 91–2
Harrison, Martin, 70
Hayek, Frederick A., 105, 113–14, 115, 117, 182–3; *Law, Legislation and Liberty*, 167–8; *The Mirage of Social Justice*, 144, 145
Healey, Denis, 160
Heath, Anthony, 31
Heath, Edward, 2, 10–11, 14, 19, 44, 53, 63, 134
Henderson, Arthur, 81, 84, 85
Hobbes, Thomas, 174–5
Hobhouse, L. T., 183
Hobson, J. A., 183
Howe, Sir Geoffrey, 55, 160
Howell, Ralph, 105
Hurd, Douglas, 196
Hutchison, T. W., 4

Independent, 71, 200
Industrial Reorganisation Corporation, 7
Inflation, 4–5, 9, 15, 36, 96–8, 113
Institute of Economic Affairs, 3, 90

Jaguar, 99, 100
Jay, Peter, 16
Jenkins, Roy, 8

Index

Johnson, Lyndon B., u.s. President, 3, 52, 57–8
Jones, Aubrey, 7
Joseph, Sir Keith, 14, 27, 32, 94, 169

Kaldor, Nicholas, 6–7, 21
Kaunda, Kenneth, 133
Kennedy, John F., u.s. President, 3, 52
Keynes, John Maynard, 90, 111, 112, 113, 116–17, 119, 120, 162; *The General Theory*, 109
King, Anthony, 15, 18
Kinnock, Neil, 67, 70, 72, 73, 80–81, 186
Kirkpatrick, Jean, 134

Lange, David, 114, 135
Lansbury, George, 81
Lawson, Nigel, 107
Lerner, A. F., 114
Lloyd, Selwyn, 5
Lloyd, Trevor, 66
Lloyd George, David, 44, 53
Locke, John, 149
Low, David, 84
Lyttelton, Oliver, 58

McAlpine, Lord, 71
McCallum, R. B.: *The British General Election of 1945*, 65
McCarthy, Joseph, 166
MacDonald, James Ramsay, 70, 81, 177
Machiavelli, Niccolò: *The Prince*, 56–7, 59, 63, 64, 133
McKibbin, Ross, 85
Macmillan, Harold, 6, 19, 25, 26, 44, 53, 55, 57, 134, 186

Maine, Sir Henry, 182
Malthus, Thomas, 174, 181
Mandelson, Peter, 67, 74
Market Failure, 109–11, 147–51
Marquand, David, 3, 21, 22
Marshall, Alfred, 183
Marshall, T. H., 155
Marx, Karl, 128, 130, 132, 175–6, 177, 178, 181
Matthews, Kent, 96, 97, 98, 99, 101
Maudling, Reginald, 6, 8, 9
Mayhew, Christopher, 68
Mill, John Stuart: *On Liberty*, 145
Minford, Patrick, 1, 19, 20–21, 107, 112
Minogue, Kenneth, 22
Monetarism, 15, 17, 98, 160
More, Thomas: *Utopia*, 176–7
Morrison, Herbert, 31
Mrs Thatcher, as a political leader, 18, 35, 45, 51–64, 96, 164; popularity of, 44; as a woman, 58, 134–5

Neustadt, Richard, 55, 60
News Chronicle, 69
Nicholson, Max, 6
Nott, Sir John, 55, 58, 137
Nozick, Robert, 145, 149

Observer, 72
Olson, Mancur: *The Rise and Decline of Nations*, 95, 171, 192

Paish, G. L., 5
Phillips, Morgan, 5, 68, 182
Pickles, William, 79
Pimlott, Ben, 19
Pinto-Duschinsky, Michael, 71

Policy Studies Centre, 90
Pollard, A. F., 66
Potter, Beatrice, *see* Webb, Beatrice
Prentice, Reginald, 201
Prior, James, 59, 98
Privatisation, 99–100, 157
Pulzer, Peter, 86
Pym, Francis, 55, 59

Rand, Ayn, 145
Reagan, Ronald, U.S. President, 134, 182
Reece, Gordon, 67
Roosevelt, Franklin D., U.S. President, 26
Rose, Richard, 15
Rothbard, Murray, 145

St-John Stevas, Norman, 59
Salisbury, Lord, 53
Sargent, R., 105
Schumpeter, J. A., 15, 94, 113, 115–16, 117–18, 123, 124
Sedgemore, Brian, 200
Shanks, Michael, 5
Sinclair, Peter, 8
Smiles, Samuel, 39
Smith, Adam, 21, 107, 108, 123
Soames, Lord, 59
Socialism, defined: 81, 143, 176
Southcott, Joanna, 143
Sowell, Thomas, 128
Spencer, Herbert: *The Man Versus the State*, 182, 183
Sun, The, 71

Tawney, R. H.: *The Acquisitive Society*, 184, 185
Tebbit, Norman, 98–9, 166, 167
Thatcherism: background to, 2–18,

160, 182, 185, 191–2; defined, 1, 32–3, 45–7, 94, 124, 126, 160–65; as economic theory, 113, 120, 123; as political economy, 113–18, 161–2; authoritarianism of, 22, 32–3, 146, 167–9, 208; electorate's view of, 35–48, 93
Thorneycroft, Peter, 160
Times, The, 16, 69, 71, 72
Titmuss, Richard: *The Gift Relationship*, 154–5
Tocqueville, Alex de, 174; *Memoir on Pauperism*, 178–9, 180–1
Trotsky, Lev, 177
Tullock, Gordon, 15

Unemployment, 39, 101–3, 105, 112, 118–20

Veljanovski, Cento, 99
Virginia School, the, 4, 15

Walden, Brian, 167
Wallas, Graham, 90
Walters, Sir Alan, 96, 107
Webb, Beatrice (*née* Potter), 85, 89, 183
Weber, Max, 21, 182, 192
Whitelaw, William, 55
Wiener, Martin: *English Culture and the Decline of the Industrial Spirit*, 169
Wilson, Harold, 2, 6, 7–9, 11–12, 13, 17, 19, 44, 53, 55, 57, 81, 160
Worsthorne, Peregrine, 32
Wyatt, Woodrow, 68

Young, Hugo, 174
Young, Lord, 102, 105